The Caring Relationship

Elderly People and their Families

Hazel Qureshi

Alan Walker

MACMILLAN

First published 1989

Published by
MACMILLAN EDUCATION LTD
Houndmills, Basingstoke, Hampshire RG21 2XS
and London
Companies and representatives
throughout the world

Typeset by Footnote Graphics,
Warminster, Wiltshire

Printed in Hong Kong

British Library Cataloguing in Publication Data
Qureshi, Hazel
The caring relationship: elderly people and their families.
1. Great Britain. Old persons. Care. Role
of families. Social aspects.
I. Title. II. Walker, Alan
362.6'0941
ISBN 0–333–41947–2 (hardcover)
ISBN 0–333–41948–0 (paperback)

*To the elderly people and
their relatives who gave
us their time so generously*

Contents

List of Tables and Figure

Tables

Figure

Preface

This book is about elderly people and their families. Although it has a particular focus upon the care given to elderly people in case of disability or other need, and is thus perforce largely about family care, it will be obvious that we would disown any inference that disability and dependency is the inevitable lot of those who achieve old age, or that becoming a 'burden' is the most likely consequence. The majority of people aged over 74 in the study we report led full and independent lives, and many others were better seen as interdependent than dependent.

The book begins with a description of the overall sample of elderly people, and goes on to discuss the patterns of contact which they have with their relatives and the variety of needs and sources of help which are identified. The second half of the book focuses upon those who receive regular assistance with practical tasks and discusses how choices are made about who will help within the family, what effects increasing disability and dependency are seen to have on relationships, and how statutory help is seen in relation to family help. We conclude with a discussion of the ways in which our improved knowledge of the informal sector might be better taken into account in the policy and practice of the formal sector of care. The policies of central and local government on pensions, benefits, housing, transport, health and social services all set the context in which exchanges of care within the family take place, but it is the services provided by the last of these which seem most often to be considered to be a possible substitute for family care.

The evidence we advance is based on a survey of around 300 people aged 75 or more, living in the community in Sheffield in 1982/3, and follow-up interviews with some informal carers. The elderly people interviewed were a representative sample drawn with the help of the Sheffield Family Practitioner Committee's central age/sex register. We are grateful to the staff of the Family Practitioner Committee (FPC) and to the Sheffield GPs who co-operated with us.

We are aware that the restriction to one geographical area places limits upon the generalisability of the detail of our results. However, we see no reason to believe that families in Sheffield are greatly unlike families in other British cities. Readers will be aware that Sheffield has a reputation for a prevailing political commitment to collectively provided services coupled, as will become clear, with a widespread traditional view of family responsibilities.

Many people contributed to the successful implementation of the research. In particular, we wish to acknowledge the invaluable contribution of the other individuals who were at various times members of the research team: Josephine Green and Ken Simons who played important parts in the study of carers and in computing and data processing; Eileen Austin, Barbara Bell, Jean Bloor, Margaret Harrison and Nancy Pavey who undertook much of the interviewing of elderly people; and Margaret Jaram and Gloria Walton who were project secretaries. Margaret Jaram was primarily responsible for preparing the manuscript for publication. Nigel Johnson (on an Economic and Social Research Council linked studentship) and Mick Bond (on placement from the University of Surrey) also contributed to the research effort.

The research was funded by the Joseph Rowntree Memorial Trust and a special debt of thanks is owed to the then Director of the Trust, Robin Guthrie, who provided help and support considerably beyond that normally expected from funding agencies. Valuable advice and support were also received from Michael Bayley, Ron Middlestorb and Eric Sainsbury.

The research on which this book is based represented the fulfilment of a long-standing personal ambition for Alan Walker. His desire to conduct an enquiry into the family system of care stemmed both from his practical experiences in working with elderly people as part of his secondary school task force and the early years of his research career spent analysing data on elderly people from Peter Townsend's survey of household resources and living standards. This commitment was reinforced by xii *Preface*

his subsequent disappointment with the lack of penetration of sociological research on elderly people into the field of social policy (with the notable exception of the pioneering work of Peter Townsend). Hazel Qureshi came to the project, as Research Officer, from a background in social work and research into the community care of elderly people.

Alan Walker thanks Carol, Alison and Christopher for bearing so stoically the sacrifices necessary for the completion of this book. Hazel Qureshi thanks Martin and Imran for emotional support and distraction.

Our final and warmest thanks go to the elderly people and their carers who gave up their time to be interviewed and received us with such courtesy and friendliness. We hope that this book is a worthy reflection of their views.

Manchester   HAZEL QURESHI
Sheffield   ALAN WALKER

1
Introduction

> But it all really starts in the family, because not only is the family the most important means through which we show our care for others. It's the place where each generation learns its responsibility towards the rest of society . . . I think the statutory services can only play their part successfully if we don't expect them to do for us things that we could be doing for ourselves. (Margaret Thatcher, 1981, p. 3)

The subject matter of this book lies at the heart of current debates about both the development of modern society and the future of the welfare state. As the population ages the issue of the provision of help, assistance and care to the growing number of elderly people in need is directly, and sometimes painfully, confronting more and more families. However, while some light has been shed in recent years on the costs that providing such care can entail 'Equal Opportunities Commission' 1980; Nissel and Bonnerjea, 1982; Joshi, 1987), very little research has been conducted into the social foundations of the caring relationship itself. Why do families (and, within them, women in particular) care for elderly relatives who are in need? On what is the caring relationship founded? Can the family be expected to go on caring for elderly relatives for longer and longer periods? These questions prompted the survey on which this book is based. The answers to them have major implications for the state, as well as millions of individual elderly people and their families.

Since the family is, by a long way, the main unit within which care is provided, there has always been an uneasy relationship between it and the state. As long as public provision for elderly and other people with disabilities has existed there have been

1

concerns expressed, largely from within the state, about the 'danger' this poses to the family (Anderson, 1977; Flandrin, 1979). These concerns have been particularly forcefully expressed under the Thatcher governments of the 1980s, which have combined neo-monetarist stringency in the public sector with an aversion to state welfare and a belief in 'Victorian' family values (Bosanquet, 1983; Walker, 1987a).

Many years ago, in his classic book *The Family Life of Old People*, Townsend (1963, p. 13) noted this official concern about the growing numbers of old people and the belief that many of them were isolated from their families and from the community:

> It was widely believed that the ties of kinship are much less enduring than they once were and that as a consequence the immediate family of parents and unmarried children, of which the individual is a member for only part of his lifetime, has replaced the larger family of three or four generations, of which the individual is a member for the whole of his life, as the fundamental unit of society.

In the mid-1970s Moroney (1976, p. 125) found that, in the opinion of 'scores' of civil servants and social welfare practitioners throughout England and Wales as well as in Denmark and West Germany, families were less willing to care. Civil servants and planners cited the increases in the demand for social services as an indication of the reduced willingness to care on the part of families. This was also the theme running through a series of speeches by successive Secretaries of State for Social Services in the 1980s (Jenkin, 1981; Fowler, 1984; Moore, 1987) the latest of which, on the future of the welfare state, expressed fears about increasing dependency and reliance on the state.

This research shows, in common with a long line of authoritative historical and contemporary studies, that these fears are misplaced. Contrary to the views strongly held by some politicians there is no *evidence* whatsoever of a significant unwillingness to care on the part of families. Indeed we were struck, first, by the universal nature of the acceptance of their primary role in the provision of care for elderly relatives (particularly by the female kin) and, second, by the tremendous normative pressure on them to do so; which meant that, in some instances, they were forced into a caring relationship which was psychologically damaging to both elderly person and carer. While we are saying, on the basis of evidence detailed in the rest of this book, that the fears of Right-wing politicians are largely unfounded (and appear to reflect a preoccupation with restricting the size of the public sector rather than ensuring the best care for elderly people) we must also be clear we are *not* suggesting that the family system of care can be regarded any longer as being able to cope, largely alone, with the consequences of an ageing population.

In the first place, the number of very elderly people requiring care is expanding rapidly and a significant proportion of them do not have families. Second, for various reasons, there exists a 'care gap' between the needs of some elderly people and the provision of informal care. Third, as we demonstrate in Chapters 5–8, the responsibility for, and the physical act of, caring are unequally distributed between the sexes and (partly as a result) this often places undue strain on both the carer and the cared for. Alternative policy responses are required to overcome this unfair and, in some instances, intolerable position. The possible policy responses are considered in Chapter 9. Here we discuss briefly the relevant demographic changes and the growing care gap, before going on to describe the survey and sample on which this research is based.

Ageing and dependency

The unique late twentieth-century phenomenon of an ageing population is common to all advanced industrial societies. As Table 1.1 shows, in just 50 years (1931–81) the numbers of people aged 65 and over more than doubled, while those aged 75 and over nearly quadrupled. Furthermore current projections show that the population aged 65 and over is set to increase steadily, apart from a slight decline between 1991 and 2001, until well into the next century. The largest rises, however, are expected in the numbers aged 75 and over and 85 and over: 18 per cent and 63 per cent respectively between 1988 and 2021.

The significance of population ageing, for individual families and social policy alike, lies mainly in the rising incidence of disability in successively older age groups, particularly beyond the age of 70 (see Townsend, 1979, p. 706). The need for assistance

Table 1.1   *Numbers of elderly people in Great Britain 1901–2021 (000s)*

Year	65+	%*	75+	%*	85+	%*
1901	1734	4.7	507	1.4	57	0.15
1931	3316	7.4	920	2.1	108	0.24
1951	5332	10.9	1731	3.5	218	0.45
1971	7140	13.2	2536	4.7	462	0.86
1981	7985	15.0	3052	5.7	552	1.03
1988	8697	15.8	3736	6.8	757	1.4
1991	8795	15.9	3844	6.9	757	1.4
2001	8656	15.3	4082	7.2	1047	1.9
2011	8911	15.7	4053	7.1	1187	2.1
2021	9956	17.2	4401	7.6	1230	2.1

*Percentage of total population of Great Britain.
Source: Population projections by Government Actuary. Mid-1981 based projections (from Henwood and Wicks, 1984, p. 4).

and care, both informal and formal, associated with disability is discussed in detail in Chapter 4. But one example of the national challenge facing families and social policy over the next 30 years is that the numbers aged 65 and over who are unable to bath/shower or wash all over alone will increase by 40 per cent, and the numbers aged 85 and over unable to do so will rise by 110 per cent (Phillipson and Walker, 1986, p. 7).

While statistics such as these should be taken seriously by policy makers there has been a tendency for responses to take the form of alarmist statements rather than carefully constructed plans of action. Descriptions such as 'the growing burden of dependency' and 'the rising tide' create a misleading impression of both elderly people and the nature of the challenge facing the social services (see Health Advisory Service, 1983). Moreover, such fears are chiefly expressed about the potential demand on the public sector, whilst few official voices of concern are raised about the implications for families. Official alarm at the public sector consequences of an ageing population is not new (Titmuss, 1963) but it is important to distinguish the facts from the rhetoric if responsible policies, aimed at helping families to care, are to be constructed within limited resources.

In the first place, as we demonstrate in Chapter 4, the majority of elderly people are *not* in need of care and are able to look after themselves without assistance from either relatives or the social services. Nationally more than half of those over 65 have no disabilities and a further 20 per cent have only slight ones. Even among those aged 75 and over nearly half experience only slight or no disablement.

Second, as we show in Chapters 2 and 5, when it comes to elderly people needing care the state is the last resort. The image of infinite demand for social services which some politicians portray is false. Where elderly people in need of care have families, all available kinship sources of help are usually exhausted before recourse to the state.

Third, as Titmuss (1963, p. 56) pointed out, it is paradoxical to conceive of increases in the numbers of elderly people as a threat or burden when this should be a cause for celebration of social progress and, particularly, the achievements of public welfare in putting an end to many of the causes of premature death which prevented earlier generations reaching advanced old age.

Fourth, alarmist statements about the burden of dependency have hindered an understanding of the true nature of dependency in old age. Rather than assuming that the social problem of dependency is necessarily associated with old age and that the problem is growing because the numbers in a particular age group are increasing, it is important to recognise that dependency is a social relationship rather than a biological rule. Dependent status is socially and not biologically constructed. It is partly the product of a particular social division of labour and structure of inequality rather than a natural concomitant of the ageing process (Walker, 1980, 1981b, 1982c; Townsend, 1981a). Of course this is not to say that people do not grow old and suffer from disabilities, some of which might entail physical dependency, but rather that what we regard as dependency and, for that matter, old age is manufactured by society and not a function of the ageing process (this issue is discussed further in Chapter 4).

The community care gap

This book is about the caring relationship between elderly people and their families. This relationship is the bedrock of 'community care', whether this is used to mean care *by* the community or care *in* the community (Bayley, 1973). According to P. Abrams (1977, p. 125) 'community care' is the 'provision of help, support and protection to others by lay members of societies acting in everyday domestic and occupational settings'. To the extent that care *by* the community can be said to exist, then it is overwhelmingly families, and female kin in particular, who provide it (see Chapters 4 and 8). Outside the family there is little evidence of substantial inputs of care by lay members of the 'community' (Chapter 8; Wenger, 1984). In practice, therefore, community care consists of care *in* the community. This may be provided 'informally' through kinship networks and also, for the less arduous and less personal tasks, by friends, neighbours and volunteers, or 'formally' by the statutory social services. This 'community care' might be defined more generally, as 'the help and support given to individuals, including children, people with disabilities and elderly people, in non-institutional settings' (Walker, 1982b, p. 5). For most of the post-war period the state has tended to apply the term 'community care' to the activities of the personal social services in the domiciliary field, although in recent years it has been attempting to redefine the central thrust of the policy from care *in* to care *by* the community (Walker, 1986; Bulmer, 1987, pp. 10–16).

In the same way that the term 'community' conjures up misleading images of precisely who it is that provides care and on what basis, so the term 'care' is equally value laden and problematic. In fact the bulk of what is actually done in the name of care should more exactly be labelled as assistance, personal aid, help and support or 'tending' (R. Parker, 1981, p. 17). However, although we use some of these terms interchangeably with 'care', we do not want to lose sight of the fact that care comprises a social relationship as well as a physical task. In view of the confusion associated with the notion of 'community care' it is tempting to conclude that it should be abandoned (Wilson, 1982), but its currency is too wide and, for some, too compelling to make this a serious proposition.

Community care has been one of the centrepieces of social services policy over the whole of the post-war period. But it is the failure of successive governments, during that time, to meet the needs of the rising numbers of elderly people (Phillipson and Walker, 1986) which gives rise to serious concern about the preparedness of the welfare state to respond to the challenge of population ageing over the next 40 years. There has been a long-standing community 'care gap' (Walker, 1982b, 1985c) between rising needs and the public resources allocated to meet them. This has been exacerbated by increasingly wide variations between local authorities in the services they provide. There is a danger that, unless action is taken to ensure enlarged caring resources, the gap between the need for care on the part of elderly people and the supply of both informal and formal care will widen. The main points may be summarised.

First, more and more elderly people are surviving into advanced old age without any children or other relatives. A large number of elderly people, particularly women, are outliving their spouses, but in addition a significant number of elderly people have never had children. Second, the pool of potential family carers has shrunk because of declining fertility in the 1920s and 1930s. Even when elderly people do have children, therefore, there are fewer of them than in previous times. Third, because people are living longer many of those caring for the over-75s and over-85s are themselves elderly and, therefore, less able to withstand the rigours of caring work. Fourth, there are a range of factors – such as divorce, the growth of poverty and unemployment and the continuing upward trend in women working outside the home – that might limit the propensity to care (Walker, 1985c, p. 13). When these factors are considered against a backcloth of continuing restrictions on the social services which should be supporting the caring activities of families, coupled with more exhortations for the community to care, it is obvious that the caring relationship is going to experience increasing strain. It is on the strength and durability of that relationship that the community care of elderly people in need rests and that is why it is the subject of our investigation.

The survey

In order to investigate the role of the family in the provision of help and care for elderly relatives, and the relationship between elderly people and their family carers, it was considered necessary to conduct interviews with both sides of the caring relationship. Thus a two-stage survey was carried out in Sheffield, in 1982/3. In the first stage, a sample of 306 people aged 75 or more were interviewed. This group constituted the primary sample because elderly people were regarded as the best source of information about their own needs and attitudes towards the different forms of care they might be receiving. Moreover there was a worry that some contemporary research, in the full flush of its rediscovery of the importance of the informal sector, was in danger of regarding older people as merely the anonymous recipients of care (Nissel and Bonnerjea, 1982; Finch, 1984). Certainly some politicians in their (largely rhetorical) enthusiasm for carers had begun to give this impression (Jenkin, 1981; Fowler, 1984).

In the second stage, interviews were carried out with 57 people who had been identified during the first stage as providing elderly respondents with regular weekly practical assistance on an informal basis. A decision was made to interview only helpers living *outside* the elderly person's own household. This was not the result of any underestimate of the importance and interest of the situation of those caring within households, but rather a reflection of the desire to focus upon the kind of everyday, often (but not always) routine, assistance which forms the bulk of informal caring activity, and perhaps to identify some of the factors affecting the formation of, or failure to form, joint households. Also much in-household care is by *spouses*, and a study of carers living in the same household would have to be quite differently focused in order to discuss their perceptions of caring as opposed to the perceptions of other family members, and to distinguish the help given to elderly relatives from all the other responsibilities and tasks associated with caring for other household members. It was known that the situation of carers within households was under study elsewhere (see, for example, Nissel and Bonnerjea, 1982), but an intensive look in the same study at both out-of-household helpers, and the elderly people who were helped, seemed to be a new departure, certainly on this scale.

Source of the sample of elderly people

The sample of elderly people was drawn from the Family Practitioner Committee's central age/sex register, from the lists of six different practices in Sheffield. This was not strictly a random sample because the practices concerned were not randomly selected. One criterion

Table 1.2 *Comparison of achieved sample with census data residents in private households, Sheffield Metropolitan District 1981 census: small area statistics*

Age	Males (%)		Females (%)		Totals (%)
	SWD*	Married	SWD	Married	
74–9	6	15	25	10	56
80–4	4	5	17	3	29
85+	2	1	11	†	15
Total	12	21	53	14	100 (31 104)

Family care of the elderly sample

Age	Males (%)		Femalcs (%)		Totals (%)
	SWD*	Married	SWD	Married	
74–9	6	14	25	11	56
80–4	5	5	16	2	28
85+	2	1	11	2	16
Total	13	20	52	15	100 (306)

*Single, widowed and divorced.
†Less than 0.05%.

for choice was a belief that the GPs concerned would be willing to collaborate in research on elderly patients. However, a considerable attempt was made to ensure both a geographical spread of patients and an appropriate distribution of the sample among areas with differing socio-economic characteristics. Details are given in the Appendix.

It became possible to check the composition of the achieved sample against 1981 census data and this showed that the age, sex, marital status and household composition of respondents was very close to that of the total population aged 75 and over in Sheffield (see Table 1.2).

The sample of carers

The second-stage sample of carers was found by asking the elderly people for the names and addresses of friends, neighbours and

relatives who provided regular practical assistance. The identification of one 'principal carer', although it could be quite clear in
many cases, was not always simple. The definition of a 'carer'
certainly varies across studies, with some (for example, the
Dinnington research) including many types of activity, such as
social visits, whilst others consider only those who provide intensive personal care.

To identify a principal carer as 'the person who does the most'
can be problematic in two ways: first, since total care needed is
variable, a 'principal carer' so defined might be providing 24-hour
intensive assistance, or a once-a-month tidying of the garden;
second, since caring tasks are qualitatively different it may well be
extremely difficult to weigh up one person's contribution against
another's. Frequency, intensity and type of task may all vary. The
interviews with elderly people determined 'who helped' by asking
this question repeatedly in relation to particular tasks, rather than
asking what specific people did. The range of tasks undertaken by
each relative could then be constructed from the answers to task-
related questions. It was then intended, subsequently, to make
whatever distinctions between carers seemed appropriate for a
particular piece of data analysis.

However, it was necessary for interviewers to make a decision in
the field about whether to ask for a particular relative's name and
address in order to be able to include them in the carer study. (The
unsatisfactory, and probably unworkable, alternative was to expect interviewers to ask in some cases for the names and addresses
of all prominent members of the older person's network.) Also, a
series of questions about identified principle helpers was included
in the schedule, and these had to be asked irrespective of whether
the helpers lived within the household or not. Since we did not
wish to ask these questions in relation to friends or relatives giving
only small infrequent amounts of assistance, the criterion used in
the field was that the person should give *sustained practical
assistance involving the complete performance of tasks such as
laundry, shopping or housework at least once a week, or lighter
tasks such as cooking and light housework at least three times a
week*. It was specified that this assistance should not be part of
routine household duties, such as were performed by many elderly
wives for their non-disabled spouses. In the vast majority of instances the identification of principal helper proved unproblematic

but such a criterion excludes, for example, carers who share caring tasks on a fortnightly basis with other relatives (there was one such case). There is further discussion of this issue in Chapter 5.

At least one carer outside the household was identified in 103 cases (33 per cent). The elderly person refused to give (or did not know) their address in 26 instances, and in 8 instances the carer could not be traced from the address given. Among those carers whom we were able to approach for interview 75 per cent agreed to take part in the study. There were 58 carer interviews in all. Further details of methodology, and an assessment of the representativeness of the achieved sample of carers is given in the Appendix.

The achieved sample of carers was representative of informal carers living outside the household and providing assistance. Although most of those interviewed in the carer study were daughters, this is a very clear reflection of the composition of the population of informal carers of interest in this case. Equally, the proportion of non-relatives is also consistent with what would be expected. (Detailed discussion of how and why particular network members came to be the ones who were providing help is to be found in Chapter 5.)

Interviews with elderly people

The first stage schedule, used for the interviews with elderly people, was a structured interview in which a number of questions were left open for verbatim responses to be recorded. The interview fell broadly into three main sections. The first concentrated on the elderly person's family, the second on health, disability and help received and the third on support systems used and their interaction. A conscious decision was made to ask questions about the circumstances of family members before seeking information about the provision of help or assistance. The majority of elderly people, after all, were not receiving intensive assistance from relatives and it seemed desirable initially not to approach the discussion of family relationships and contacts from that perspective.

In the section of the interview schedule about the family a list of relatives was made, and information was sought about the present circumstances of each, especially those not living more than two hours' journey away. Further details about this process will be given later. The level of contact with each relative was ascertained, and special intimacy with particular individuals was noted. Following this an attempt was made to discover to what extent the 'family' functioned as a whole for that particular individual. A brief family history was sought with a focus on intra-family helping in the past, particularly in relation to key life events such as retirement or bereavement. This section also contained a brief assessment of other, non-family, social contacts. The main analysis of this section of the questionnaire is contained in Chapter 3.

Under health, disability and help there were simple checklists of common physical conditions, and symptoms of forgetfulness, confusion, depression and anxiety. There were also two scales to assess aspects of morale. One was that used by M. Abrams (1978), namely the acceptance-satisfaction scale; the other was derived from the Philadelphia Geriatric Centre Morale Scale (PGCMS) and covered the individual's reaction to ageing. Loneliness and difficulty passing time were dealt with in separate questions. With regard to physical disability, the functional disability scale was based on the work of Townsend (1962), S. Sainsbury (1973) and Walker and Townsend (1976) and was integrated with questions about the sources of help which attempted to compensate for different aspects of functional disability. This sub-section gave rise to a list of helpers and an assessment of their relative importance. Details of help given by the elderly person to others were also recorded. Information from this section is to be found primarily in Chapter 4, with more detailed analyses of different patterns of informal care and the factors underlying them in Chapters 5 and 6.

In the third section, support systems used, there was a common core of questions on reactions to disability, and on likely (or actual) sources of help in a variety of (not too improbable) situations. For those who were receiving help from home-help or warden services there was a short series of additional questions designed to determine satisfaction with the service and whether formal helpers had taken on informal roles. People receiving regular informal help were also asked a series of questions in relation to their informal helpers, including questions about the history of helping. Respondents were also asked about preferences regarding different sources of help, including financial or material help. Material from this section of the questionnaire is contained mainly in Chapter 7.

At various points in the interview information was sought on the elderly person's own financial and material circumstances, housing conditions and feelings about old age.

The interviews with carers

In contrast to the interviews with elderly people, the smaller numbers involved made it possible to use a less structured approach in relation to carers. Although there was a core of structured information to be collected about circumstances and help given, the major part of the interview was conducted as a focus interview, using tape recordings which were later transcribed. The topic areas in the interview guide were: how helping began, perceptions of alternative sources of help both within and outside the family, degree of flexibility for helper and felt indispensability, the quality of the relationship with the elderly person and considerations of reciprocity, the opportunity costs helping, norms about caring and expectations about the future.

Information about relatives

Each elderly person was asked to give detailed information about up to 10 relatives, to include all children, any other relatives with whom there was at least monthly contact and up to three siblings (even if contact was less than monthly). Since it was accepted that elderly people might feel emotionally or psychologically close to relatives with whom they had infrequent physical contact, they were also invited to include any relative to whom they felt especially close. People listed just over four relatives on average, giving a total of 1,221 relatives in all.

Although independent grandchildren were listed separately, information about dependent grandchildren and spouses of children was included with the information about the relevant child. Thus, if a person listed only one relative, there might be other family members in the elderly persons' network. In calculating the size of the family network, spouses of children were counted separately.

In order to facilitate analysis, the 1,221 relatives were sometimes treated as a group: a sample of relatives of people aged over 74.

This is of course quite distinct from the carer sample. In the latter our information was obtained from direct interviews with carers, whilst basic information about all relatives and the extent and methods of contact with them was obtained through the report of the elderly person only.

Plan of the book

This book is primarily intended to report the findings of our survey of the family care of elderly people. As a result the central section of it (Chapters 3–8) concentrates on the key dimensions that the research set out to illuminate: the social contacts between elderly people and their families (Chapter 3), elderly people's need for care and assistance (Chapter 4), determinants of the supply of care within the family (Chapter 5), responses to both receiving and giving care (Chapter 6), reactions to increasing disability and dependency (Chapter 7) and the role of other sources of informal and formal care (Chapter 8). As far as possible in these central chapters we try to allow the elderly people and their carers to speak for themselves. In Chapter 9 we draw together some conclusions from the research and suggest some possible policy responses. In the following chapter we set the scene for subsequent analyses by examining the role of family care for elderly people in a broader policy context.

2
Family Care and the State

Since social policy is concerned with the collective organisation of welfare provision, both public and private, it tends to concentrate on the activities of the formal bureaucratic social services. The paradox facing social policy with regard to the care of elderly people is that, although they are the major consumers of the public social services, the vast bulk of the care they receive does not come from the public sector but from their own families. Within the family it is female kin who are by far and away the main providers of care (Land, 1978; Finch and Groves, 1980; Walker, 1981a, 1982a). Although a significant change has taken place recently in the official recognition of the role of family and other formal carers (see, for example, DHSS, 1981b; Fowler, 1984), in the past an overemphasis on the public social services, by policy makers and policy analysts alike, helped to create a misleading impression of elderly people as welfare dependants and an equally misleading rigidity in the distinction between the formal and the informal sectors. Both of these false constructions are clearly exposed by an examination of the care of the elderly people, as is the inadequacy of a social policy analysis based only on the public services. In practice the formal and the informal sectors are interdependent. On the one hand, the formal sector depends on informal carers: if only a small proportion of those with major caring responsibilities for frail elderly people – in excess of one million people (Henwood and Wicks, 1984, p. 12) – metaphorically downed tools and ignored their emotions the personal social services would be swamped. On the other hand, the caring capacity of the informal sector is partly a function of the availability and distribution of social services as well as of the broader social and economic policies of the state (Walker, 1982b).

15

The main purpose of this chapter is to examine the relationships between the family and the state in the provision of care to elderly people in order to provide a context for the subsequent examination of the caring relationship in action. We discuss the nature of family care, the impact of state policies (particularly in the personal social services) on the care provided by families, the role of other informal carers and recent government policies on community care. Discussion of a possible alternative basis for policy, which does not exploit the duty felt by families and female kin in particular to provide care for elderly relatives, is reserved for the concluding chapter. At the heart of this analysis is the ostensible conflict between elderly people and carers. We argue that, in so far as a conflict can be seen to exist, it derives primarily from the failure of the state to meet the needs of *both* elderly people and carers adequately and to strike a balance between these needs.

The family system of care

As we pointed out in the previous chapter with regard to the general situation in Britain, and as we demonstrate in Chapter 4 on the basis of our own data from Sheffield, the need for care by elderly people is increasing. In itself this should not be a cause for alarm; however, when coupled with the substantial existing short-fall in both informal help and formal service provision (Walker, 1982b, pp. 20–1; and see also Chapter 4) we believe that there should be serious public concern about the adequacy of care for elderly people in need. In addition there are two other factors which contribute to the urgency for a radical reappraisal of present community care policies: on the one hand, various social and economic changes outlined in Chapter 1 are resulting in a contraction in the pool of potential carers, and on the other hand there is the continuing (grossly unequal) gender division in tending and caring.

In the field of social care the terms 'community' and 'family' have for too long masked the fact that it is female kin who carry out the bulk of caring and tending (see Chapter 5). This means that, in addition to doing most of the unpaid labour involved in tending or caring for elderly people, women bear the main burden of guilt and worry which usually accompanies the ties of love and affection involved in caring *about* close relatives (Graham, 1983; Ungerson, 1983a, 1983b). A postal survey of carers by the EOC (1980, p. 9) found that there were three times as many women carers as men. A recent study of elderly people using short-term residential care found that 85 per cent had female carers (Allen, 1983). A detailed study of a very small group of families caring for severely disabled elderly relatives found that the average time spent on care activities on weekdays was 3 hours 24 minutes, of which 3 hours 11 minutes was spent by wives and 13 minutes by husbands (Nissel and Bonnerjea, 1982, p. 21). Fifteen of the 22 wives spent at least two hours a day caring for their elderly relatives, but none of the husbands spent this amount of time on caring work. These gender inequalities were even greater with regard to those activities which are the most arduous and difficult and which put the greatest stress on those doing the caring. On average wives spent 2½ hours on these 'primary' care activities and husbands only 8 minutes.

The burden of care falling on women appears to be increasing despite the upward trend in women's participation in the labour market. In a survey of women's employment, Hunt (1968, p. 109) found 5 per cent of women aged 16–64 were responsible for the care of at least one elderly or infirm person in their household and 6 per cent were responsible for at least one person outside the household. In the recent Office of Population Censuses and Surveys study of women's employment, 13 per cent of all women aged 16–59 were found to have caring responsibilities for sick and elderly dependents, a proportion that rose to 21 per cent among those aged 40–59 (Martin and Roberts, 1984, p. 112).

Caring and tending tasks include physical work, particularly where incontinent relatives are involved, such as lifting, extra washing, cooking, cleaning and shopping. Then there is the mental effort involved in dealing with sometimes confused elderly people. Finally, there is the burden of bearing the total responsibility for the provision of care and medication with little help from other relatives or statutory services (Deeping, 1979). Although many of these caring tasks are similar to ordinary housework it cannot be assumed that they can be performed simultaneously with other tasks. For example, the elderly person may not live with the relative or may require special treatment, such as a diet. Moreover all caring and other household tasks may require greater time and effort because of the need constantly to keep an eye on the elderly relative (EOC, 1980, p. 15). Providing care to older family members often has a disruptive impact on family life and òn other members of the family. One study of the family care of elderly relatives found that four in every five families were experiencing problems and two in every five severe problems. Half of the families found that their social life was restricted (P. Sainsbury and Grad de Alarcon, 1971). This picture of tension between members of the nuclear family was confirmed by Nissel and Bonnerjea (1982), who found that in two-thirds of families there was considerable tension. As well as anxiety, physical and mental stress and interpersonal conflict the provision of care often results in a lack of privacy and strained relationships with any children because less time can be devoted to them. Moving an elderly relative into the family home in order to care for them can result in cramped accommodation for everyone, lack of privacy and increased tension between family members (EOC, 1980, pp. 32–3).

It is now well documented that for women acting as principal carers, often married women with children, caring and tending can involve considerable economic, physical, emotional and psychological costs (see Walker, 1982a, pp. 24–5; G. Parker, 1985, pp. 42–65; Joshi, 1987). But, of course, caring involves a relationship between at least two people. Descriptions of caring from the perspective of the carer tend to concentrate, not surprisingly, on the often considerable burdens that caring entails and sometimes present a picture of the elderly person 'taking over' the household (see, for example, Nissel and Bonnerjea, 1982, p. 40). While important advances have been made recently in documenting the previously latent role of carers (Oliver, 1983), we still know very little about caring from the perspective of the elderly person being cared for. This deficiency has been redressed to a considerable extent by the present research.

Elderly people do not give up their independence easily; with few exceptions they are reluctant subjects in caring and dependency. Determination often overcomes severe physical handicap (Townsend, 1963, p. 60): indeed this resilience may itself be the cause of some strain in caring relationships. Elderly people desire, often more than anything else, the preservation of their independence yet, at the same time, they usually want to remain in contact with their relatives. This common attitude has been described, in a famous phrase, as 'intimacy at a distance' (Rosenmayer and Kockeis, 1963). Two-or three-generation households require considerable adjustments on the part of elderly people as well as their kin (Williams, 1979, p. 49) especially, as we show in the following chapter, since it is as likely to be kin who join the elderly person's household as vice versa. In addition the flow of care and tending is not only one way towards elderly people; they are themselves the providers of care for other elderly people and sometimes for younger people (see Chapter 4). Thus in one study it was found that 30 per cent of the elderly were receiving help from others of their generation (Green, Creese and Kanfert, 1979). Elderly people also provide a great deal of practical help to their children, including child care, shopping, cleaning and cooking (see Chapter 4 and Townsend, 1963; Butcher and Crosbie, 1978; Hunt, 1978). Indeed reciprocity remains an important feature of the relationship between elderly people and their families, and inability to reciprocate creates a reluctance to accept help (see Chapters 4 and 6 and Townsend, 1963, p. 70).

The dual approach to the analysis of caring we have adopted in this book suggests that it can be a difficult and rewarding experience for *both* carers and elderly people. Rather than concentrating on the needs of one group over the other – which can result in inequitable policy proposals (see, for example, Finch, 1984) – this sort of analysis indicates that both share a common interest in opposing the current organisation and practice of 'community care' which is instrumental in imposing dependency on carers and elderly people alike (Walker, 1982c). The failure to provide alternative sources of community-based care, or to support the caring activities of families adequately, removes any effective choice for carers and elderly people and increases the likelihood of tension between relatives and breakdown on the part of carers. The majority of elderly people are opposed to residential accommodation which, not surprisingly, they associate with loss of independence (Chapter 7 and Tobin and Lieberman, 1976, p. 19). But as long as the whole responsibility for care continues to fall on one person, this prospect is likely to face increasing numbers of elderly people. For their part, women have borne the often considerable physical and mental strain of caring and tending alone for far too long. In order to understand why this unsatisfactory pattern of care has developed it is necessary to examine the role of the state in the care of elderly people and the promotion of family care. As a first step we look at the relationship between the formal sector and the informal sector of care.

The formal and the informal systems of care

Of the four sectors from which welfare services might be obtained – statutory, voluntary, informal and commercial sectors (Wolfendon, 1978) – the informal sector (the world of relatives, friends and neighbours) is distinguished most sharply from the other sectors both in terms of principles of organisation and also its suitability for fulfilling different types of need. Indeed, P. Abrams (1978a) suggested that the differences between the formal and informal sectors were so great as to place considerable difficulties in the way of attempts to integrate the two.

First, he pointed to the differences in the criteria for eligibility for services: informal care is directed towards a particular person on the basis of their social relationships with others – care for a mother, a sister or a friend, for example – whereas formal (statutory or voluntary) care is organised to be delivered to all people in particular, defined categories of need.

Second, in the formal sector, acceptable types of intervention and outcome are prescribed, whereas in the informal sector these kinds of intervention are more diffuse and less well specified. Of course, this does not imply that there are no 'rules' operating in the world of informal care. On the contrary, it is clear that there are complex sets of social expectations and obligations which influence much of the activity in the informal sector and which will be considered at more length later. But it is characteristic of the rules of such social exchange that they are not well specified (in particular they are not found in written form), and that, although social sanctions may be imposed upon those who do not comply, there are no formal procedures for obtaining redress against those felt to have failed to discharge their obligations.

The disadvantages of formal services are those associated with large bureaucratic organisations: developing rigidity of approach, inflexibility (particularly with atypical cases), difficulties in achieving a quick response and the professionals' usurpation of power. At the same time, of course, the resources and expertise of such organisations are often valued by consumers. Typically within bureaucratic structures there are rules decreeing equal treatment of equal cases, and agents of the organisation, or bureau professionals, do not enter into direct exchange relationships with clients or, strictly, perform additional services for some clients only (P. Blau, 1964).

The personally-directed nature of informal care provides the key to both its advantages and disadvantages in comparison with formal care. Since such care is specifically directed towards certain people, others with similar needs may receive no assistance. So, for example, P. Abrams (1978a, p. 3) suggested that by the standards of the providers of formal sector services the world of informal care is 'something of a disaster' because it does not secure equal provision for all cases in particular categories of need, and neither can it adequately meet the needs of all those who do receive its services. However, P. Abrams (1977, 1978a) expounded the theme that care provided by the informal sector is qualitatively different from (and superior to) formal sector care. He argued that because informal care is embedded in pre-existing social relationships it has a different meaning (from formal care) for recipients. Caring for someone in a practical way is seen as an expression of caring *about* them as an individual. Furthermore, although there may be no obvious difference in the extrinsic benefits supplied in a particular caring exchange – commodities such as meals, shopping, cleaning and so on – it is likely that those who receive services will have preferences among the suppliers of such commodities which will depend on the *intrinsic* benefits – such as emotional warmth, affection, interest – expected from potential suppliers.

One implication of this distinction is that, unless no importance at all is attached to consumer preferences, the appropriate relationships between different sectors of welfare provision cannot be determined without taking account of the importance to recipients of intrinsic benefits to be derived from receiving services from one source rather than another. Equally the existence of such intrinsic benefits also places limits upon the applicability of any framework based strictly upon economic exchange. But an acknowledgement of the effects of their existence is essential to an understanding of informal sector provision. In short, the 'mixed economy of welfare' is nowhere near as simple as the economic model its advocates have in mind (Beresford and Croft, 1984; Walker, 1984b).

As we indicated earlier, the assertion of the superiority of family care cannot be accepted without question. In the first place family care entails a grossly unequal gender division in tending and caring activities (a point we return to in the next section).

Second, it must be acknowledged that within families it is possible for people to experience the most damaging and emotionally destructive relationships, which can have lasting negative effects upon their lives. As we show in Chapters 6 and 7 the past history of the relationship between an elderly person and their children may not always have been one of mutual exchanges of assistance and affection. Family care can be among the very best or the very worst experiences that human beings can devise for each other (see the example on p. 248).

Third, there is some evidence that elderly recipients of state-provided services see these as an expression of caring *about* them. For example, a study of meals-on-wheels from the point of view of the elderly recipients concluded that the symbolic function (that of demonstrating that people were cared *about*) was the main function being fulfilled by the service (M. L. Johnson, 1981). It is also the case that agents of the state can provide the intrinsic rewards of affection and interest. The home-help service is often mentioned in this respect (Hunt, 1968; Bayley *et al.*, 1983), when accounts are given of the development of personalised commitment to individual clients. This includes such activities as returning to or from work and taking the elderly person into the worker's own home. These examples should make clear, however, what appears to be an important distinction between effective rewards and the more instrumental activities that form the basis of the contract between home helps and their employers. It may be that, to be recognised as genuine, the affective benefits offered in the caring exchange must be given freely rather than being coerced or required as part of the job. If warmth or affection are seen to be expressed in the expectation of some promised reward then this compromises the genuineness of such expressions (P. Blau, 1964). However, it is most likely that home helps behave in this informal way only with selected clients: they personalise their service to these few only, and thus only by stepping outside their formal role as agents of the state (in which all clients should be treated equally) can they offer genuine informal social rewards.

Since the value of intrinsic benefits associated with any caring exchange depends on the meaning attached to such activity by the recipient (and this crucially depends on the perceived motivation of the giver), does it follow that such benefits can only be generated as a by-product of state services and never directly generated by any third party? The belief that this is the case has contributed to arguments against the professionalisation or 'colonisation' of the informal sector (Caplan, 1974; P. Abrams, 1980; see also Bayley, 1982), on the grounds that to formalise the informal destroys those features which make it so uniquely valuable to recipients. But, as we have indicated already, affective benefits are sometimes associated with formal service delivery. Moreover it is not necessary for practical services to be delivered by informal network members in order for such affective benefits to be received. Affective benefits can be delivered independently even though, within a particular caring relationship, the expressive and instrumental aspects of caring may be inextricably mixed. Warmth, affection and interest do not have to come wrapped around practical tasks, and neither is the performance of practical tasks necessarily accompanied by such expressions in either the informal or the formal sectors.

The survey of people aged 75 or over and their carers in Sheffield provides a number of examples which illustrate that there is no necessary relationship between the quality of family relationships and the provision of practical assistance (Chapter 6). Certainly there were children who helped despite reporting a poor relationship with their parent, both in the present and in the past, although there is evidence (supported by similar results in Levin, Sinclair and Gorbach, 1985) that this is experienced as a particularly stressful situation by carers, and is more likely to end in the parents' admission to residential care (Gilleard *et al.*, 1984).

On the other hand, there were also examples where people did not provide help despite feeling that they had a generally good relationship. This might be a consequence of the result of differing expectations about the appropriateness of family help within particular tasks. One in three middle-class people over 74 in Sheffield were employing paid domestic helps and perhaps felt, as one commented: 'I wouldn't expect my family to provide domestic help.' Of course, to argue that feelings towards someone and the provision of practical help *may be* independent is not to deny that involvement in the process of helping may change the feeling of helpers and helped over a period of time.

The state and family care

How can the state influence the provision of tending by families?
A variety of direct methods exist, varying from outright coercion
(for example, prosecution for neglect of children) through to the
provision of incentives, such as tax allowances or additional
benefits for those caring for dependents. The state can influence
family help less directly by the way it organises and provides
services to individuals in need and the assumptions it makes about
the nature and availability of such assistance (Moroney, 1976;
Land, 1978; Walker, 1981a). Finally, the state's general economic
and social policies set the framework of material and social
conditions within which individual families find themselves. It was
a recognition of the importance of the social and economic context
within which caring relations are reproduced which led one of us to
conclude that care *by* the community depends to some extent on
care *for* the community (Walker, 1982b).

In the field of the care of the elderly coercion has rarely proved
successful. The idea that the state could compel families to offer
love and gratitude to their elderly parents was given little credence
even by the administrators of the Poor Law. They commented,
regretfully, on the fact that even the most obvious needs of elderly
people failed to call forth sufficient informal support, despite
coercive measures:

> if the deficiencies of parental and filial affection are to be
> supplied by the parish, and the natural motives to the exercise of
> those virtues are thus to be withdrawn, it may be proper to
> endeavour to replace them, however imperfectly, by artificial
> stimulants, and to make fines, distress warrants, or imprison-
> ment act as substitutes for gratitude and love. The attempt
> however is hardly ever made. (Checkland, 1974, p. 115)

This emphasises the fact that if informal care is unwillingly given
it loses its special qualities and can no longer claim to be a superior
form of care. Indeed in this situation it can become rapidly
destructive of relationships, inducing resentment and guilt in both
giver and receiver.

The impact of formal care on relationships

The state occupies a central role in the maintenance of the present pattern of care which is dominated by the family. Despite the existence of community care policies for the last 30 years, the direct involvement of the state in the caring functions of the family is still relatively small. Social services departments are primarily concerned with crisis intervention, short-term support and, in cases of severe breakdown, long-term residential care. The state is obviously committed to a system whereby the bulk of support for the disabled elderly is provided by relatives (DHSS, 1978, p. 6; Fowler, 1984; Moore, 1987). In doing so it tacitly supports the gender division in caring. Without alternative forms of community-based care and while work and caring roles are still strictly divided by gender, women are effectively coerced into caring, often because of guilt.

From the late sixteenth century to the nineteenth century, the primacy of family responsibility was enshrined in the Poor Laws; and the fear that state help, if too easy to obtain, would undermine family relationships was ever present. The words of an Assistant Poor Law Commissioner in 1834 have a familiar ring today 'social ties ... [are] now in the course of rapid extinction by the Poor Law' (for present-day comparison see p. 2). From his study of the evidence Anderson (1977) reached the opposite conclusion: 'the [legal] obligation to assist was often a source of tension between parents and children throughout the nineteenth century. The "quality" of relationships was thus clearly worsened in these cases'; whereas: 'The removal of tension-inducing cash support functions, enables the family to provide effective and idiosyncratic functions which are difficult to bureaucratise.'

Most American studies have revealed a preference that long-term financial assistance to the elderly should be provided by the state. However, the concern that 'state interference' may threaten family ties by taking over the functions of the family seems to have persisted even in the area of financial help (see, for example, Kreps, 1977). Like the earlier Poor Law fears this appears to be based on the assumption that intergenerational dependence is essential for the maintenance of family ties. Similar concerns have affected the construction of social policies in Britain: how to strike

an appropriate balance between assuming too many responsibilities, and thus weakening family ties, or offering too little help,
thus causing the family to collapse under the unrelieved burden of
providing care (Land and Parker, 1978). The result is that the
organisation and distribution of social services has played a key
role in reproducing traditional dependencies within the family,
based on age and gender.

Community care and elderly people

An explicit policy of 'community care' for elderly people with
disabilities has been in operation for more than 25 years. In 1958
the Minister of Health stated that the 'underlying principle of our
services for the old should be this: that the best place for old
people is in their own homes, with help from the home services if
need be' (quoted in Townsend, 1962, p. 196). This principle has
been reaffirmed by successive ministers and official documents
(see, for example, Ministry of Health, 1963; DHSS, 1981a). In
practice, however, this policy was compromised from the outset by
the absence of strategic planning to achieve it, the failure to devote
sufficient resources to achieve it and the reluctance of the state
genuinely to share care with families (Walker, 1982b). Today the
allocation of resources by residential care, which takes over half of
the annual budget, compared with the one-fifth spent on community care. The mid-1970s DHSS guidelines on community care
services (which are themselves below independent estimates of the
need for services) are nowhere near being achieved. For example,
the supply of home helps for those over 65 is only half of the
guideline figure of 12 per 1 000 population. Provision has increased
over the post-war period, but not in line with need: the jam has
been spread thinner (Henwood and Wicks, 1984; Walker, 1985a).
For example, an expansion in the coverage of the home-help
service has been carried out at the expense of the amount of
service received by each elderly person. In the official survey
carried out in 1976, 42 per cent of the elderly had home help visits
more than weekly compared with 64 per cent in 1962 (Bebbington,
1980).

In 1976, 12 per cent of those elderly people living in the
community classified as being in moderate, considerable or severe

need were not receiving a home-help service; 16 per cent did not receive a visit from a community nurse at least once a fortnight; and 15 per cent did not receive meals on wheels at least once a week (Bebbington, 1981, pp. 66–7). Furthermore, the definition of 'need' in this instance included only those living alone and who did not already get help with domestic care and, therefore, excluded all those elderly people being cared for by relatives and others. The results of these shortfalls in services, the failure to increase resources in line with need and the assumption that if elderly people are being cared for they do not need statutory services, is that female relatives continue to be the main – and usually the sole – source of care for disabled elderly people.

The state occupies a dual role in relation to community care: it may provide direct support where this is absolutely necessary, but its main concern is to ensure the continuance of the prime responsibility of the family for the support and care of its own members. So, as Moroney (1976, p. 213) has pointed out, by presenting traditional family responsibilities for dependents and the division of labour between the sexes and between generations as 'normal' or 'natural' 'the state supports and sustains these relationships without appearing intrusive, thus preserving the illusion that the family is a private domain'. Thus women and families continue to bear the social costs of dependency and the privatisation of family life protects 'normal' inequalities between family members (Land, 1978, p. 213) and constrains the demand on public social services. In contrast to the constant public debate about expenditure on the social services, the privatised costs of caring to the family are rarely discussed publicly.

As well as giving implicit support to the gender division of caring, the state operates more openly to sustain it by the differential distribution of social services support (Finch and Groves, 1983). Regarding social security too, excluding domestic tasks from the attendance allowance and, until 1986, excluding married women caring for their husbands from receiving the invalid care allowance, reinforces the social division of care and ensures that many carers do not receive any payment for doing so. Two assumptions underlying social policy with regard to the family, as Land (1978, p. 268) has shown, are that men are not expected to look after themselves as much as women are and that men are not able to look after elderly infirm relatives. This aspect of what has been referred to as the 'naturally negotiated' relationship between the old and young in the family (M. L. Johnson, 1972) consequently takes place within the context of the firm expectation that female relatives will be the principal carers. Underlying the construction of dependency relationships within the family, therefore, is a fundamental conflict between women and men (Walker, 1983a).

Recent developments in community care and other government policies are likely to increase the burden of care that falls on the family while, at the same time, reducing the capacity of families to provide care (for a full account see Walker, 1982b, 1985b). The Conservative government's response to the major expansion in the need for care outlined in Chapter 1 has been, on the one hand, to reduce the proportion of public expenditure going to the personal social services and so restrict the ability of these services to cope with increasing demand and, on the other hand, to emphasise the traditional role of the family and to encourage the expansion of voluntary and other unpaid help and private formal provision. The words of the Prime Minister with regard to the family were quoted on p. 1, and echoes of it can be found in recent speeches by three successive Secretaries of State for Social Services (Jenkin, 1981; Fowler, 1984; Moore, 1987).

This anti-welfare state ideology has been translated directly into policy towards the elderly: 'it is the role of public authorities to sustain and, where necessary, develop – but never to displace' informal and voluntary care and support; and 'Care *in* the community must increasingly mean care *by* the community' (DHSS, 1981a, p. 3). While it is placing a great deal of reliance on the family to provide care to elderly relatives, the government's own economic and social policies are undermining the ability of families to provide care and reinforcing the gender division of care. In particular the growth of poverty and advent of mass unemployment are putting family ties and relationships under enormous strain. The conflict between the family and the state, or more specifically, between elderly people and female kin and the state, is now more explicit than at any previous period in Britain's post-war history.

False assumptions underlying social policy

Two implicit assumptions underlying the relationships between the family and the state in the provision of care and tending require critical scrutiny. It is assumed that state help, once offered, would inevitably be preferred (at least by those giving help); and, second, that the voluntary sector can fill the care gap created by the failure of the personal social services to keep pace with need.

In practice, those elderly people receiving services from their families are *not* anxious to apply for state help instead. In our survey of elderly people and their families less than 10 per cent of those in receipt of weekly practical assistance from relatives or (in a few cases) neighbours said that they would prefer such tasks to be performed by a home help (see Chapter 8). Most people preferred their existing family help even if a home help would have been available. What of those few who would have preferred a home help? Most frequently these elderly people did not exactly prefer formal help but wished to relieve a perceived burden upon their family carer. Most elderly people felt (and their carers agreed) that family members were the right people to help them.

Upon what basis are decisions made that informal help is too much trouble for family carers and therefore potentially damaging to the quality of relationships? Clearly in each individual case a complex of normative and structural factors are at work. Those factors identified by carers were: the personal capacity of the potential carers in terms of physical and mental health and necessary material resources; the pressure or absence of other prior informal obligations, such as a sick husband, child or dependant parent (in the case of a daughter-in-law); and the quality of the relationship with the elderly person. Where there is a choice between family members, decisions about who should help will incorporate normative judgements based on gender-role expectations about the appropriateness of the particular tasks required, and the importance which may be attached to other informal obligations. For example, it may be that a man's obligations to his immediate family are assumed to include remaining in full-time employment, whilst a woman's may not be (see Chapter 5).

This brief summary of analyses in Chapters 5 and 6 should serve to convey the fact that seeking formal help is only the final stage of a dynamic process in which the available sources of informal assistance have all been considered, and the costs associated with them evaluated, *before* any approach is made to statutory services for assistance. Moreover, judgements about the quantity of informal help available are made by those with the most detailed and exhaustive knowledge of the informal network: that is, the members themselves.

Current allocation practices in the social services show little respect for, or insight into, these prior processes in the informal sector. We have noted already that statutory services are often delivered, and to some extent rationed, on the assumption that other family members, particularly daughters, should help in preference to agents of the state, especially in tasks where no recognised professional expertise is required. Such services as home help and auxiliaries to assist with bathing have been denied to, reduced or withdrawn from elderly people who have local relatives, particularly daughters, available (Hunt 1978; and Chapter 8). Also it has been clearly shown that elderly people living with relatives are less likely to receive statutory help, no matter what their level of dependency (Charlesworth, Wilkin and Durie, 1984; Levin, Sinclair and Gorbach, 1985).

Although every effort should be made to counter the disadvantages of bureaucratic service delivery, it is important not to lose sight of the fact that the provision of state services can strengthen family ties. Furthermore, it is important to remember that many statutory services are highly valued by recipients. One example is given in the National Institute for Social Work study of people caring for elderly mentally infirm relatives or neighbours (Levin, Sinclair and Gorbach, 1983). Carers who received practical help in the form of home help day care or community nursing services were *less* likely to suffer stress and more likely still to have the dependent person at home than people who did not receive such assistance. Additionally, it should be noted that the impersonal nature of help delivered through a bureaucratic structure may be seen as an advantage by some of those receiving help. Agents of an outside organisation are detached from past family quarrels or disputes, and have no future expectations of return for services rendered. Equally, from the point of view of carers, there are sometime, situations in which an elderly person behaves less reasonably towards family members than towards agents of the state. A number of carers in the Sheffield study indicated occasions on which their elderly relative 'put on a different face', generally a more co-operative face, for people from outside agencies. Other evidence (Boyd and Woodman, 1978) suggests that this can be carried to the extreme in situations in which an elderly person's capacity for, or willingness to display, independence drops dramatically as soon as they are returned from a hospital or residential home to the care of their relatives.

We are not suggesting that only relatives promote dependency, whilst statutory services encourage independence. On the contrary, some domiciliary services are delivered in a way which does create dependency and effectively hinders people from functioning independently (Walker, 1981a; 1982c; Carpenter and Paley, 1984). Thus improving the quantity and quality of care for elderly people is not simply a matter of increasing the amount of statutory services.

Turning to the second assumption underlying policy, particularly recent developments, it is clear that the potential of the informal sector to take on additional caring responsibilities has been over-estimated. Within the family those regarded by both elderly people and carers as the most appropriate persons to provide help are already doing so and often working beyond their normal capacity. Beyond the family, friends, neighbours and volunteers are undoubtedly an important resource for care, but they cannot be regarded as a *substitute* for either family care or formal services. In some close-knit communities the contribution of friends and neighbours to care can be significant, but even in this setting it is secondary to the contribution of the family (Seyd *et al.*, 1985; Wenger, 1984). Other research in more typical locations confirms that neighbours and friends rarely fulfil a principal carer role for disabled elderly people needing considerable daily support (Charlesworth, Wilkin and Durie, 1984; Tinker, 1984; and Chapter 8). Similarly volunteers are not an adequate substitute for family or formal care and, in fact, formal services are required in order to make the most of voluntary help (Hatch, 1980).

Conclusion: the conflict between family and state

The recent direction of government economic and social policy has increased the likelihood of female kin being expected to care for elderly relatives in need. At a time when the numbers of very elderly people requiring care are rising and the pool of family carers shrinking, albeit slowly, the government has reduced the already meagre resources for community-based formal care. In addition to a growth in the coverage of family care the burdens on individual carers are likely to be increased. We are witnessing the heightening of a major conflict between the state and the people. The needs of both elderly people and family carers are not being adequately met by policy. The strains and tensions that exist in a caring relationship which is imposed on two relatives or which is conducted in an atmosphere of great physical and emotional tribulation, affect *both* sides of the relationship. While the state sustains a casualty-orientated system of care it is effectively supporting the unequal division of labour in care and the detrimental impact this has on carers and elderly people alike. The starting-point for the development of responsible policy, which seeks to provide an alternative to this unacceptable approach to the care of elderly people, is a better understanding of the caring relationship. That is the task we embark on over the next six chapters, and we return to the public policy issues in Chapter 9.

3

Elderly People and their Families

The structure of an elderly person's family – including such factors as marital status, number of siblings, number of children and grandchildren and the age and sex of children and other relatives – is fundamental to an understanding of the pattern of family relations within which the elderly person is located (Townsend, 1963, pp. 232–55). Thus in a large-scale study of elderly people in Britain, Denmark and the USA, family structure was found to be more important than cultural factors in explaining variations between different families in their organisation and behaviour (Shanas *et al.*, 1968, p. 165). Moreover, the availability of family care for sick or disabled elderly people is a function of family structure and the sort of family relations that partly arise out of it. (This is not to say that family structure determines precisely *who* it is that provides care to an elderly relative, which is the subject of Chapter 5.) Thus answers to questions such as how often elderly people see different relatives should be of direct relevance to policy makers and planners interested in assessing the potential supply of family care and, in turn, demand for formal services, as well as to sociologists and others interested in ageing and the nature of family relations in old age.

The changing structure of the family and the implications of these changes for social policy were discussed in Chapters 1 and 2. Our purpose here is to review the structure of the families of elderly people and to examine its relationship to social contact between elderly people and their relatives. This is a necessary preliminary to the discussion of family care in subsequent chapters because in order to provide this care there must, of course, be contact; in general, the provision of help and care by relatives is preceded by and built on a history of family relationships and contacts.

33

The main focus of this chapter turns first to a description of the size, structure and organisation of the extended family, and this is followed by an assessment of the extent to which the extended family is integrated. Finally, we examine the factors that influence patterns of contact between elderly people and their families.

Family size and composition

The method by which information was collected about the 1 221 relatives of the elderly people in the sample was outlined in Chapter 1. All children and up to three siblings had to be included irrespective of the degree of contact with, or feelings about, them on the part of the elderly person. Among other relatives, those with no contact or no close relationship were selected out. Details of all relatives obtained in this way are shown in Table 3.1. More sisters were listed than brothers, but this is understandable in the light of differing death rates. It is less obvious why nieces should outnumber nephews by two to one. A similar gender difference was observed for cousins. The latter result does seem to imply a greater propensity to keep up contact with, or feel close to, female relatives. In the case of brothers-in-law and sisters-in-law, where death rates might also be relevant, brothers-in-law were out-numbered by four to one.

Children were the largest group of relatives listed and, as we shall see in subsequent chapters, they were by far the most

Table 3.1 *Relatives listed by elderly people*

Relationship	Total number	Listed (%)
Child	498	41
Sibling	363	30
Grandchild	96	8
Nephew/niece	97	8
Stepchild	28	2
Step sibling	13	1
Sibling-in-law	70	6
Cousin	33	3
Other	23	2
Total	1 221	100

Table 3.2 *Elderly people and their children*

Children	Elderly people number	(%)
None	79	26
One daughter only	37	12
One son only	46	15
Daughters only	26	9
Sons only	13	4
At least one daughter and one son	98	33

important group of care-giving relatives. One in four elderly people had no living children (this is somewhat lower than the proportion nationally), and only just under half (46 per cent) had more than one child. Table 3.2 gives an idea of the family types encountered.

It should be evident from Table 3.2 that just over half of all elderly people (54 per cent) had at least one daughter, and one-third of elderly people had at least one child of each sex. Over 80 per cent of those with children listed other relatives as well as their children, but this meant that one in five of all respondents listed children as their only relatives. Seven people (2 per cent) listed no relatives at all.

With respect to class and family size similar results were found to those reported in the three-nation study (Shanas *et al.*, 1968). Middle-class (non-manual) elderly people were more likely to have no children (36 per cent) than working-class (manual) ones (23 per cent). They were also less likely to have more than one child (33 per cent compared with 52 per cent).

In all the elderly people listed 526 children. This included 28 step-children whom the elderly people thought of as their children. It seemed that the adult children of a partner married later in life might not be listed as the elderly person's relatives, especially if contact was infrequent (this became evident in one carer inter-view). Clearly the extent to which obligations are transferable in reconstituted families is an area of considerable interest, but little except anecdotal evidence can be derived from the present study because numbers are small and evidence (for example, of the length of periods of co-residence) is insufficiently detailed. The average age of children was 48 years. The youngest child listed was 21, the oldest 69. Seven per cent of children were themselves over 60 years of age.

The majority of children were in some form of employment although daughters were more likely than sons to work part time (26 per cent compared with 2 per cent). Conversely 71 per cent of sons were in full-time employment compared with 28 per cent of daughters. About 5 per cent of children were themselves retired. One-third of daughters were described as housewives. In a small number of cases (7 per cent) the elderly person did not know the employment status of their child. One in ten sons were unemployed but, of course, unemployment, or the threat of redundancy, also affected some daughters, sons-in-law, daughters-in-law and grandchildren.

Household structures and family relationships

Table 3.3 shows the different kinds of households that elderly people lived in according to their age, sex and marital status. This gives a first indication of the organisation of the elderly person's immediate family. Before going on to examine the proximity of

Table 3.3   *Percentage of elderly people living in different types of household*

| Age, sex and marital status | Lone person | Couple | Joint households | | Total | Number |
			Single person + other(s)	Married couple + other(s)		
Age						
75–9	44.0	41.7	11.4	3.0	100	168
80–4	60.5	21.0	9.9	6.2	100	81
85+	65.1	18.6	16.3	0.0	100	43
Sex						
Male	28.0	54.8	9.8	7.6	100	93
Female	62.8	22.1	13.5	1.5	100	199
Marital status						
Single person	56.5	4.3	34.8	4.3	100	23
Married	—	90.3	1.0	8.8	100	103
Widowed, divorced or separated	83.6	—	16.4	0.0	100	165
All elderly people	51.6	31.7	12.9	3.9	100	306

the extended family it is important to look at these types of household in more depth.

Living alone: is the family breaking up?

The majority of elderly people in our sample were living alone. In common with other national and international research, Table 3.3 illustrates the tendency for people to be living alone as age advances and, to a lesser extent, for them to live with relatives other than a spouse (Hunt, 1978, p. 14; Shanas *et al.*, 1968, p. 154). The main factor here was the impact of the loss of a spouse on household composition: nine out of ten single-person households were the result of bereavement.

This also had a direct bearing on the marked gender difference in types of household, with women being much more likely to live alone than men. The larger proportion of elderly single-person households in Sheffield than that found by Hunt in 1976 for the country as a whole (38.4 per cent) is the result of two main factors. The percentage of single elderly women in Sheffield is higher than in Britain as a whole. Second, largely due to the availability of a substantial stock of single-person council accommodation, single people in Sheffield are more likely to live alone than the average for the whole country.

There is a widespread trend in all industrial societies for fewer elderly people who have children to live with them. In 1962 Shanas and her colleagues found that just over two-fifths of single, widowed and divorced people aged 65 and over were living alone (Shanas *et al.*, 1968, p. 156). For those with living children the proportions varied between one-third and one-half depending on the number and sex of the children. A significantly higher proportion of elderly people lived with their children in Britain (42 per cent) than in Denmark (20 per cent) or the USA (28 per cent). More recent research has found that joint households consisting of elderly people living with their children are an increasingly rare phenomenon, a finding that appears to be common to all industrial societies (Troll 1971; Fengler, Danigelis and Little, 1983, p. 358).

Differences in living arrangements do not necessarily imply differences in the experience of loneliness, and neither does living alone mean that old people do not remain in close contact with their children and other relatives. Despite the fact that the evidence points in the opposite direction, it is the change in household composition during the post-war period that has led to claims that the family is breaking up and the myth that elderly people are being abandoned by their families to cope alone (see Chapter 1). These are very widespread and influential beliefs (Hendricks and Hendricks, 1977, p. 287) holding sway, not least, among policy makers, planners and practitioners in several different countries (Moroney, 1976, p. 125; Shanas, 1979).

The false assumption underlying these myths – that changes in household structure over time mean changes in social relations and emotional bonding – has been exposed by an important series of research studies in the 1950s and 1960s, starting with those by Townsend (1963) in the Bethnal Green area of London and Shanas (1962) in the USA. This research showed that, rather than being outcasts from the family, where they could afford to elderly people *chose* to live alone in order to maintain both their own and their children's independence. At the same time, while living in the same household less often than hitherto, children were likely to settle nearby to their parents and to keep in regular contact with them. Thus the myths that elderly people have become alienated from their families is based partly on a simple confusion between 'household' and 'family'. Separate households may be more common than in the past but this does not mean that family members are less close emotionally or less happy. As Shanas (1979, p. 3) has bluntly pointed out, 'Some old people, with or without children, even have the temerity to live alone.' Of course, as we noted in Chapter 2, demographic changes over the same period have meant that more and more elderly people, and particularly elderly women, are surviving without any living relatives. But for those elderly people with children, the phrase coined by Rosenmayer and Kockeis (1963) more than 25 years ago has summed up the consistent finding of research into the attitudes of elderly people towards the family: their preference for 'intimacy at a distance'. Whether or not this still holds true will be discussed in the latter half of the chapter; for the moment it is important to emphasise that the large number of single-person households among elderly people is a function of demographic changes and single or widowed elderly people's preference for living alone.

Living togethèr: the false assumption of dependency

Given the expressed preference of elderly people for independence and the long-term decline in the proportion living in joint households, an interesting question posed by Table 3.3 is why did some elderly people share their household with someone other than a spouse? Just over one in six elderly people in our sample were living in joint households. Four of them shared with someone who was not related, but by far the most common situation encountered (nine out of ten) was sharing a household with relatives. Again this is a phenomenon surrounded by assumptions about the 'burden' of increasing dependency that elderly people present to their relatives and, therefore, the similar burden they imply for society at large, the common assumption being that when elderly people become too disabled to care for themselves, or the burden of providing care from outside the household becomes too great, they move in with relatives (where space allows) to receive informal 'residential' care. In fact, as the following data show, a move by a disabled elderly person to join relatives was the *exception* rather than the rule in determining the formation of joint households.

Table 3.4 shows the different types of joint household we encountered. Men were slightly more likely to share a household than women but, because women so greatly outnumber men at this age, it was still the case that in three out of five joint households the elderly person was female.

How did elderly people come to be sharing a household with others and, in four out of five instances, sharing with children or grandchildren? Over half of all joint households started as all or part of the elderly person's nuclear family household; most often where a child (or more rarely, children) was still living in the parental home. The most common type of shared household, comprising one in three of such households, was a widowed elderly parent living with a single son or daughter (in one case, a single grandchild who had been brought up by the elderly person). In three instances the child living at home was mentally handicapped and unlikely ever to be capable of independent living.

Turning to the remaining group of shared households (just over two-fifths) which did not originate in the elderly person's nuclear

Table 3.4   *Percentage of elderly people living in different types of joint household*

Type of household	Percentage of people in joint households
Married couple	
with one or more children	20.4
with child and grandchild	2.0
Single, widowed or divorced	
with one child (or one grandchild)	34.7
with children	6.1
with married children	4.1
with child and grandchild(ren)	12.2
with same generation relatives	12.2
with non-relatives	8.2
Total	100
Number	49

family household, a move by the elderly person to join relatives was still *not* the rule. In fact it was more common to find that relatives had moved to join the elderly person (over half of those living with relatives). Four elderly people lived with non-related friends and two had moved at the same time as their relatives to a place which was new to both parties. In only 16 per cent of joint households (representing only 3 per cent of all elderly people in the sample) had the elderly person moved to join their relative's household. This contrasts with the small non-random study of shared households by Nissel and Bonnerjea (1982, p. 31) in which all the elderly people had moved to join their relatives.

What precipitated the formation of joint households? The most frequently mentioned event was the death of the elderly person's spouse (mentioned by two-fifths of elderly people whose joint household resulted from the amalgamation of two previously separate households), followed by the divorce of the relative (one-fifth of such households). Ill health of the elderly person was mentioned in only one case (4 per cent of amalgamated households and 2 per cent of all joint households).

According to those elderly people living in shared households, this arrangement had been proposed most frequently by relatives, next most often by others, such as a hospital social worker, and least often by the elderly people themselves. Moreover, nearly one in ten joint households were regarded as temporary rather than permanent.

Shared households thus resulted from a variety of social factors and needs and only rarely from the direct need for care or assistance on the part of elderly people. The mere observation that an elderly person is living with relatives cannot be taken to imply the existence of any particular pattern of care or interpersonal dependency within the household. Joint households do not mean that the elderly person is dependent on within-household relatives, although living with relatives might have some impact on the extent to which elderly people need assistance (p. 75; and Walker, 1982c, p. 127), and will certainly influence the delivery of formal services (see below and Chapter 8). Indeed, it appears that the most common form of dependency is that of relatives on elderly people for shelter. Shared living arrangements are not, in general, necessarily the end result of a process of increasing incapacity on the part of elderly people.

Although the formation of the majority of joint households was not the result of incapacity and the need for care or assistance on the part of the elderly person, differences in the pattern and receipt of care between recently formed households and those originating in the nuclear family household suggest that the former were in part a response to such needs. In the majority (55 per cent) of recently formed households most household tasks were done by other members of the household, compared with only one-third of long-standing households. While 73 per cent of those elderly people in households which started as the nuclear family household received at least weekly informal practical assistance of some kind, the proportion of those in more recently formed households was 95 per cent.

Whether or not the elderly person lived in a joint household with relatives was also a significant factor in the distribution of formal care. Only one elderly person in a joint household of any kind received any weekly statutory assistance, and in this case the person was sharing with someone who was not related.

Who were elderly people in joint households sharing accommodation with? Nearly three-quarters of relatives (excluding young grandchildren) were their own children. The majority of these (59 per cent) were daughters, the remainder being either sisters (and one sister-in-law), older independent grandchildren or the spouses of children.

Within shared households care and assistance was as widely divided between the sexes as that revealed in other studies (see, for example, Nissel and Bonnerjea, 1982, pp. 39–41). Female relatives were much more likely than male relatives to be providing assistance with personal care: 28 per cent of women compared with 5 per cent of men. They were also more likely than male relatives to be providing assistance with household tasks: 64 per cent compared with 31 per cent.

Attitudes towards joint households

The extent to which people are satisfied or dissatisfied with shared living arrangements deserves extensive study in its own right because with increasing age there is not only an increase in the proportion of people living alone, but also in those living with younger people (Hunt, 1978, p. 17). Thus, although they are a minority of all households containing elderly people, they are likely to increase in number in the future. In the context of our long main-stage interview it was not possible to probe in depth the elderly person's levels of satisfaction with joint living arrangements. In all but two cases, shared living meant precisely that: all meals were taken together and the elderly person had no separate sitting room or cooking facilities. There was only one instance, however, where the elderly person had to share a bedroom.

When questioned about the advantages and disadvantages of joint living for themselves and their families, very few respondents mentioned any disadvantages. One elderly person regretted the loss of independence, and the reduced contact with friends. In particular, she regretted that the money obtained from the sale of her home on widowhood was no longer, several years later, sufficient to enable her to purchase another home in which she might be independent. This is one illustration of the way in which the formation of a joint household can be an inflexible way of coping with a temporary period of incapacity and need for care. What starts as a temporary arrangement may be forced, by external factors, such as the inflation in house prices, into becoming a permanent one.

In order to gauge the strength of the respondent's desire to remain independent of their family's household(s) – that is, the distance across which intimacy has to be maintained – we asked those with at least monthly contact with any relative whether or not they would contemplate the idea of going to live with relatives. Excluding those with no living relatives or no regular contact with a relative (13 per cent), just over half said that they did *not* like the idea. Only one-fifth said they would not mind living with relatives, but one-third of those qualified the answer in some way, such as, 'only in the last resort'. Of the remainder, 9 per cent were already living with relatives and 7 per cent had mixed feelings.

Not surprisingly the proportion of those living with others (in most cases relatives) who said that they did not like the thought of living with relatives was much lower than for other types of household (20 per cent, compared with over half of those living alone or with a spouse). Partly as a result of this difference based on household structure there were significant differences in response according to marital status: 30 per cent of the single elderly people said they did not like the idea of living with relatives compared with 52 per cent of the married and 45 per cent of the widowed. There was no difference between men and women in their reluctance to live with relatives. However, there was some indication that this reluctance waned with increasing age (for both sexes). The strong desire to remain in a household independent of their relatives was also constant across all degrees of disablement. Perhaps most important as far as social policy is concerned was the fact that there was no significant enthusiasm on the part of severely disabled elderly people to live with their relatives: most wanted to remain spatially independent of them.

Proximity of the extended family

In view of the small proportion of elderly people living with members of their extended family, a better guide to the current structure of the extended family is the proximity of relatives in general and children in particular. Previous research has indicated that although joint households are now less prevalent than they were in the past (see p. 37 above), they have given way to a 'modified extended family' form in Western industrial societies (Troll, 1971) in which a high proportion of elderly people live near their relatives and especially their adult children. The three nations study, for example, found that while two-fifths of elderly people in Britain in 1962 shared the same household with an adult child, a further two-fifths were living within 30 minutes' journey time (Shanas *et al.*, 1968, p. 193). This tendency for children to live near to their elderly parents was strongest among working-class families (Shanas *et al.*, 1968, p. 240), with some adult children of middle-class parents tending to live much further away than those of working-class parents. The marked tendency for children to settle in the vicinity of their parents' home was also noted in the late 1950s (Rosenmayer and Kockeis, 1963, p. 413).

More recently Willmott (1986) has distinguished three main patterns of contemporary kinship outside the nuclear family: the 'local extended family' in which key relatives, especially women, are in daily contact; the 'dispersed extended family' comprising regular and fairly frequent contacts and the provision of support when needed; and the 'dispersed kinship network' which rests on the ties between relatives, such as parents and children, but the contact is less frequent than in the other two types and maintained by telephone or letter and by stop-over visits. Members of this last type of network do not give regular support but might be called upon in times of crisis (Willmott, 1986, pp. 26–7).

The results of our research show that, although elderly people are less likely to live with their children than they were 20 years ago, the extended family has not dispersed, and where children in our sample had moved away from the parental home they had not gone very far. Caution is necessary in comparing the results of the Sheffield research with the earlier cross-national survey not only because the former was based in one locality, but also because it concentrated on those aged 75 and over whereas the latter included all those aged 65 and over. Nevertheless we encountered a remarkable spatial concentration of relatives around the elderly person's place of residence. This applied particularly to children: 84 per cent (including 23 per cent living in the same household) of elderly people with children had their nearest child living within 30 minutes' journey time and a further 6 per cent between 30 minutes and one hour. But it also extended to other relatives as well: one-third of elderly respondents had all their listed relatives – that is, all children and step-children, up to three siblings or step-siblings and other relatives with whom the elderly person had at least monthly contact or felt especially close to emotionally – living within half-an-hour's journey time from them. Moreover, this clustering was notable for its depth as well as its coverage. Thus two-fifths of *all* children lived within 15 minutes' journey time from their elderly parents and nearly two-thirds within a 30 minute journey. Furthermore, three-quarters of all listed relatives lived in Sheffield or South Yorkshire.

This close proximity of relatives and elderly people can be explained partly by the fact that South Yorkshire is an area with lower than average levels of migration, where moves tend to be made within the county rather than out of it (South Yorkshire County Council, 1979, p. 87). Seven out of ten of the population of Sheffield have lived at their present address for at least five years. This compares with just over six out of ten of people in Great Britain as a whole (OPCS, 1973, p. 149).

Migration is highly correlated with social class and age (Harris, 1967) and, therefore, it was not surprising that the low level of migration was even more apparent among very elderly people: 70 per cent of those in our sample had lived in Sheffield all their lives (although some did not consider themselves to have been born in Sheffield: rather the city boundaries have been extended gradually until they were included). Those not born in Sheffield had lived there for an average of 50 years. This does not mean that the majority of respondents had lived in the same residence for all or virtually all their lives but, on average, people had lived in their present house or flat for 20 years.

Impact of moving on social contact

Geographical mobility, even within the same city or county, is assumed to have an adverse impact on social contact and, therefore, may be detrimental to the provision of care within the family (Moroney, 1976, p. 23). These assumptions have not been tested thoroughly and, although there are a number of anecdotes in circulation about the provision of care and assistance over great distances (including midnight or weekend dashes to the aid of elderly relatives) and the difficulties encountered by such relatives in being long-distance carers must not be minimised, these do seem to be confined to a small number of (primarily middle-class) families. They might be expected to cope better with the inconveniences in financial terms than less well-off families. Hard evidence about the experience of the bulk of families providing care and assistance to elderly relatives has been much less easy to find. Our data shows that for the majority of elderly people who have moved residence this has *not* resulted in a diminution of contact with relatives. Indeed, one important reason for moving is the desire to be nearer to relatives.

We asked those elderly people who had moved in the last 20 years whether, as a result, they now lived closer to or further away from their relatives. Nearly nine out of ten said that they lived the same distance away as before the move or nearer. Only 12 per cent said that the move had taken them further away from their relatives, representing 7 per cent of the total sample of elderly people. More importantly, a similarly large proportion (86 per cent) reported that they had more contact or about the same level of contact with relatives after they moved. Only 14 per cent of the movers – 8 per cent of the total sample – reported less contact after moving. The main reason given for lower levels of contact was the greater distance to travel in order to visit following the change of residence.

Percentages can be deceptive, of course. If we extrapolate these findings to the population of South Yorkshire as a whole some 5 000 people aged 75 and over, and nationally nearly a quarter of a million are in the position of experiencing less contact with relatives as a result of moving residence. Moreover, for the reasons outlined earlier, the national figure is likely to under-estimate the size of the problem. There is no doubt, then, that for a significant number of people (if only a small proportion of the total population over 75) moving can result in a reduction in social contact with relatives. The impact on the elderly people involved can be gauged from the discussion of data on loneliness below.

While moving home did not have much impact on the proximity to or levels of contact with relatives of the majority, it did seriously disrupt the elderly person's contact with their neighbours. It is this form of social contact, therefore, that is most affected by official slum clearance and rehousing policies. One-quarter of elderly people said they had more contact with neighbours following their move, two-fifths about the same and just over one-third reported less contact. The main reasons given for lower levels of contact with neighbours after moving were that the new neighbours or environment inhibited it or that the elderly people did not want to have any contact with their neighbours. In (rare) defence of environmental planners it can be pointed out that nearly twice as many elderly people (17 per cent of those who have moved and 8 per cent of the total sample) said that their new environment promoted contact with neighbours as those who felt inhibited by it. The fact remains, however, that for a significant proportion of elderly people, moving home had reduced their neighbourly contacts. This will have had some impact on the quality of social life experienced by those elderly people as well as reducing the pool of potential helpers in the neighbourhood. The fact that some of those who were rehoused by the council, following redevelopment or at the elderly person's own request, were allocated purpose-built accommodation with other very elderly people means that opportunities for such support were likely to have been reduced still further. In 1976 elderly people (65 plus) in Yorkshire and Humberside were twice as likely as those in most other regions to have moved to their present neighbourhood because that is where the council offered them accommodation (Hunt, 1978, p. 92), which is a reflection of the high proportion of public housing in the region.

In view of the importance of moving to the degree of contact of a small section of elderly people with their relatives and that of a much larger group with neighbours, the reasons for the elderly person moving in the first place are of some interest. These indicate a rather different focus to the analysis of occupational and social mobility which usually accompanies discussion of the 'breakup' of the family. Employment is an important factor in children moving away from their parents but, in the case of elderly people, if a change of address is not enforced it is likely to be made to facilitate contact with relatives or to enable the elderly person to continue to manage independently. The main reason given for moving by the three-fifths of elderly people that had done so in the previous 20 years was the demolition of their previous accommodation (28 per cent). One in six elderly people who had moved had done so to be nearer relatives. Similar proportions had moved because of their own or their spouse's health or because their previous house had been too large for them.

Notwithstanding the purely local factors – relatively low migration and the bus service – the clusters of elderly people and their children were remarkably close geographically. Thus the distances over which intimacy had to be maintained were not great. We now turn to the discussion of how far the opportunities for social contact provided by geographical proximity were taken up.

Social contact within families

The amount of contact elderly people have with their relatives is an important indicator of both the structural integration of elderly people within the extended family and, in turn, the potential for emotional and material assistance and support. We examine the content and quality of relationships in Chapter 5 and 6; here we concentrate on the quantity of contact as the first step in unravelling the caring relationship between elderly people and their families.

The frequency with which elderly people are visited by relatives has been shown previously to be higher in Yorkshire and Humberside than in any other region of England. In 1976 Hunt (1978, p. 95) found that 65 per cent of those aged 65 and over were visited at least weekly be a relative, compared with a national average of 54 per cent. Some years earlier Shanas and her colleagues (1968, p. 24) reported that 94 per cent of those in the same age group in Britain as a whole had seen either a child or, where no children were living, another relative during the previous week. On the face of it, therefore, there does seem to have been a decline in the amount of contact between elderly people and their relatives between the early 1960s and mid-1970s. But, by the early 1980s, we found no evidence that this had declined further and, on the contrary, encountered *higher* levels of social contact within families than Hunt had done in 1976.

For each relative listed (see p. 13) elderly people were asked the usual frequency of direct, face-to-face contact and indirect contact by letter or telephone, as well as the number of hours of contact during the previous week. More than one in three elderly people had at least one relative (excluding spouses) with whom they had daily contact (five times a week or more). A further two in every five had at least one relative with whom they had contact weekly. So, in all, three out of four elderly people had a minimum of one relative with whom there was face-to-face contact at least once a week. By this measure therefore, the majority of elderly people were not socially isolated.

This is a crucial finding because it suggests that the extended family remains almost as highly integrated, in terms of social interaction, as it was in the early 1960s, despite the decline in joint households and the assumed detrimental effects of occupational and social mobility. We know that research based on Sheffield will not be representative of every area of the country, but once local variations are taken into account there are sound reasons for believing that the findings of our research provide a better indication of the current state of family relationships in old age than did the official national survey conducted in the mid-1970s.

In the first place, the apparent discrepancy between the levels of social contact revealed by Hunt's (1978) national study and our own research cannot be explained by the unrepresentativeness of the latter. The close correspondence between our sample and census data was shown in Chapter 1. But if our results are representtive of Sheffield, is Sheffield unrepresentative nationally? We have already noted that social contact between elderly people and their relatives is higher than the national average in Yorkshire and Humberside. But the difference is not very large. In fact the main deviations (downwards) from the national average (54 per cent) were Greater London, where 45 per cent of elderly people received visits at least once a week, and the coastal 'retirement areas' where the proportion was 40 per cent (Hunt, 1978, p. 95). In other parts of the country between one-half and three-fifths received visits at least once a week.

Second, our research along with that of Shanas and her colleagues (1968) revealed a greater degree of contact with relatives than Hunt's research because the former collected information about *all* such contacts, whereas the latter was concerned with separate visits made by relatives and elderly people. Although information was collected by Hunt (1978, p. 101) on visits made by elderly people to relatives – and just over one-quarter of those aged 75 to 84 did so at least once a week – there are no data on total social contact. However, even if we assume a high proportion of reciprocal visiting, the overall amount of contact was likely to be somewhat higher than the estimate based solely on visits to elderly people made by relatives. Thus, for example, in common with the three-nation and Sheffield studies, Mark Abrams' (1978) large-scale survey of four contrasting urban areas in England also collected information on all social contacts and found a similarly high level of contact between elderly people and relatives. Thus 73 per cent of those aged 75 and over saw one of their children at least once a week, and this level of contact varied from 62 per cent in the south coast town of Hove to 87 per cent in the Midlands industrial town of Northampton (M. Abrams, 1978, p. 22, 25). An adjustment in the national survey results to take account of face-to-face contact resulting from visits by *both* relatives and elderly people would probably bring the total level of contact up to that revealed by other research, including our own.

Third, there were differences between the two surveys in the collection of data on social contacts. The information sought by the Sheffield study was more detailed than that in the more general national survey and, because of the differences in focus of the two studies, greater efforts were made by us to establish the precise amount of contact between elderly people and their relatives. Specific questions were asked about the frequency of contact, method of travel and journey time for each relative in turn; whereas in the national survey respondents were simply asked, 'How often do any of your relatives manage to visit you?' It is not clear how far elderly people distinguished between formal 'visits' and other forms of social contact (for example, joint outings for purposes such as shopping, or 'popping in'). Moreover, some elderly people may have regarded children and other relatives differently and therefore not included them in response to this question. The painstaking approach adopted by the Sheffield research is more likely to have uncovered all forms of contact than the more general one necessitated by an all-purpose national enquiry. The fact that the main difference in the frequency of social contact reported by the two studies was in weekly contacts rather than more frequent contacts reinforces the suspicion that the national survey did not record all forms of interaction with relatives.

Fourth, there were important differences in the composition of the two samples, which were likely to have influenced the findings about social contact. Most importantly elderly people in the Sheffield sample were older than those in the national one. Although the national study reported that age (and sex) made little difference to the frequency with which visits were received

(Hunt, 1978, p. 94), this is not borne out by other research (Shanas *et al.*, 1968, pp. 212–13; M. Abrams, 1978, pp. 22, 26). The main factor here is the tendency, demonstrated by the national survey itself (Hunt, 1978, p. 95), for widowed people to receive more visits from children than other groups. Because we concentrated on older age groups, the widowed and single elderly comprised a larger proportion of our sample than they did in Hunt's research based on the 65 and overs.

Together these factors help to explain the discrepancy between the results of Hunt's research in 1976 and that of Shanas and her colleagues in 1962, M. Abrams in 1977 and our own in 1982/3. They suggest strongly that the national survey underestimated the amount of social contact between elderly people and their families and that it is a particularly poor guide to such contacts between very elderly people and their families.

The results of this research demonstrate that the close geographical proximity of members of the extended family to elderly people is matched by a high frequency of contact between them. In quantitative terms at least it would appear to be the case that elderly people are highly integrated within their extended families and particularly so with their children. Thus we are able to establish the fact that findings of research carried out in the early 1960s and mid-1970s (Shanas *et al.*, 1968; M. Abrams, 1977) concerning the close contact between elderly people and their families still held good in the early 1980s. Moreover, we are able to go further than previous research in assessing the strength of the integration between elderly people and relatives by examining the nature of the relationships involved, and this is the subject of Chapters 5 and 6. But on the evidence presented so far it can be seen that, although the generations prefer to live apart, they still maintain frequent contact.

Variations in the frequency of contact with relatives

Within the general picture outlined in the previous section it is obvious that there will be variations between different groups of elderly people. For example, those living in the same household as their children in all probability will have a much greater amount of face-to-face contact than those living apart. The purpose of this

Table 3.5 *Frequency of contact between different groups of elderly people and their children (%)*

Characteristics of elderly person	Same household	Daily	3–4 per week	Children's frequency of contact 1–2 per week	1–2 per month	2–4 per year	Annually or less	Total	Number of children*
Marital status									
Married	5.3	11.6	4.8	26.1	21.7	20.3	10.1	100	207
Widowed, single, divorced	1.6	22.9	9.4	29.9	11.5	16.2	9.4	100	314
Age									
75–9	4.0	13.5	7.6	28.1	18.1	19.9	8.9	100	327
80–4	2.2	23.0	7.4	27.4	12.5	19.3	8.2	100	135
85+	0.0	32.8	6.3	26.6	7.8	11.0	15.6	100	64
Sex									
Male	5.6	18.6	6.8	20.3	14.7	22.0	11.8	100	177
Female	1.7	18.1	7.7	31.5	15.7	16.9	8.3	100	349
Social class									
Professional, managerial	(4.3)	(17.0)	(12.8)	(23.4)	(7.1)	(21.3)	(6.4)	100	47
Skilled, non-manual	1.3	13.9	6.3	24.1	12.7	31.6	10.1	100	79
Skilled manual	4.9	18.9	6.7	22.6	19.5	16.5	11.6	100	164
Semi-skilled and unskilled	1.8	19.6	6.7	34.7	13.8	16.0	7.6	100	225
Disability									
None	7.1	20.0	5.9	34.1	14.1	8.3	10.6	100	85
Slight	1.0	17.6	8.8	14.7	24.5	25.5	7.9	100	102
Minor	2.9	14.7	5.9	32.4	14.8	22.8	6.6	100	136
Appreciable	4.5	18.8	7.1	33.0	12.5	12.5	11.6	100	112
Severe	0.0	18.5	11.1	22.2	13.0	22.3	13.0	100	54
Very severe	(0.0)	(27.0)	(8.1)	(24.3)	(8.1)	(21.6)	(10.8)	100	37

*Total number of children of elderly people in the sample.

section is to examine the main factors underlying variations in the amount of contact between elderly people and their families. Family structure, age, sex, physical incapacity and social class have been shown previously to have some influence on the frequency of contact between elderly people and their families (Shanas, *et al.*, 1968, pp. 210–21; Hunt, 1978, p. 85), and we discuss each one in turn. The main details concerning contact between elderly people and their children are set out in Table 3.5.

Family structure and composition

As expected, single people had substantially less family contact than the married or widowed. Their average contact in the week prior to interview was 4.5 hours, compared with 11.5 hours for the married and just over 12.5 hours for the widowed (these figures exclude those elderly people who were living with relatives). Also predictably, total weekly contact hours for those without children were much lower than for those with children. In fact children were overwhelmingly the most important source of family contact for elderly people in the sample.

As Table 3.5 shows, face-to-face contacts between children and elderly parents were very frequent indeed: three in ten children of elderly people in the sample saw their parent three times a week or more, and well over half saw their parent at least once a week. These contacts were more frequent among the children of the widowed than those of the married elderly. This supports the findings of some previous research that widowed elderly people are certainly not more socially isolated than their married counterparts and, on the contrary, may have closer relations with their children (Lopata, 1979; Kohen, 1983).

If, in past times, one reason that parents had children was as a form of economic insurance against their own ill health or old age (Flandrin, 1979), it is clear today that if individuals want to look forward to frequent family contact in old age then having children is the surest way to realise that goal.

There has been very little research on sibling relationships in old age and especially little about the factors affecting the frequency of contact and closeness between siblings (Chappell, 1983, p. 81). We found that siblings were an important source of social contact, but frequency of contact with siblings was substantially lower than contact with children. Thus only 6 per cent of siblings were in daily face-to-face contact with their elderly brothers and sisters in the sample, and just over a quarter were in contact at least once a week. This corresponds to the finding in the USA that three in ten older people (65 and over) had seen a relative other than a child in the last week (Shanas, 1979) and underlines the point that, although contact with children is high, siblings are still an important source of social contact in old age.

Again there were differences in the frequency of contact between married and widowed, single and divorced elderly people and their siblings (see also Shanas, 1973) but not so marked as the differences in contact with children. Just over two out of ten of the siblings of married elderly people were in direct contact with them at least once a week compared with three out of ten of the siblings of the widowed, single and divorced.

There was no evidence that those with low frequencies of contact with children had more contact on average with siblings. It does not appear, therefore, that contact with siblings compensates to any degree for lack 'of contact with children. (It is worth emphasising that a similarly high proportion of the elderly person's siblings as their children lived in Sheffield or South Yorkshire: 70 per cent and 75 per cent.) It is clear, furthermore, that where the frequency of social contact is concerned, children occupy a quite a different position from that of siblings: a proposition that we explore with regard to the quality of relationships in Chapter 5. This suggests, in turn, that the quality of interaction might have been different and, in line with some previous research perhaps, that the obligation to help was not as great for siblings as it was for children (Scott, 1983, p. 61). The fact that those siblings who had never been married tended to have more frequent contact with their elderly brothers and sisters does seem to support the argument that sibling ties (including any obligation to provide help or support) are weakened by marriage. Contrary to the suggestion of some previous research in the USA (Shanas, 1979, p. 7) widowed elderly people were not in more frequent contact with brothers and sisters than single and married people. But this does not mean that the *quality* of relationships between widowed people and siblings are not different from those between married people and siblings (Powers and Bultena, 1976; Kohen, 1983).

If social contact rests primarily on children, then in practice it is daughters rather than sons who are likely to see their elderly parents most frequently. Hours of contact in the previous week were highest for those elderly people who had daughters only. But there was evidence that kinship obligations can override some differences based on sex: among elderly people with only one child, there was no difference in the average level of contact for sons and daughters. In addition, daughters-in-law were no more likely to visit independently than sons-in-law (about one-third of each group did so), and the average hours of contact with children-in-law showed no sex difference.

Sex and age of elderly person

In comparing patterns of visiting and frequency of family contact experienced by elderly men and women it has to be borne in mind that their circumstances are different in some important respects. Most women over the age of 74 are widows, while most men of this age are married. Elderly women are more likely to suffer disability than men (primarily because they live longer) and on average they have lower incomes. These factors are likely to reduce the level of social contact experienced by elderly women.

The average weekly hours of family contact for elderly women did not differ greatly from the average experienced by men; in fact the contact hours for men were, on average, very slightly higher than those for women. But there were differences in the breadth of the family contact networks of elderly men and women, an indication perhaps of differences in the potential for substitution among relatives and, therefore, in the security of such contacts. For one in three elderly women compared with one in four men, social contact was likely to be equally shared between two or more relatives. In addition a higher proportion of men (17 per cent compared with 10 per cent) had no relatives whom they saw more than three or four times a year. As far as siblings were concerned, those of elderly women were slightly more likely to see their sisters at least once a week than were the siblings of elderly men (29 per cent compared with 22 per cent).

In line with previous research (Shanas, *et al.*, 1968, pp. 212–3) we did not find marked differences in the frequency of direct contact experienced by elderly people of different ages. However, as Table 3.5 shows, when viewed from the perspective of the elderly person's children there was a substantial increase in the proportion who saw their parent on a daily basis as the age group of the elderly person increased. As in the three-nation study, we found that there were marked differences in the frequency of contact with siblings and other relatives as age increased. These differences are accounted for by different survival rates: very elderly people are less likely than younger people to have sur- viving siblings. Again, when viewed from the perspective of the surviving siblings, there was a very slight increase in both their daily and weekly contact the higher the age of their brothers and sisters (24 per cent of the siblings of those aged 75–9 saw their elderly relative at least weekly compared with 28 per cent of the siblings of those aged 85 and over). So, if the elderly person was lucky enough to have siblings, they remained an important source of contact in advanced old age.

Disability

As Table 3.5 shows, there was not a large variation in the frequency of contact between children and elderly relatives related to differing degrees of disablement. Although there was some decline in the frequency of contact in the middle range of disability, the children of those with severe disability are just as likely to see their parent on a weekly basis as the children of those with no disability. This means that the children of some of those with disabilities were compensating for their parent's inability to visit independently by increasing the frequency of their visits to their parent's home. Contact with siblings was only marginally higher where the elderly person was severely disabled compared with the non-disabled (30 per cent of the siblings of those with no disability were in contact at least weekly compared with 35 per cent of the siblings of the severely disabled).

Social class

Previously observed differences in patterns of contact between elderly people in different social classes were confirmed (see, for example, Shanas *et al.*, 1968, pp. 245–6). Even in an area of relatively low mobility, the family networks of middle-class elderly people were geographically less densely concentr measured by the proportion of listed relatives living within half-an hour's journey). Second, the middle classes made more use of indirect forms of contact (such as the telephone and letters) while in working-class family networks there was a higher level of face-to-face contact. Social and (accompanying it) geographical mobility were important factors here because, where middle-class children lived locally, their level of face-to-face contact was not significantly lower than the contact of local working-class children, although their frequency of non-face-to-face contact remained higher. In addition the higher level of indirect contact by relatives of middle-class elderly people reflects at least partly their possession of greater material resources and the different styles of interaction these facilitate. (We found a high level of correlation between social class and savings and a less strong one between class and income.) While all those elderly people in social class I possessed telephones, the proportion fell steadily to only 24 per cent of those in class V (measured on the Registrar General's 5-point scale: I Professional, II Intermediate, III Skilled, IV Partly Skilled, V Unskilled).

What about the influence of social mobility within the family on patterns of contact? Where the elderly parent and all of their children were working class, levels of face-to-face contact were highest: nine out of ten elderly people in this type of family had at least one relative whom they saw weekly, and just over two-fifths had at least one relative they saw on a daily basis. The corresponding proportions for middle-class families were 57 per cent (at least weekly contact) and 21 per cent (at least daily contact). Contact figures for working-class parents with middle-class children fell between these two extremes: 72 per cent (weekly) and 29 per cent (daily). Thus, social mobility between the generations is not the major disrupting influence on family relations it is popularly believed to be: the lowest level of daily face-to-face contact was among the middle class, where indirect forms of contact were more prevalent. But even where children are willing to live apart from their parent's home this is apparently not out of any desire to dissociate themselves from their parents, but in order to pursue careers (Hendricks and Hendricks, 1977, p. 264).

Patterns of visiting between elderly people and relatives

We were able to analyse the patterns of face-to-face contact between elderly people and relatives. Excluding those with whom direct contact was not maintained and those who lived more than two hours' journey away from the elderly person we were left with data on some 860 relatives. As Table 3.6 shows, the majority of elderly people in the sample were not simply the passive recipients of visits from relatives but were engaged in a two-way flow of visits, even if some needed fetching and bringing back. However, there were important differences in the patterns and styles of interaction based on social class. Middle-class elderly people played a much more active role in maintaining direct contact with their relatives than working-class elderly people. Over half of the relatives of middle-class elderly people engaged in active mutual visiting (where the elderly person was able to visit without being fetched by the relative), compared with 34 per cent of the relatives of working-class elderly people.

The class differences in visiting patterns shown in Table 3.6 are even wider if we focus on mutual visiting between parents and children only. Three-fifths of the children of middle-class elderly people received as well as made visits, compared with just over one-third of the children of working-class elderly parents. Those in class V were much less likely than other groups to visit

Table 3.6   *Patterns of visiting by relatives (%)*

Social class of elderly person	Relative visits only	Mutual visits only if elderly person fetched	Mutual visiting	Elderly person visits only	Total	Number of relatives
Middle class (non-manual)	29.2	9.1	53.5	8.2	100	243
Working class (manual)	45.5	11.9	34.2	8.4	100	620
All	40.9	11.1	39.6	8.3	100	863

independently (nearly two-fifths visited only when fetched compared with less than one-fifth in the other classes), and mutual visits were much less common in classes IV and V than other classes.

These different patterns of visiting are partly explained by differential access to transport. Middle-class elderly people were more likely (but still not very likely) to own a car and to make use of taxis. Second, as we show in more detail in the following chapter, although working-class elderly people were not more likely to be disabled, once they were disabled their lower level of resources meant that they were less able to compensate for the restricting effects of disability by, for example, using taxis for transport.

The tendency for relatives to visit elderly people increased with the severity of the elderly person's disability. To take, for example, visiting between elderly people and their children: only 11 per cent of the children of the non-disabled made visits to their parent without receiving any in return, compared with 38 per cent of the children of those with minor disablement and 70 per cent of the children of the very severely disabled. Correspondingly the incidence of mutual visiting was much less common where the elderly parent was very severely disabled: 7 per cent compared with 71 per cent among the children of the non-disabled.

Factors affecting the frequency of contact with children

The 306 elderly people in the sample had 526 children living: 268 daughters and 258 sons. Of these, 28 were step-children whom the elderly people considered as their children. During the course of the second-stage carer interviews it was discovered that some relatives who were technically step-children had not been listed as relatives in the first stage. Where an elderly person had married in later life, and the new partner's children had already left home, then it seems the elderly person had often not considered these step-children as their own children at all. Thus our analysis of contact with children includes step-children only if they were thought of as children by the elderly person. Detailed questioning about children's circumstances was restricted to the 83 per cent who lived within two hours' journey of the elderly person's home.

Elderly people were asked whether their children were

experiencing any particular problems which were occupying them a good deal at the time of the interview. The main problem areas were ill health on the part of the relative, relative's spouse or child, the need to care for the spouse's parents and unemployment in the family. Elderly people reported at least one such family problem for 42 per cent of the children in the sample.

It might be expected that those who saw most of their children would know more about any problems they were experiencing. Nevertheless there were some clear patterns of association between level of direct contact in the past week and particular problems being experienced by members of the extended family. Factors associated with a lower than average level of contact were: the presence of another elderly person requiring care (5 per cent of children were in this position and their contact time was only half the average level); second the child's own poor health resulted in lower than average contact time and one in ten children were affected in this way. In contrast, where a grandchild was in poor health (4 per cent of children) levels of contact were actually higher than average: a clear pointer to the elderly person fulfilling an important supportive function within the family (perhaps allowing a daughter to remain in employment).

Those for whom actual or impending unemployment or redundancy was mentioned as a problem had about an average level of contact, similar to that enjoyed by those said to have no particular problems. This suggests that family ties are not broken by the anxiety created by the threat or experience of unemployment in the child's family, although they may be strained by it.

Further analysis of the influence of the child's unemployment status on social contact revealed that if worry about impending or actual unemployment in his or her family did not appear to have a direct impact on the amount of social contact, the *actual* experience of unemployment was clearly associated with reduced contact. Eleven per cent of sons and 2 per cent of daughters were unemployed at the time of interview. (It should be noted that those who were worried about unemployment or redundancy were not exactly the same group as those who were actually experiencing it: for example, the impending or actual unemployment of a daughter's husband might be entered as a current problem, but the daughter herself might be employed, or described as a housewife.) In contrast to the often popularly voiced expectation that unemployment should provide opportunities for social interaction and support for relatives in need, average hours of contact between elderly people and unemployed children were substantially *lower* than with those in full-time employment. This remained true when the comparison was restricted to male children only.

In line with the familiar findings of research on the personal impact of unemployment – the experience of loss, stigma, ill health, social isolation, depression and reduced social and economic status (see, for example, Marsden and Duff, 1975; Jahoda, 1979; Showler and Sinfield, 1981) – the lowest contact levels were with those children who were unemployed, together with those who were permanently sick or disabled (7 per cent and 2 per cent of children respectively). There is no doubt, therefore, that rather than creating more opportunities for social contact within the family, unemployment weakens some of the psychological and economic foundations on which such contacts are based (for a discussion of this point see Walker, 1982b, p. 33)

The important influence of employment status on the level of social contact between elderly people and their children was underlined by the fact that those children who were retired (a small minority of 4 per cent) had the highest contact levels, followed by those described as housewives (17 per cent). This provides further evidence of the qualitative difference between the experience of unemployment and retirement (Walker, Noble and Westergaard, 1985) and the fact that, regardless of other calls on their time, women are likely to be most actively in contact with elderly relatives: a point that we turn to next.

Gender divisions in social contact provide the first concrete illustration of the major differences in the roles of male and female kin in relation to elderly people. Average hours of contact were higher for daughters than for sons. Moreover this difference was not explained by the greater likelihood that sons were in full-time employment; daughters in full-time employment still had substantially more hours of direct contact per week on average than sons. So this research substantiates the point – frequently made but about which there is very little supporting evidence – that even when women are in full-time jobs they still bear the brunt of responsibility for family members, both young and old (see, for example, Land, 1978; Wilson, 1982; Finch and Groves, 1983). It was also clear that in general daughters visited more frequently than sons: 61 per cent visited weekly compared with 45 per cent of sons. Whether or not these differences between the sexes in the frequency of contact were also reflected in differences in the provision of care and support will be discussed in subsequent chapters.

Investigation of the geographical spread of children's residences showed that over 70 per cent of both sons and daughters lived in Sheffield and South Yorkshire, and approximately two-thirds of each group lived within half-an-hour's journey of their parent. Thus, although sons were slightly more likely to live more than two hours' journey away (17 per cent did so, as opposed to 12 per cent of daughters), the differences in patterns of contact could not be explained by any tendency for daughters to live closer to their parents.

Finally, there was the possible influence of divorce on the frequency of contact between elderly people and their children. Only 31 listed relatives and only two elderly people were described as divorced. (Undoubtedly other children had been divorced in the past but had been remarried and thus were described as 'married' by their parents.) These numbers were not large enough to make any generalisable comparisons. However, it is of interest that in only one case of a divorced child was any contact at all maintained with the child's ex-spouse (a suggestion, if no more, that divorce can severely disrupt kinship contact networks). Among divorced children, daughters had higher than average contact with their parent in the previous week, while divorced sons (with the exception of one person who shared a household with his father) had lower than average contact (compared with other sons).

The family relations of elderly people: independent household, intimate family

Elderly people were unlikely to live with their relatives and when asked about the possibility of doing so they were inclined to express reluctance. What stands out from the responses of elderly people to questions about social contact with relatives is the strong desire to remain in their own independent household but at the same time to be socially integrated with their families. Thus, as we have shown, the increased trend towards elderly people living alone – which has encouraged a gloomy prognosis about the break-up of the family – is wholly compatible with the sustained high frequency of contact with relatives, especially children. Consequently the assumption that elderly people who live apart from their children are neglected by them has been dismissed by the evidence presented here.

Of course this does not mean that all elderly people are in regular contact with relatives; some do not have any surviving relatives, others are isolated from some or all of those they do have. Elderly people without children (27 per cent of our sample) are particularly vulnerable to isolation, and more so in advanced old age following the onset of disability and if they experience widowhood. Notwithstanding these important exceptions we found no evidence of widespread isolation from their families among those aged 75 and over. Even among the over 85s such isolation was relatively rare. Frequent direct and indirect interaction was more common than not.

It may be, however, that what matters most to an elderly person's experience of old age and to their general well-being is not the quantity of contacts they have with relatives, but the *quality* of those contacts (Shanas, 1979; Connor, Powers and Bultena, 1979). This aspect of family relations is undoubtedly of most relevance to the care of elderly people and public policy, and is the main preoccupation of subsequent chapters. As an introduction to the evaluation of the family relations of elderly people we examine the attitudes of the elderly towards their families and the extent to which loneliness was experienced. Are elderly people on as intimate terms with their relatives as the frequency of contacts between them would suggest?

Isolation and loneliness

It is assumed in the gerontological literature that social interaction, especially with family members, is important to the well-being of elderly people and their adjustment to old age (see, for example, Chappell, 1983, p. 78). Were the elderly lonely despite frequent contact with relatives?

Loneliness may be distinguished from living alone and social isolation. People may feel lonely despite frequent social contact (Tunstall, 1966, p. 96), perhaps because of the loss of a marriage partner. Loneliness may be confined to particular parts of the day or, most common in old age, to the night. Frequency of social contact may be taken as an indicator of social isolation (Townsend, 1963, pp. 166–72) and, as we have seen, the majority of elderly people were not isolated from their families. Thus less than one in five (18 per cent) had not seen at least one relative in the previous week, while 38 per cent had seen one or more in the last five days.

The very elderly (85 and over) were slightly more likely than younger people not to have seen a relative in the past week. Single people were much less likely than others to have seen a relative in the last week: 30 per cent compared with 19 per cent of married people and 14 per cent of the widowed (further confirmation that the elderly widowed were not more isolated than others). Elderly people with very severe disabilities were markedly less likely than the non-disabled to have seen a relative last week (32 per cent compared with 8 per cent). But there was no difference between them in the proportion who had seen a relative on six or seven days in the last week (two-fifths). Those in social classes I and II were less likely than the semi-skilled and unskilled to have seen a relative in the last week.

As a further indication of isolation we asked if there were any days in the past week when they did not see anyone; an overwhelming majority, four-fifths, said no and the majority of the rest said they had not seen anyone on one, two or three days. This left 7 per cent of the sample who had not seen anyone on four days or more in the previous week and who, therefore, may be described as being severely isolated in that week.

Respondents were asked if they ever felt lonely and, if so, how often. Two-thirds of them said no, only 5 per cent said they felt lonely all the time and 7 per cent most of the time. There were variations in reported loneliness based on age, sex, marital status, social class and disability. Those over 85 were slightly more likely than other age groups to say they felt lonely all or most of the time (17 per cent). As a result of this age factor and the demographic tendency for women to survive men, women were more likely than men to be lonely (43 per cent compared with 25 per cent), and three times as likely to say they were lonely all the time. It follows that widows were more likely than married elderly people to be lonely (48 per cent compared with 21 per cent). None of those in social classes I and II said they were lonely all the time compared with 6 per cent of those in classes IV and V. Elderly people with severe and very severe disabilities were more than twice as likely as those with no or only minor disabilities to be lonely and even more prone to be lonely all the time.

The vast majority of elderly people (75 per cent) said that they never experienced any difficulty passing the time, and only 9 per cent said they often had difficulty doing so. As with loneliness, those over 85 were more likely than younger elderly people to say they often had this difficulty (12 per cent compared with 7 per cent of those under 80). There was no significant difference between those living alone and those living with others in reporting difficulty in passing the time.

Integration and reciprocation between elderly people and their families

In order to begin to form a picture of the quality of relations between elderly people and their families, respondents were asked to identify any relative they felt emotionally close to (apart from a spouse) and then if they saw enough of that relative. Three out of five did nominate one or more relatives and two-fifths of those said they saw enough of them. The main reason for insufficient contact was illness of the elderly person: 30 per cent of those not seeing enough of their closest relative(s). Again very elderly and single people were least likely to be seeing enough of their intimate relative, which is a further indication that while the majority were satisfied with the extent of their contact, there was a small isolated minority whose desire for greater interaction with relatives was frustrated to some extent.

An indication of the overwhelming emotional importance of the family in the lives of elderly people can be obtained from answers to a similar question about emotional closeness to anyone outside the family. More than two in three said there was no one, 17 per cent identified a friend and 10 per cent a neighbour. The family – and within it children and among them daughters – is the prime source of emotional interaction and support in old age.

When asked whether or not they would describe their family as a close one, nearly two in three elderly people said yes, one in four said it was not close but on good terms, only one in 25 said they were distant and none said they were on bad terms. Not surprisingly those living with others (overwhelmingly relatives) were more likely than those living alone or with a spouse only to say they regarded their family as close. Single people were least likely to have close families (52 per cent) and widows were most likely to (69 per cent). Both married and single elderly people were more likely than widows to regard their families as distant, but only 5 per cent of both groups felt like this.

Next, elderly people were asked how important the family was to them at the present time. Of those with surviving family members over two-fifths said it was very important and only 5 per cent said it was not very important or unimportant. Marital status and the living arrangements which follow from it were again influential: the proportion of those living with others who said their family was not important was four times that for the married and those living alone (8 per cent and 2 per cent). Single people, who were therefore without children, were the least likely to say that their family was the most important thing in their lives: 13 per cent compared with 37 per cent of the married and 47 per cent of the widowed (further indication of the compensation the family provides for widowhood, in this case emotional compensation).

As well as asking people to describe their feelings towards their family we sought information about actual interactions to see how far practice matched attitudes. As with the data on frequency of social contact, answers to questions about reciprocity suggest a high level of structural integration between elderly people and their extended families. As a further guide to reciprocity within the family, respondents were asked if they ever helped members of their family financially, with money or goods. Three-quarters did not provide any assistance of this sort. On the other hand, three-quarters did not receive any such help from their family. Of course, as reported earlier in this chapter, a major contribution made by a minority of elderly people to their children was to provide shelter by sharing their household with them.

There was a strong social class influence on the provision of financial help by elderly people. Just under half of class I and II, compared with one-fifth of classes IV and V, provided help of this sort. Those in the higher classes were more likely than others to give money. Similarly men were more likely than women to make gifts of money, and women were more likely than men to give goods. This is a sure sign of the continuing strength of the economic division of labour between men and women, and the dominance of the male 'breadwinner' over the family finances.

As well as questions about financial exchanges, we asked a long series about the help and support that elderly people themselves provide for others (the full results are reported on p. 99). A significant proportion of people were providing help and support to others, though not necessarily members of their own family. For example, 5 per cent were performing personal care tasks, such as washing, bathing and dressing for another person (half were caring for spouses) and 20 per cent were providing emotional support and company.

Family get-togethers were reported by seven out of ten people, the most common occasions being Christmas, followed by funerals. As a concrete illustration of such occasions we asked where the elderly person spent last Christmas. Just over half had been to the home of a member of their family (usually a child). The very elderly (85 plus) were less likely than others to go to their family's home, largely because they were less likely to have surviving relatives. Widows spent Christmas at the home of their family more often than single and married people. Similarly those in the manual socio-economic group were more likely to spend Christmas at their family's home than the non-manual, and the unskilled were most likely of all to do so (64 per cent). Elderly people with very severe disabilities were unlikely to go to their family for Christmas (29 per cent compared with 50 per cent of those with no disability or less severe disabilities).

This account of the quantity of social interaction between elderly people and their families, and some qualitative and subjective aspects of contact from the perspective of the elderly people, shows that currently the family life of elderly people is characterised by a high degree of mutual interaction. We found many practical demonstrations of goodwill between family members. This cohesion and integration between elderly people and their relatives, and especially their children, has been demonstrated by the continuing existence of frequent social interaction between the generations and the exchange of mutual services. Intimacy rather than isolation still characterises the relations between the generations, as seen through the eyes of the elderly. Moreover, this interaction is *not* based on any need for care or support on the part of the elderly because contact is high, indeed higher, among the non-disabled and their families. Neither are elderly people a passive group depending on visits or gifts from relatives, and where physical mobility and geographical distance allow there is a large amount of reciprocal visiting and a significant number of exchanges of money or goods. In other words, the majority of people aged 75 and over, at least in England's third city, led a full and active family life. At the same time, however, there is a small minority who are socially isolated (usually lacking close relatives) who will need special consideration in the formation of policy.

4
The Need for Care

It is commonplace to describe the implications of our ageing population in terms of increasing *dependency*. This has had the twin effects of contributing to the construction of the stereotype of old age as a universal experience of senility and, in turn, attributing the causes of dependency to individual pathology rather than to social and economic factors (Walker, 1980, 1983c; Townsend, 1981a). It has also helped to devalue the social and economic status of older people and dismiss their contribution to family and society. We have noted already that policy makers and practitioners are a major source of this stereotype of old age. Recently their restricted descriptions of old age have turned to alarmist and denigrating warnings about the 'growing burden of dependency', 'social disaster' and 'rising tide' (see, for example, Health Advisory Service, 1983). This sort of caricature of old age is at complete odds with the facts of ageing, as we show below. Before doing so, however, it is necessary to distinguish between dependency and disability.

The term dependency has, confusingly, been used in at least five different senses in the social policy literature: life-cycle dependency, physical and psychological dependency, political dependency, economic and financial dependency and structural dependency (Walker, 1982c). Our primary interest here is with the second form, in which dependency is often equated with disability. This application of the concept of dependency is found most frequently in studies of elderly people in receipt of social services where a service provider's or practitioner's perspective is dominant. For example, in research on elderly people living in residential institutions, information on self-care, mobility, continence and other personal characteristics is often collated and assumptions made about levels of dependency (see, for example, DHSS, 1975; Mooney, 1978). Unfortunately the link between disability and dependency is neither as clear-cut nor as uniform as this kind of exercise would suggest (Walker, 1985a).

There is, of course, a correlation between disability and dependency but, for any given degree of disability measured in functional terms, physical dependence on another person for care and tending will vary betweeen individuals according to the interaction of disability and environment (S. Sainsbury, 1973; Carver and Rodda, 1978). In fact the degree and impact of both, over much of their range, is determined to a significant extent by social and environmental factors. For instance, a severely disabled elderly person living in purpose-built accommodation and using a wide variety of expensive aids to daily living may not be very dependent on another person for care. Within the social services, particularly the residential sector, one of the most important environmental influences on elderly people is the care staff themselves. They might underestimate the capacity of residents to look after themselves and manage their own affairs, adopt summary judgements about residents' abilities or mental states or limit freedom in order to maintain an orderly regime and thereby *increase* the level of dependency experienced by elderly people in their care (Townsend, 1962). It is possible that families, too, may create or enhance dependency by taking over tasks that elderly people can perform for themselves. A full discussion of reactions to dependency on the part of both elderly people and carers is contained in Chapter 6.

Physical dependency implies a social relationship and, therefore, its exact form and degree rests on interaction with at least one other person. Disability, equally, is a function of social and environmental factors (Walker, 1980). In contrast to the service-oriented application of dependency, research on the health status and capacity for self-care of elderly people living in the community is more usually analysed in terms of disability. Thus it is possible to measure disability objectively without making assumptions about the degree of reliance, if any, of the disabled person on another. The drawback to using measures of dependency outside the particular needs of the residential setting is that dependency is an indicator of the receipt of assistance rather than of the need for it. In view of what we have already said about the social construction of dependency this distinction is crucial. Because dependency is a matter of judgement it is very difficult to measure it precisely. Moreover, indicators of dependency tell us very little about the sufficiency of care in relation to need. For these reasons we concentrated attention on the assessment of disability rather than dependency.

There is a strong correlation between disability and advancing age (Townsend, 1979, p. 705). The proportion of the population suffering from a limiting long-standing illness is 26 per cent among both men and women in the 45–64 age group, and 44 per cent and 56 per cent among men and women aged 75 and over (OPCS, 1982, p. 140). In fact the vast majority of people with disabilities are over retirement age and nearly one in three are aged 75 and over (Harris, Cox and Smith, 1971). Despite the preponderance of people with disabilities among older age groups, the concept of disablement has not been applied systematically to this group in order better to understand the problems of ageing, to define the scale of need in old age and to organise the best policies and services to meet these needs (Townsend, 1981b). One indication of the official failure to acknowledge disablement among the elderly is the absence of any record of which supplementary pensioners suffer from a given degree of disability and who, therefore, might be incurring additional costs.

The readier application of a concept of disability will better enable policy makers to understand the experiences of elderly people and their families and to develop more effective policies to meet their needs. With this aim in mind information was collected from elderly people on both objective and subjective indicators of need. The first, objective approach comprised two elements: on the one hand, a list of conditions which troubled elderly people or limited their activities, such as arthritis, heart trouble and poor hearing; and on the other hand, an assessment of the elderly people's capacity to look after themselves in their own homes and the activities with which they require assistance. Previous research had validated and successfully applied a measure of functional capacity based on an index of self-care and household management activities (Townsend, 1962, 1979; S. Sainsbury, 1973; Walker and Townsend, 1976). It was designed to ascertain individual need for help and support on the assumption that incapacity to look after oneself in a home of one's own can be defined only in relation to the activities and roles which are commonly regarded as 'normal' for people in society. The index consists of nine items representative of those essential for personal care (such as washing all over and cutting toenails) and household management (such as going shopping, doing housework and preparing a hot meal). A score of two was recorded if the subject was unable to carry out a particular activity and of one if he or she was able to undertake it only with difficulty. The maximum score was 18 and scores were grouped into the following categories of severity: none, slight, minor, appreciable, severe and very severe.

Subjective indicators of need in the survey included self-assessments of health status and, for each of the full list of personal care and household management items, respondents were asked whether or not they got all the help they wanted. If a person replied 'no' – that they did not receive enough help with that particular activity – this was taken to be an expressed need for help in that area.

The need for care and tending

Paradoxically the application of the concept of disability to old age reveals the continuing *abilities* of many very elderly people. Thus the majority of those in our sample either had no physical disability (17 per cent) or experienced only minor disablement (47 per cent). Those with appreciable or more severe disabilities – the main focus of policy makers' interest – comprised only 36 per cent of the population over 75. This is an important fact to bear in mind because it conflicts with the popular stereotype of very elderly people. Even so, these figures indicate that as many as 1.2 million people aged 75 and over in Great Britain suffer from appreciable, severe or very severe disablement.

This picture of activity in advanced old age was confirmed by information about mobility. Seven out of ten of the elderly went out of doors without assistance and a further one in eight were able to go out with help. Only 14 per cent were permanently housebound and 3 per cent temporarily. However, as age advanced activity declined dramatically: four-fifths of those aged 75–9 were able to go out, compared with less than one-third of those aged 85 and over. Only 7 per cent of those aged 75–9 were permanently bedridden compared with 41 per cent of the 85 and overs. The index of capacity for personal care and household management revealed a similarly inexorable trend. Thus there were more than five times as many people aged 85 and over who were classified as very severely disabled compared with those aged 75–9. Because of this age distribution of disability women were more likely than men to suffer from disablement, especially severe disablement. Thirty-two per cent of men and only 9 per cent of women had no disability, while 24 per cent and 43 per cent respectively had appreciable or more severe disabilities.

Our survey provided further evidence that disability is closely associated with other forms of social deprivation (see, for example, Disability Alliance, 1975; Walker, 1976; Townsend, 1979; Walker and Townsend, 1981). Severely disabled elderly people, for instance, were more likely than the non-disabled to live in poverty: three-quarters had incomes under £2 500 per annum compared with two-fifths of the non-disabled; 4 per cent had incomes over £3 500 per annum compared with 18 per cent of the non-disabled. The severely disabled were much more likely than the non-disabled to have little or no savings: two-thirds of the former and two-fifths of the latter had less than £300. Despite this clear association between poverty and disability and, as we show in this chapter, the demonstrably greater needs of the severely disabled, there is no special social provision for the disabled elderly; indeed, they are denied such items as the mobility allowance which is available to younger people.

Partly related to this material deprivation was the greater social isolation of the severely disabled compared with the non-disabled. Twenty-nine per cent of the severely disabled said that they were lonely all or most of the time, a response given by only 6 per cent of those with no disability. One-half of the severely disabled and three-quarters of the non-disabled said they were never lonely.

While severe disablement was confined to a minority of the population, the incidence of chronic illness and disability was widespread. Thus only 9 per cent of elderly people did not suffer from at least one chronic condition that affected their everyday activity and 57 per cent suffered from three or more conditions. The most common complaints were trouble with feet or legs (47 per cent) and arthritis (46 per cent); next came poor eyesight (34 per cent) and poor hearing (33 per cent); then bouts of dizziness (26 per cent), bronchitis (22 per cent), stomach trouble (20 per cent) and high blood pressure (18 per cent). Surprisingly, one of the groups that presents the greatest difficulty to carers – those suffering from incontinence – were not necessarily the most severely disabled but were spread across the range of degrees of severity from minor to very severe. Eleven per cent suffered from bladder incontinence and 6 per cent from bowel incontinence. The majority of the incontinent (66 per cent) experienced problems of control at least daily; overall, however, less than one in ten of the elderly suffered daily or more frequent incontinence. Neither were those with daily or more frequent problems of bladder or bowel control concentrated in the high receipt of care categories, a fact that may be explained by the absence of a direct correspondence between incontinence and severity of disability and the tendency for those experiencing acute incontinence to be women in the 80 plus age group. As we show below, elderly women were less likely than men to get care if they needed it.

Indicator of the need for care

Since our assessment of disability was based on self-care and household management activities, the proportions of elderly people with different degrees of disability (as given earlier) are broadly indicative of the need for care and tending. But we also wanted an indication of need across the whole range of self-care, household management and maintenance tasks which have to be performed if elderly people are to remain independent in the community. For this purpose we constructed a need for care indicator which included, in addition to the items making up the disability index, such other activities of daily living as light housework, gardening and decorating. After people had been asked about the degree of difficulty, if any, they experienced with these tasks, they were then asked whether or not they received any assistance, and finally, whether they received enough help. The need for care indicator is based on the same approach as the disability index: a score of one was recorded where respondents reported some difficulty in carrying out a task and two where they could not do it. If a person replied 'no' – that they did not receive enough help with that particular activity – this was taken to be an expressed need for help in that area. This is not a refined index but an indicator of the existence of need for care and tending. Table 4.1

Table 4.1 *Percentage of elderly people requiring care*

Characteristic of elderly person	Degree of need for care				Total	Number
	None	Some	Moderate	Substantial		
Age						
75–9	8.1	70.3	12.2	9.3	100	172
80–4	2.4	47.5	22.0	28.1	100	82
85+	(6.7)	(20.0)	(20.0)	(53.3)	100	45
Gender						
Male	11.3	65.0	6.2	17.5	100	97
Female	4.0	52.3	20.8	22.8	100	202
Marital status						
Single, divorced, separated	(4.0)	(64.0)	(24.0)	(8.0)	100	25
Married	8.7	63.5	13.5	14.4	100	104
Widowed	5.3	51.2	16.5	27.0	100	107
All	6.4	56.2	16.4	21.0	100	299

shows the distribution of need in relation to age, gender and marital status. Subjective, expressed needs are discussed in the final section of this chapter.

The need for care and tending increased dramatically in advanced old age, along with the increased incidence and severity of disability. The greater likelihood of women than men experiencing substantial or severe need is largely attributable to the fact that those in the older age groups are likely to be women and, in turn, widows were much more common than widowers. But when the gender groups were standardised for age it was noticeable that gender differences were much less apparent among those over the age of 80. So 39 per cent of women aged 80 and over had a substantial need for care compared with 32 per cent of men.

There was also a slight tendency for working-class elderly people to be more often in very severe need compared with those in the middle class, probably due to the influence of the various factors which depend on social class, including income and housing. Thus, for example, 23 per cent of low income elderly people (those with incomes under £2 000 per annum) were in severe or very severe need compared with 13 per cent of those with higher incomes (£3 000 or more per annum). What was surprising, perhaps, was that there were not greater differences between the needs reported by middle- and working-class elderly people. This suggests that, among this age cohort at least, social class had a diminishing impact on disability and the need for care as age increased. Advanced old age in this limited sense does appear to be a leveller, although inequalities based on severity of disability were widened.

Interestingly, too, there was no difference in the need for care between those living in owner-occupied and council housing. Similar proportions were assessed as being in very severe need (12 per cent of owner-occupiers and 11 per cent of council tenants). One indication of the family's response to the need for care was that those elderly people living with others were more likely than those living alone to demonstrate moderate or substantial need for care (45 per cent compared with 36 per cent).

The need for care indicator is useful in identifying gross categories of need among the elderly: just under one-fifth of the sample were classified as being in substantial need of caring and tending support. Applying this proportion to the population of Great Britain aged 75 and over we estimate that some 672 000 people are in gross need of care and tending, with a further 525 000 in moderate need. It must be emphasised that, since we are not using a refined and validated index, these figures can only be taken as a rough guide. We can be much more precise in our estimate of the need for care and tending by breaking down this broad indicator into its constituent items. This sort of information is also more helpful than overall indicators of need in describing precisely which activities elderly people were most likely to need help in performing, and where formal services are necessary to support the activities of informal carers. Table 4.2 shows the detailed picture of the need for assistance with different self-care and household management activities.

There are four important findings contained in Table 4.2. In the first place, it confirms the fact that, with one exception, the majority of elderly people did not need assistance and were capable of looking after themselves in their own homes with, at most, minimal support. The exception was the need for help with chiropody. Not surprisingly the day-to-day household management tasks that proved most taxing and where most help and support were required were those demanding strength and sustained effort: heavy housework, shopping and laundry.

Second, however, it reveals that underneath this surface capacity

Table 4.2 *Need for and receipt of assistance with various activities*

Activity	No difficulty		Some difficulty		Cannot perform		Number*
	Received assistance	Did not receive assistance	Received assistance	Did not receive assistance	Received assistance	Did not receive assistance	
Washing all over	0.3	80.3	4.6	6.3	8.3	0.0	300
Getting in/out of bed	0.0	83.7	1.7	11.6	3.0	0.0	301
Going up/down stairs	0.4	56.9	1.9	34.8	0.7	5.2	267
Cutting toenails	3.0	41.9	7.3	18.8	27.1	2.0	303
Heavy shopping	8.0	25.0	17.7	11.3	37.3	0.7	300
Light shopping	5.9	57.2	4.5	4.8	27.5	0.0	269
Preparing and cooking hot meals	27.5	50.5	7.0	4.9	10.1	0.0	287
Heavy laundry	13.7	34.1	16.3	7.4	28.5	0.0	270
Light laundry	8.6	64.5	4.7	5.5	16.8	0.0	256
Heavy housework	13.7	22.9	17.0	9.8	29.1	1.0	306
Light housework	12.9	67.1	4.9	5.6	8.7	0.7	286
Decorating	7.7	9.1	14.0	2.5	59.6	7.0	285
Gardening	5.2	35.1	16.6	9.0	30.8	3.3	211

*Numbers differ because answers to some questions included the categories 'don't know how to' (e.g. cook a meal), or 'no facility' (e.g. garden).

to cope there was a substantial degree of latent need for help with important household management functions. On the face of it this seems to confirm the fears of some politicians and policy makers that there is a vast pool of unmet need among the elderly such that, if more resources were put into community care and support and rationing procedures were consequently released, the result would be an upsurge in demand for help which would end up swamping the social services (see, for example, Moroney, 1976; Land and Parker, 1978). But for the most part this need was confined to those functions which elderly people reported some difficulty in carrying out and, therefore, these were not cases of severe need. What appears to be required is not full-time replacement support but occasional help with specific tasks such as heavy housework and shopping. This could be met by a combination of formal and informal care and tending and suggests that fears about a flood of unmet need are misplaced. However, this does not mean that action is not required on the part of policy makers. Significant proportions of people who experienced difficulty with self-care functions – for example, in washing all over, getting in and out of bed and cutting toenails – were not getting any help.

Third, the table shows that most of the severe cases of need were getting care and tending, from either the formal or informal sectors. With the slight exceptions of heavy shopping and housework, most self-care and household management tasks were being done for those unable to do them for themselves. There was a consistent need for help in cutting toenails, though not necessarily requiring the expert attention of a fully qualified chiropodist. The remaining areas where further help was required were not in the realm of tasks usually performed by formal care staff, such as home helps. A small group of elderly people were unable to climb stairs and received no assistance. Nationally they represent some 166 000 people aged 75 and over. This points to the need for aids, including chair lifts, adaptations and ground level housing provision. Then there were two small groups who were unable to decorate their homes or do their gardens. There appears to be substantial scope here for voluntary help with decorating and gardening. Volunteers are not able to provide sufficient sustained input of personal care to substitute for formal or family care (Hatch, 1980; Wenger, 1984), but there is a major role for volunteers in meeting occasional needs such as decorating and gardening.

Finally, there were significant proportions of elderly people who received assistance when they said they did not need it. Here 'assistance' consisted predominantly of family-based interaction and exchange rather than tending for someone with a physical disability. In some cases this amounted to indirect financial support rather than physical tending. Often, however, it was a matter of spouses, particularly wives, performing their customary household duties for their husbands. For instance, the differences between elderly men and elderly women who were getting hot meals cooked for them on a daily basis were striking. Although the proportion receiving this assistance grew for both groups as age increased, for every one woman in each group getting a meal cooked for her daily there were at least six men. There was no sign whatsoever of any significant general overprovision by the formal services; for example, none of those who were receiving help in preparing and cooking hot meals when there was no ostensible need for it got this help from the social services: the vast bulk of such help came from relatives. But, as we show later, there were some instances where the social services were providing help when there was no apparent need for it.

There were clear variations based on age and gender as well as disability in the need for help with the various personal care and household management activities. A few examples illustrate the general picture. Let us take the need for assistance with washing first. The proportion of those unable to wash all over and getting help was nearly five times greater among those aged 85 and over compared with those under 80 (24 per cent and 5 per cent). Most of those who experienced difficulty washing but were not getting assistance were concentrated in the over-80 age group. Again, related to this age distribution, there were twice as many women as men who could not wash and were getting help to do so. Widowed people were much less likely than married people to get help with washing if they had some difficulty: 9 per cent compared with 2 per cent of married persons. Need for help with washing was also closely related to overall degree of disability: 96 per cent of those unable to wash and getting assistance were very severely disabled.

When it came to washing hair the ratio of those in the under-80 and 85-and-over age groups who could not do it for themselves and got help was 1:3 (8 per cent and 22 per cent). The gender differences in need for assistance with washing their hair were obviously strongly influenced by culturally determined gender divisions in roles and consumption. Thus 91 per cent of men and 62 per cent of women reported no difficulty and were getting no assistance with washing their hair. Widowed people were, again, less likely to get assistance if they experienced some difficulty washing their hair (8 per cent) than were married persons (4 per cent).

Need for help with cutting toenails was also a function of age: 17 per cent of those under 80 and 40 per cent of those over 80 could not cut their toenails and were getting help to do so. Women were twice as likely as men (32 per cent compared with 16 per cent) to be unable to cut their toenails and be receiving help. However, among those experiencing some difficulty the over 85s were the least likely to get assistance: three out of ten were in this position. Furthermore, unlike other personal care functions, need for assistance with cutting toenails was spread across nearly the whole disability range, although the majority were concentrated in the most severe groups. All of those classified as very severely disabled who experienced some difficulty with cutting their toenails were receiving help, but not so in the less severely disabled group: between one-fifth and three-tenths of those with minor, slight, appreciable and severe disabilities received no help when they experienced difficulty. Also, unlike most other personal care activities, there were variations based on social class, probably resulting from the existence of a large private sector in chiropody. Thus those in social classes IV and V were *less* likely than those in classes I and II to get help if they needed it. For example, 23 per cent of those in the top two classes who reported some difficulty in cutting their toenails received no assistance compared with 31 per cent of those in the bottom two classes.

The need for help with heavy laundry revealed a similar pattern of variation with respect to age as the previous personal care functions. However, a significant gender difference was apparent in the *response* to this need. Men who experienced some difficulty in doing their heavy laundry were more likely to get assistance than women experiencing similar difficulty (90 per cent of men compared to 64 per cent of women). Moreover, men who experienced *no* difficulty at all with heavy laundry were nearly three times more likely than women in the same position to be getting assistance (21 per cent and 8 per cent). In other words, regardless of whether or not need for help with heavy laundry existed, men were more likely than women to be getting assistance. Women were nine times more likely than men *not* to be receiving help with heavy laundry if they needed it. A similar gender-based pattern of inequality was revealed in respect of heavy housework, light housework, light laundry, cooking, shopping and decorating. This confirms the fact that men in these age groups are not expected to do housework, and that women are expected to do housework for men as well as themselves. The result is that elderly men are the recipients of an *excess* of care and tending in relation to need, whereas women suffer a shortfall of care. This point may be emphasised with regard to the preparation and cooking of hot meals: men were more likely than women to have meals cooked for them, even in the oldest age group. Two-fifths of men and less than one-fifth of women received help with cooking meals when they did not need it. One in ten men had seven hot meals cooked for them each week, whereas among women the proportion was one in 200.

The provision of and receipt of care

The previous section was concerned with the objective assessment of need, and now we turn to the sort of care received by elderly people, the amount of care and the main sources of care. In order to get a picture of the total package of care, both informal and formal, being received by people aged 75 and over we constructed a receipt of care index. From the answers to the series of questions about capacity to perform and help received with activities of daily living we were able to determine, first, whether or not assistance was being received, and second, the degree of difficulty with which help was associated. On this basis the total amount of all forms of care received was calculated and the results are set out in Table 4.3. Discussion of the relationship between the need for care and the receipt of care indices is reserved for the final section.

Table 4.3 reinforces the point made in Table 4.1: namely, that most people aged 75 and over do not require significant amounts of care and tending. Thus to register a 'low' input of care on our receipt of care index a person only had to be receiving occasional assistance with just one of the activities of daily living, such as

Table 4.3   *Percentage of elderly people receiving different amounts of care*

Characteristics of elderly person	Total of care inputs					
	None	Low	Medium	High	Total	Number
Age						
75–9	8.1	79.1	4.7	8.1	100	172
80–4	3.7	63.4	20.7	12.2	100	82
85+	(2.2)	(42.2)	(17.8)	(37.8)	100	45
Gender						
Male	6.2	75.2	6.2	12.4	100	97
Female	5.9	66.4	13.4	14.3	100	202
Marital status						
Married	3.8	76.9	5.8	13.5	100	104
Widowed	6.5	63.5	15.3	14.7	100	170
Single, divorced, separated	(12.0)	(76.0)	(4.0)	(8.0)	100	25
Disability						
None	18.0	82.0	0.0	0.0	100	50
Slight	6.7	93.3	0.0	0.0	100	60
Minor	5.1	88.6	6.3	0.0	100	79
Appreciable	1.8	56.4	32.7	9.1	100	55
Severe	(0.0)	(33.3)	(29.6)	(37.0)	100	27
Very severe	(0.0)	(0.0)	(7.1)	(93.0)	100	28
All	6.0	69.2	11.0	13.7	100	299

shopping, laundry or chiropody. At the other end of the spectrum, to be classified as a receiver of high inputs of care and tending respondents must have been receiving some help with at least 16 activities, substantial assistance with at least eight tasks or some combination of these inputs of different degrees of care. The figures in Table 4.1 indicate that there are around 430 000 people aged 75 and over in Great Britain receiving substantial inputs of care. As with the need for care there was a close relationship between receipt of care and age and disability.

Which activities of daily living did elderly people require most frequent help with? The answer to this question begins to uncover the extent of the demands on informal carers and paves the way for the discussion of the social division of labour in caring in the rest of this chapter and the following one. Where help was being provided with personal care and household management functions it was usually done on a very regular basis, often with an extremely high level of frequency. Of those in receipt of care and tending the most frequent forms of help were with light housework (82 per cent of this help was given at least three times a week), light shopping (65 per cent), preparing and cooking hot meals (58 per cent), heavy housework (64 per cent), heavy shopping (31 per cent), washing all over (23 per cent) and light laundry (20 per cent). Within these totals a significant proportion of help with three of the daily living activities essential for elderly people to remain in the community was provided on a *daily* basis: light housework (64 per cent), preparing and cooking hot meals (40 per cent), light shopping (25 per cent) and washing (18 per cent). This suggests that for a significant minority of carers the commitment of time involved was substantial. Having said that, the striking fact remains: whenever care and tending was being received it was, for the most part, on a frequent and regular basis. There were only two personal care and household management functions where the bulk of support was received *less* frequently than weekly – namely washing hair and cutting toenails – which were also the two activities in which the private sector played an important role in providing assistance to the elderly.

We spoke to carers as well as elderly people about the frequency with which they provided help. Assistance with an elderly person's personal care and hygiene was given at least once a week. Only a very small proportion of carers (5 per cent) provided help with washing nearly every day. This picture contrasts with some previous research, such as that by Nissel and Bonnerjea (1982) which was based on a small group of in-house carers, because it is based on a more representative group of carers, the majority of whom did not live with the elderly person concerned (see Chapter 3). Help was given more frequently with household tasks. For example, most carers did shopping for their elderly relatives once or twice a week, with one in six doing it four or more times a week. One-fifth of carers cooked meals for the elderly person at least four times a week. Two-fifths of them checked that their elderly relative was all right four times a week or more frequently.

As with the aggregate data on the need for care, information on the receipt of care is valuable in giving an overall picture of the total supply of care and tending to elderly people. Of course these totals are made up from the activities of a range of different carers in both the informal and formal sectors, and it is essential to look behind these totals at the contributions made by these different carers to the needs of elderly people. We were able to identify the principal helper(s) for each of the activities of daily living which elderly people were asked about and Table 4.4 shows the results.

84

Table 4.4 *Percentage of elderly people receiving care from different sources*

Activity	Percentage receiving care	Informal		Volunteer	Formal			Total	Number
		Relative	Friend/ neighbour		Local authority	NHS	Commercial		
Washing all over	13.4	(35.0)	(5.0)	(0.0)	(2.5)	(55.0)	(2.5)	100	40
Getting in/out of bed	4.7	(71.0)	(0.0)	(0.0)	(14.0)	(7.0)	(7.0)	100	14
Washing hair	29.4	26.7	3.5	0.0	0.0	12.8	57.0	100	86
Cutting toenails	37.1	21.1	3.7	0.0	0.0	19.3	56.0	100	109
Sewing	19.7	84.7	8.5	0.0	6.8	—	0.0	100	59
Heavy shopping	63.2	78.8	12.2	0.0	7.4	—	1.6	100	189
Light shopping	33.8	77.2	13.9	0.0	7.9	—	1.0	100	101
Heavy laundry	60.2	70.9	5.6	0.0	8.9	—	14.5	100	179
Light laundry	33.8	82.5	5.8	0.0	7.8	—	3.9	100	103
Heavy housework	65.6	54.4	3.6	0.5	26.7	—	15.4	100	195
Light housework	26.4	82.3	1.3	0.0	12.7	—	3.8	100	79
Preparing and cooking hot meals	45.5	79.2	4.0	6.4	6.4	—	4.0	100	125
Gardening	37.5	74.8	11.7	1.0	0.0	—	12.6	100	103
Decorating	80.6	51.5	4.6	0.4	0.0	—	43.5	100	239

Principal source of care

Table 4.4 provides clear evidence of the two fundamental characteristics of care in old age. The bulk of care, particularly personal care, is self-care (Walker, 1983a, 1985a). Elderly people reluctantly relinquish the arduous physical activities of daily life as their strength and stamina declines, but they sustain, often fiercely, their own personal hygiene as well as those aspects of household management which they can do for themselves without undue strain. This is an important finding because it emphasises the commitment of elderly people to what is sometimes described as independence, but which is more properly regarded as interdependence, within which they might preserve areas of complete independence (particularly in personal care) while accepting other forms of non-personal assistance. This contrasts with the increasingly common tendency in the discussion of old age to stress dependency and the demands on formal and informal carers. Our research, like that conducted by Shanas and her colleagues more than 20 years ago (Shanas *et al.*, 1968, p. 115) and more recently by Hunt (1978) and Wenger (1984), shows that the elderly value independence very highly and will strive, sometimes obstinately, to preserve it.

Second, for those elderly people who need it the family is by far and away the major source of care and tending. There were only two exceptions to the primacy of family care: hairdressing and chiropody. In contrast to some official and popular perceptions of the roles of the family and public services in the provision of care and tending – for example, Moroney (1976, p. 125) found that in the opinion of scores of civil servants and social welfare practitioners in England, Wales, Denmark and the Federal Republic of Germany, families are less willing to function as the primary, first-line caring institution – there is no evidence here of services, other than the specialist ones of nursing, chiropody and hairdressing making any inroads into the primary caring role of the family. Neither should we regard these services as entirely replacing the role of the family in these spheres. To some extent a formal comprehensive service may be replacing an informal, perhaps rough-and-ready, one but for some people there was no family available to provide care (see Chapter 3). Moreover, these specialist services are *different* from those provided by the family: they are sought out (demanded) and preferred precisely because of their professionalised nature and the specialised skills and training which that entails, in contrast to the informal care of the family which is unskilled in these areas. As

Shanas and her colleagues have pointed out, the growth of specialised medical services did not attract the criticism that it displaced the skills of the family; what is true of medicine should be no less true of professional nursing, chiropody and, for that matter, hairdressing: 'The evolution of skilled services does not so much *displace* the functions that the family performs as refine and complement them' (Shanas *et al.*, 1968, p. 117).

A comparison of the results of the Sheffield study with those from the three-nation research conducted in 1962 demonstrates the absence of a major redistribution of care over the last 20 years, although the coverage of the social services does appear to have increased. In 1962 some two-thirds of elderly people (aged 65 and over) in Britain were receiving it from relatives (Shanas *et al.*, 1968, p. 118) and 12 per cent from the social services. In 1982, in Sheffield, 54 per cent of those aged 75 and over who were getting help in doing heavy housework were receiving it from relatives and 27 per cent from the social services. Much of the difference between these two sets of findings can be explained by the different age groups in question, with those aged 75 and over having fewer relatives available to care than those aged 65 and over, the spread of the personal social services over the period in question and the higher-than-average provision of home helps in Sheffield. The most surprising aspect of this comparison, however, was the fact that in 1962 only 13 per cent of those aged 65 and over who had difficulty in doing heavy housework were receiving assistance whereas in 1982 the equivalent proportion had risen to 19 per cent.

Table 4.4 shows the division of labour between the different sectors of care. Particularly noteworthy, in view of the great reliance placed by the government (DHSS, 1981a; Fowler, 1984) on their role in the future development of community care policy, was the relatively small contribution of friends and neighbours (yet Sheffield is widely regarded as an extremely friendly and neighbourly city, as signalled by its description as the largest village in the country) and the even smaller role played by volunteers. Volunteers did not make much of an impact even on the gardens of elderly people. In the formal sector the NHS, in the form of district nurses, made significant contributions to the personal hygiene of severely disabled elderly people; while the local Family and Community Services Department was helping a large minority of elderly people, predominantly through the home help service (which in Sheffield had tended to concentrate on cleaning) and home wardens. There was a small but none the less significant contribution being made by the private sector.

Relationship between formal and informal care

Were the different sectors of formal and informal care combining to meet the needs of elderly people? Table 4.4 shows the distribution of help given by different principal carers, but we also collected information on other subsidiary carers and it is possible to describe the different patterns of collaboration between carers. There has been a great deal written about informal caring networks (Collins and Pancoast, 1976; Froland, *et al.*, 1981; Gottlieb, 1981; Whittaker and Garbarino, 1983; Yoder, Jonker and Leaper, 1985) and about the need for professionals and formal care staff to mesh their activities with the informal support network already in existence (Barclay Committee, 1982). The case for such 'network sensitivity' (Walker, 1985b) and the need for formal services to support the caring activities of the family (Walker, 1982a) has been established in theory but not often translated into practice. The relationship between the family and the formal sector is examined in Chapter 8; here we take a preliminary look at whether or not the formal services were supporting the caring activities of the family.

The most important fact to emerge from this analysis was that there were very few subsidiary carers; in most instances there was only one person doing the caring and tending and, as we have already shown, the vast majority of these carers were relatives. For many elderly people, therefore, there was no caring network. Nearly all of the 75-and-over age group had living relatives, and three out of four had daily contact with at least one relative (see Chapter 3), but the majority of relatives were not active in caring and tending.

Second, where there was more than one active carer it was usually another relative supporting the relative who was acting as principal carer. The main exceptions, which provide initial evidence of collaboration between formal and informal sectors rather than the displacement of the family, included washing and bathing, whereby the small number of second helpers were relatives supplementing the specialised skills of the district nurse. Then, in those cases in which there were second helpers with heavy laundry and heavy housework, there were a few instances of relatives supporting the activities of local authority workers. The largest number of secondary carers were found doing heavy shopping and preparing and cooking hot meals. Three out of four of those providing secondary help with heavy shopping were relatives supporting other relatives. There is a similar picture concerning the preparation and cooking of hot meals, but in this case there were instances of relatives supplementing the contribution of the local authority and vice versa.

Third, although neighbours and friends were only rarely fulfilling the role of principal carers, they were evident in a back-up capacity to relatives particularly in heavy shopping, heavy housework, preparing and cooking hot meals and gardening. For example, in doing heavy shopping one in four second helpers were neighbours of friends complementing the principal caring activities of relatives. So there was some indication of collaboration between the formal and informal sectors as well as within the informal sector (for further discussion see Chapter 7).

More information on the presence or absence of a caring network was gained from interviews with principal family carers themselves. It is important to emphasise here that the label principal carer does not necessarily mean that this person assisted their elderly relatives with every activity of daily life – the bulk of tasks were still performed by elderly people themselves – or that he or she was the principal carer in respect of every activity with which the elderly person required help. Indeed, on a number of the personal care and household management functions the majority of principal carers were *not* providing any help. These included toilet (90 per cent of carers were not helping), bathing (85 per cent), incontinent laundry (85 per cent) and transport (78 per cent). As regards other activities – such as shopping (12 per cent), laundry (31 per cent), cleaning (40 per cent) and social calls (16 per cent) – the proportions of carers not providing assistance were much smaller. Principal carer means the person doing most overall to care for the elderly person. With regard to toilet and bathing the majority of carers who were giving help were in fact supporting other main carers, in most cases a district nurse. When it came to incontinent laundry, in most cases where elderly people had carers help was not necessary because this was done by the elderly people themselves. The remainder were split equally between carers who had no help, those who provided assistance with another carer and those who were supplementing another main helper with incontinent laundry.

Turning to household management activities, there was a wide range of levels of involvement on the part of principal carers which supports the evidence adduced earlier from elderly people of collaboration in some aspects of care. For example, of those carers who did provide help with shopping just over one-fifth were the only people doing this but, in addition, similar proportions were main helpers getting some assistance; equal helpers with another person; and helping another person who did most of the shopping. This is a clear indication that the majority of those performing most of the caring and tending activities for their elderly relatives were able themselves to call on support, in some aspects of their caring role, from a wider caring network; two-thirds of principal carers were receiving help from at least one other person in doing the shopping for their elderly relatives. Let us be quite clear, we are *not* saying that the majority of elderly people were surrounded by a caring network which was operating in close co-operation to meet their needs: most of those providing help, support, assistance and care to elderly people were doing so alone, at least at the point of contact with the elderly person. But when it came to the more severely disabled needing substantial inputs of care and tending there is evidence from carers themselves that they were being assisted in performing at least some of these caring tasks. In most of the household management functions principal carers were most likely *not* to be assisting because the elderly coped by themselves, or to be playing a secondary role either to their elderly relative or to another person, usually another relative. Just over half of carers either did not help with laundry or merely assisted the elderly person who did most of it. The case was similar for six out of ten carers with regard to cooking meals. As far as cleaning the elderly person's house was concerned, two-thirds of carers either did not help or were assisting either the elderly person or another main cleaner, usually a local authority home help.

Carers were more often coping single-handedly with the administrative and social aspects of care and tending. For example, in cases where transport was provided for social visiting, regular checks that the elderly person was all right were being made or the elderly person was being accompanied outside, the principal carer was most likely to be the sole or equal main helper. Similarly, where help was provided with paying bills on time or financial administration, the principal carer was likely to be the only person involved apart from the elderly person. The one activity of daily living that carers did not consider it appropriate to be helping with was gardening. Only one in eight did any gardening for their elderly relative and none did it alone. The main reason for this was not lack of expressed need on the part of elderly people (see Table 4.2), but the strict social division of labour in caring and tending, particularly the gender division of labour, to which we turn now.

The gender division of labour in caring

We have shown that relatives performed the vast majority of caring and tending tasks, but which relatives were most likely to be carers? The two-stage answer to this question reveals a rigid division of labour based on gender and kinship, and the reasons for this division of labour are discussed in the next chapter.

In the first place, with only two exceptions – gardening and decorating – female relatives were far more likely than male relatives to be helping elderly people. Some gender divisions in caring and tending were expected from previous research (Land, 1978; Finch and Groves, 1980; Walker, 1981a; Nissel and Bonner-jea, 1982; Charlesworth, Wilkin and Durie, 1984), but even so the degree of inequality between the roles of men and women in caring was surprising. For example, in regard of light shopping the ratio of female to male relatives (excluding spouses) giving help was 6:1. In the case of heavy shopping – where men might have been expected to demonstrate their strength – the ratio of female to male non-spouse relatives giving assistance was 4:1. Differences between the contributions of male and female relatives towards helping elderly people with different activities of daily living reflected traditional gender stereotypes. So, for example, when it came to helping with heavy laundry the ratio of female to male carers was 22:1 (10:1 when spouses were included) and with light laundry it was 40:1 (13:1 when spouses were included). There was only one male relative (a husband) who helped in washing the elderly person's hair and, in the case of sewing, the only help from men was given by three husbands when their wives experienced difficulty or were unable to sew. Men, again husbands, were more likely to help with personal care than household management. Thus the ratio of female to male relatives helping with washing and bathing was just over 3:1.

Information about the ratio of female to male carers points to a differential gender response concerning the needs of elderly people. For example, female relatives (including spouses) were 33 times more likely than male relatives to be helping with heavy laundry where the elderly person was completely unable to do this. At similar levels of substantial need the ratios of female to male helpers with light laundry, heavy housework and heavy shopping were 9:1, 5:1 and 2:1 when spouses were included. There would seem to be a tendency for gender differences in helping with some tasks, such as light laundry, to be reduced when the elderly person was completely unable to perform them. Thus it might seem (uncharitably perhaps) that men, especially husbands, were being forced into caring by their spouses' disability. On the other hand it may have been that men were more inclined to play a part in caring as other female relatives including their wives were less able to manage.

While gender differences were narrowed in response to severe need for help in certain activities of daily living, when it came to the two exceptions to the primacy of female carers – gardening and decorating – differences were also reduced. In other words, when elderly people were unable to peform these functions women were as likely as men to be providing help. For instance, when elderly people reported some difficulty with decorating male relatives were twice as likely as female relatives to be providing help; whereas in cases of severe need, where elderly people were unable to decorate, female relatives were slightly more likely than male relatives to be giving the necessary help. This provides further confirmation of the point that female relatives predominated as principal carers and, although men made important contributions to some aspects of caring and tending, it was women who were most likely to be responsible for the whole range of personal care, household management and maintenance tasks and particularly so when their elderly relatives were severely disabled. It appears that with some exceptions, especially among husbands, men were able to choose which activities they helped with whereas female carers did not have such flexibility.

d, the one female relative above all others who was most
be doing the caring and tending was the elderly person's
daughter. The caring relationship was first and foremost one
between elderly mothers and younger daughters. This does not
mean that daughters were the only close kin acting as carers – the
range of relatives of the elderly person also included spouses, sons,
siblings, grandchildren, nieces and nephews, relatives-in-law and
cousins – but they were far more likely than other relatives to be
doing so. This can be illustrated with reference to three aspects of
household management. Excluding spouses, who were less frequent carers than daughters, daughters comprised three out of
every five relatives helping with heavy shopping and a further one
in ten were granddaughters or daughters-in-law; they represented
three out of five of the relatives who were helping with heavy
laundry with a further one in four being daughters-in-law; daughters
were two in every three of those relatives helping with heavy
housework and one in 12 were daughters-in-law.

Daughters were almost wholly unrivalled among those helping
with the personal care of elderly people. Thus the only non-spouse
relatives washing and bathing elderly people were daughters and
daughters-in-law. Four-fifths of those relatives helping elderly
people to wash their hair were daughters, with nearly all of the rest
being daughters-in-law and granddaughters.

Daughters were also the most likely relatives to be meeting severe
need among the elderly. Although a range of relatives was identified
as providing help with different tasks, particularly impersonal ones
that required low levels of commitment and irregular attendance
such as occasional shopping, cleaning and gardening, where the
elderly person was severely disabled in some function it was overwhelmingly daughters who were providing the necessary help.

In sum, relatives were far and away the principal source of care
and tending for the elderly. They were more likely than either
other informal carers or the formal services to be responding to
severe need. Among relatives it was primarily daughters who were
bearing the physical and mental burdens of the whole range of
caring and tending tasks.

The shortfall between need and care

Was the provision of care and tending by both the informal and formal sectors sufficient to meet the needs of elderly people? By our objective measures most instances of severe need were in receipt of care. But these figures do not reveal whether or not the assistance received was sufficient to meet fully the observed need. In order to address this question it is necessary to turn to other indicators, particularly the views of elderly people themselves about whether they received enough help. In doing so we encounter, in common with all similar attempts to assess need in old age, this paradox: by all normative standards a large proportion of elderly people can be shown objectively to be in, often considerable, need; but when the same people are questioned about unmet needs and sufficiency of existing social support their responses indicate a high level of satisfaction and low level of demand for additional services (see Walker, 1980, 1982c). This observation has contributed to the tendency noted at the outset of this chapter for some authorities to dismiss subjective opinions, or felt need and expressed needs, as inadequate guides to 'real' need.

This service – or practitioner-centred approach to need – results in narrow definitions of need which exclude the views of welfare users themselves (Foster, 1983, p. 26) or the contribution of the informal sector to meeting need. For example, Isaacs and Neville (1976, p. 13) distinguish between 'potential' need – where people are unable to perform for themselves all or some of the basic activities of daily living – and 'actual' need for social services, the difference being accounted for by the fact that many of those with potential need have their needs met by a family member or friend. The danger with this sort of oversimplified polarisation of needs and responses to need is that the interdependence of the formal and informal sectors, especially (as yet underdeveloped) role of the former in supporting the latter will be overlooked (Whittaker and Garbarino, 1983; Yoder, Jonker and Leaper, 1985). Indeed, as we show below, the assumption is frequently made by the social services that elderly people with a relative providing care and tending are having their needs fully met. This is mistaken and as we argue in Chapter 7 may, in the long run, contribute to greater demands on the formal sector as the relative, no longer able to cope alone and unsupported, suffers a breakdown. It is fundamental, therefore, for policy analysts and policy makers alike to regard all objective and subjective needs as real needs and to plan different sorts and levels of response to needs which are already being wholly or partly met within the informal sector as well as those where there is no response from informal carers.

While it is important not to dismiss subjective needs as irrelevant, it is necessary to bear in mind that for several reasons – including their depressed economic and social status, the rapid pace of change in conceptions of need over the course of their lives and the low priority given to them by social services (Walker, 1982c) – elderly people's aspirations with regard to welfare are often artificially low. Thus caution is required in interpreting subjective information about needs. It is unreasonable to expect people whose aspirations have been restricted and who lack detailed knowledge of possible welfare provision to *demand* services as if they were the idealised consumers in the perfectly competitive market place that exists only in the pages of economic textbooks. This is *not* to say that elderly people are not the best judges of their own abilities and needs (the objective measures of need used in this research relied on the opinions of individual elderly people), but that in assessing the *response* to need policy makers must take account of the factors which determine felt and expressed needs. Need is the most commonly used term in the literature on social policy and social welfare but very little attention has been given to the processes which determine need (for a full discussion, see Walker, 1980, 1982c).

The extent to which needs for care and tending were being met

The overall efficiency of the care system, especially in meeting severe need, was revealed by the fact that there was a clear inverse correlation between the need for care and the receipt of care indices. The overwhelming bulk of those with a substantial need for care were receiving a high amount of care, while a similarly large proportion of those with little or no need for care were receiving no or low inputs of care. All the same, at the margins there was a significant minority of elderly people whose needs for care and tending were not being met or met fully, and it is this group that primarily concerns us here.

Starting in general terms, there were just over one in ten elderly people in need of substantial amounts of care but who were only receiving a low input of care. On the basis of this finding we estimate that nationally some 75 000 people aged 75 and over who are in severe need are not receiving sufficient care and tending from either the formal or informal sectors. Moreover, for the reasons advanced in the introduction this is likely to be an underestimate. In contrast to this relatively small amount of unmet severe need, less severe instances did not receive the expected response from informal or formal carers. Nearly seven out of ten of those elderly people with a moderate need for care were in receipt of only a low care input. This suggests that, in the whole of Great Britain, there are more than 360 000 people aged 75 and over with moderate levels of need but receiving inadequate amounts of care and tending.

Table 4.5 provides a detailed picture of the shortfall of care in relation to need and contrasts objective with subjective indicators of need. This confirms the point (already made repeatedly) that where there was a substantial need for help or assistance this was usually being met (primarily by relatives). There were important exceptions in the area of personal care and household management, especially the considerable degree of unmet severe need in going up and down stairs and the smaller proportions of unmet severe need in sewing, cutting toenails and light housework. The column showing those in need as a proportion of the whole population points to the general incidence of need and suggests that there is a considerable shortfall: for example, one in five of those aged 75 and over were not receiving any help cutting their toenails when they needed it, and one in ten of the elderly people in need of assistance with heavy housework were not getting it. Overall, some one in six of those assessed as being in substantial need of care and tending were receiving no help at all.

It is important to note that even where the informal sector was dominant in the provision of care and tending (see Table 4.4), in activities such as shopping and laundry, there was still a significant gap between need and receipt of help. This gap was not being filled by the formal sector. On the basis of the figures in Table 4.5 we estimate that some 380 000 people aged 75 and over are in need of help with heavy shopping but not receiving it; 370 000 are in need of help getting in and out of bed but not getting it; and 348 000 need but do not receive help with heavy housework (of course, there was considerable overlap between these groups).

These comparisons are based on objective assessments of need; when we turn to subjectively expressed needs the numbers of

Table 4.5 *Percentage of elderly people needing but not receiving any or enough care and tending*

	Objective				Subjective		
	Degree of need*			Total as percentage of whole population	In need, receiving help; want more	In need, not receiving help; want some	Total as percentage of whole population
	Low	High	Total				
	% not helped	% not helped	Total				
Washing all over	(57.8)	(0.0)	(32.8)	6.3	(7.7)	(5.3)	1.3
Getting in/out of bed	(87.5)	(0.0)	(71.4)	11.6	(0.0)	(8.6)	1.0
Going up/down stairs	94.9	81.0	93.9	35.5	(0.0)	3.7	1.3
Washing hair	37.0	2.8	22.0	5.9	1.6	(0.0)	0.3
Cutting toenails	72.2	7.3	37.7	20.8	17.3	25.4	11.3
Sewing	58.3	9.7	35.8	8.2	(0.0)	(12.5)	1.0
Heavy shopping	39.1	1.8	17.9	11.9	3.0	(22.2)	4.3
Light shopping	52.0	0.0	13.1	4.8	1.2	(23.1)	1.3
Heavy laundry	31.2	0.0	14.2	6.7	2.5	(15.0)	2.0
Light laundry	53.8	0.0	20.3	5.0	1.8	(7.1)	0.7
Heavy housework	36.6	3.3	17.0	10.9	9.2	(21.2)	7.0
Light housework	53.3	7.4	31.6	6.3	(7.7)	(11.1)	1.7
Preparing and cooking hot meals	41.2	0.0	22.2	4.6	6.1	(14.3)	1.7
Gardening	30.0	9.7	20.6	9.3	16.0	(38.5)	8.7
Decorating	14.9	10.5	11.4	9.1	—	—	—

*Low = those who experienced some difficulty with the task; high = those who could not do the task.

elderly people effectively demanding inputs of care, for the reasons advanced earlier, were much lower. Overall, three in ten elderly people expressed a need for help in at least one of the activities of daily living, although a quarter of these were dissatisfied *only* with the lack of help available with gardening. As Table 4.5 shows, the most frequently expressed needs were for help with cutting toenails and with gardening, followed by assistance with heavy housework. The shortfall in chiropody services in Sheffield was widely acknowledged, and was still one of the expressed concerns of Sheffield Pensioners' Action Group in 1988. Although gardening was most often expressed as the sole 'practical' need, chiropody was most often linked with other expressed needs and it may well be that improved foot care might alleviate some of the need for help with shopping and housework.

Despite the fact that the main thrust of the formal services, particularly home helps, has been towards housework and other routine domestic help, there seems to be a substantial amount of felt need in this area. If those who required help with gardening only are omitted from the analysis then just over one in five (22 per cent of the sample) expressed a need for help with one or more of the listed activities of daily living.

Women were more likely than men to express a need for help. One in three women felt that they did not get enough help in at least one area, compared with one in six men. There was also a (not surprising) difference between those over and those under the age of 80. Four-fifths of those aged under 80 expressed no felt needs for help with the activities of daily living, compared with three-fifths of those aged 80 or more.

About one-third of home help clients identified a felt shortfall in home help type tasks, although not all of these said that they wanted more home help. One in five home help clients identified a felt shortfall in personal care, which implies that home helps were not always successfully detecting additional problems not directly relevant to their own service. One-fifth of those elderly people who did not receive home help experienced a felt shortfall in household tasks or personal care. It was clear that the needs of those elderly people who acknowledged a shortfall and felt that they needed help were not being adequately met, let alone the needs of the much larger number of people who experienced difficulties but did not express a need for help. The extent of this latent need was substantial in some cases and indicated that articulated needs are only the tip of the iceberg.

Elderly people were more likely to suggest that the help they were receiving was not sufficient to meet their need when they were clients of the formal sector. On only one of the activities of daily living – gardening – did the proportion who were receiving help from relatives and who said it was not sufficient exceed 5 per cent. But for those receiving help from the health and personal social services with washing, cutting toenails and light laundry the proportions saying that the help they received was insufficient was twice that level, and for heavy housework and the provision of hot meals they rose to 17 per cent and 25 per cent. Obviously there is a greater readiness on the part of elderly people to imply criticism of (and impose additional burdens on) formal helpers than informal ones, but there is some indication that the amount of services going to individual elderly people was not enough to meet their needs. Moreover there is a signal from a small minority of elderly people that the level of help they are receiving from relatives is insufficient to meet their needs. In short, in spite of the remarkable effectiveness of the family in responding to the needs of their disabled elderly relatives there is a significant minority of such people who are either not receiving the care they need or are not getting enough to meet their needs. There was nothing to suggest that the formal sector, particularly the public services, had fully recognised its role in meeting these two different sources of need.

It was noted earlier that in addition to those needing assistance and not receiving it there were some elderly people getting help when, on objective grounds, they did not need it. Unfortunately it was not the case that this help could simply be redistributed to those who did need it because it was provided overwhelmingly by relatives. There were very few instances of the public sector making provision when it was not needed, although the private sector – in the form of hairdressers and chiropodists – did so more commonly. In only 9 per cent of cases where assistance was received with heavy laundry when there was no apparent need for it, 5 per cent of those getting unnecessary help with light laundry and 14 per cent of such help with heavy housework was this provided by the social services department. This finding may be partly a reflection of some overestimation of their abilities by elderly people (Townsend, 1962; Isaacs and Neville, 1976: Walker and Townsend, 1976) but it may also reveal the need for more detailed assessments of need prior to the supply of home helps and home wardens.

Elderly people as carers

One of the more distorting and damaging consequences of the tendency to regard elderly people purely as dependent recipients of services is that their contribution to the life of the family and community in general, and to the care of others in particular, is often overlooked. It has already been shown that the majority of those aged 75 and over remained active and not in need of care and attention. But, in addition, many of those in need were not simply passive recipients of care but were themselves providing help and support to others.

Conscious of the role of elderly people in family and community highlighted by early research on the subject (Townsend, 1963; Shanas *et al.*, 1968) but neglected recently, we asked elderly respondents about the help they provided to others, employing a schedule of activities of daily living similar to the one used to assess the need for care. The results showed that a significant proportion were engaged in caring activities, often involving substantial commitments of time and effort. For example, 4 per cent of elderly people were providing personal care to another person, usually their spouse. All of them were in the age range of 75–9, two-thirds were married women and most of the help was provided at least once every day. In Great Britain as a whole we estimate that as many as 138 000 people aged 75 and over are providing this sort of personal care. Most of these carers had some disability and, out of the previous total, some 54 000 carers aged 75 and over have minor or more severe disabilities. Most of those giving personal care to another person were receiving some care themselves.

Nearly one in ten elderly people were providing help with housework, representing over 298 000 people in the country as a whole. Again most were in the 75–9 age band, but one-third were over 80. Half were men and half women. One in five of them suffered from appreciable or severe disabilities. Five per cent of elderly people helped another person with laundry and 4 per cent with child care.

Even larger numbers of the elderly were involved in general caring and tending activities which did not involve physical effort. For example, one in ten provided regular advice and counselling to other people, and just over one in five gave emotional support and social company. Those giving sedentary support included the most severely disabled, one-fifth of whom gave emotional support daily.

There is clear evidence here, therefore, that even the very elderly (those aged 75 and over) cannot be regarded as passive recipients of care and tending or as wholly dependent on others; on the contrary, many of them are actively engaged in caring for others.

Psychological and social needs

Thus far we have concentrated on the activities of daily living because it is clear that the performance of such basic tasks is an essential basis for survival in the community. However, the question of physical survival, although fundamental, can only be the beginning of any investigation of needs, demands and assistance. Recent studies, which have shown that up to 25 or 30 per cent of elderly people in the community are suffering from symptoms of depression (see Hanley and Baikie, 1984), emphasise the importance of considering 'higher' needs. Given that elderly people are more likely than those in other age groups to suffer bereavement and ill health (with consequent restricted mobility), they may be vulnerable to affective psychiatric disorder. The next section of this chapter investigates the psychological well-being of elderly respondents and considers the possible influences upon morale, loneliness and boredom, with particular focus upon the role which is played by family and friends.

Morale and loneliness

There were two measurements of morale. One scale measured attitude towards the effects of ageing; the other, satisfaction or acceptance of the current situation. The first was one dimension of the PGCMS as identified by Lawton (1972, 1975) and adapted to an English context by Challis and Knapp (1979). The second was used by Mark Abrams (1980) in the surveys of people over pension age conducted by Age Concern.

Attempts to demonstrate that family contact has a significant effect upon morale have been made a number of times but no convincing effect has been demonstrated (Lee and Ellithorpe, 1982). There has been a much clearer relationship between morale and measurements of health and disability, and also between morale and level of education, although this latter association may have been the consequence of an effect of unmeasured variables such as income, or other material resources.

The two measures of morale were highly correlated, but there were interesting differences: for example, women's scores on average reflected a more negative attitude towards the effects of ageing than men's, but an equal amount of acceptance/satisfaction. Of course the experience of ageing was indeed different for the two sexes, with widowhood, disability and restricted mobility being more common among women. In this respect the similar levels of acceptance are perhaps more surprising than the differing attitudes towards ageing. Neither measure of morale was significantly correlated with class, but for people living alone the level of income was related to both measures of morale, and level of savings to acceptance/satisfaction only.

The degree of contact with family did correlate significantly with both measures of morale, but not with the degree of felt loneliness. Wenger (1984) suggests that contact with friends is more important in dispelling loneliness among elderly people than contact with family; however, in the Sheffield study, degree of contact with friends was not significantly related to morale or loneliness. Nevertheless, the existence of a spouse, or someone within the family to whom the elderly person felt 'especially close', *was* significant in relation to loneliness, as was the existence of friends. This suggests that quantity of contact may not be of overwhelming importance in overcoming feelings of loneliness when compared with quality, although the fact that many elderly people wished to see more of their friends (24 per cent) and at least one of their relatives (42 per cent) suggests that they at least would have welcomed an increased quantity of contact with specific people. The distinction (Townsend and Tunstall, 1968) between loneliness as a result of restricted contact in general, and 'desolation' resulting from insufficient contact with specific people, has often been made, and such factors are undoubtedly at work here. The existence or non-existence of a specially close relationship with at least one family member was not significantly related to the way people felt about the effects of ageing, but it *was* related to their acceptance/satisfaction with their present situation.

It should probably be emphasised that two out of three elderly people said that they were never lonely, but equally one in ten were lonely all or most of the time, and one in four were sometimes or occasionally lonely.

There were differences according to household type which might be expected, with over half of those living alone confessing to some degree of loneliness compared with only one in four of those living with a spouse or others. Half of those who were widowed experienced some loneliness, but single people (that is, those who never married) were no more likely to be lonely than those who were married. About three out of four single people were never lonely.

With regard to difficulty in passing the time, differences between those of different marital status were even more pronounced. Over 90 per cent of single people had no difficulty, compared with 80 per cent of those married and 69 per cent of the widowed. There were only two elderly people in the sample who described themselves as divorced (one male, one female) and both said that they were lonely all or most of the time and 'often' had difficulty in passing their time. It seems likely that the experience of those over 74 who are divorced can be expected to be readily comparable to the experiences of subsequent generations, and certainly the number in our sample is too small for generalisation. However, other studies (such as M. Abrams, 1978) have suggested that divorced elderly people have less family contact than others. Overall, one in four elderly people reported at least occasional difficulty in passing the time although only 9 per cent in all said they felt this 'often'. Differences between people living in different household types were less pronounced than differences in felt loneliness. Between 70 and 80 per cent of those living alone or with others had no difficulty passing the time. Such difficulties were related to mobility: almost half (48 per cent) of the 44 people who were (not just temporarily) housebound replied 'often' or 'sometimes' to this question, compared with only a quarter of those who were not housebound, and there were similar differences with regard to felt loneliness and mobility.

Elderly people were asked about the activities in which they did engage and almost half (46 per cent) said that they spent more time on performing domestic tasks than any other activity. Five per cent of elderly people were unable to specify any particular activity, saying that they spent most time 'just sitting' or 'staring out of the window'.

For each person the two most frequent activities were recorded. One-third of elderly people gave 'watching television' as one of the two activities, and 57 per cent specified 'domestic tasks'. Just under one-third (31 per cent) listed 'reading books or papers' as one of their main activities. Other pastimes were going for walks (7 per cent) and visiting friends or relatives (5 per cent). Since this was an open question, not all answers could be classified and 6 per cent of replies represented individual activities which could not be classified.

How can problems of boredom, loneliness and low morale be overcome? We know that those living alone, those widowed and those disabled or housebound are most at risk. Our results, which show the link between felt loneliness and intimate relationships, indicate that to alleviate such problems it may be necessary to facilitate contact with specific people. This can be done by transport, telephones, help with letter-writing or reading if necessary, and perhaps less directly by temporarily relieving relatives of other problems, such as sick or handicapped children. If loss is a consequence of bereavement, bereavement counselling can be helpful (Barker, 1983). Increasing quantity of contact through voluntary visiting, lunch clubs or day centres might not help immediately but would provide the potential for the formation of new relationships. As we shall see, such activities did play an important role in the lives of some elderly people.

Voluntary organisations

It has been frequently suggested that volunteers could take over many statutory functions (see, for example, Jenkin, 1981) and also that agents of voluntary organisations are more able than statutory workers to play a befriending role in relation to other people.

Of course, the term voluntary activity covers a wide spectrum from the direct provision of services to mutual aid and self-help. The same form of activity – for example, organising a pensioners' club – might be seen as self-help if run by pensioners, or a service if run by a church or a voluntary organisation such as Age Concern. Let us examine services first.

Day centres. Of those who attended day centres (20 people), one in five reported that the centre was run by a voluntary organisation; however, since a further 30 per cent did not know who ran the centre they attended, this may be an underestimate of voluntary activity in this area.

Voluntary visiting. Reports of voluntary visitors were very rare: less than 2 per cent of elderly people mentioned such visitors, but of course this is almost certainly an underestimate, both because voluntary visitors may have become friends, and also because visits by church members, for example, might not be perceived by the elderly person as visits from a volunteer. Just under one in six elderly people reported friends who came regularly 'for a chat'.

Let us now consider participatory activities.

Attendance at clubs. Fifty-one people (17 per cent) attended clubs for elderly people, and about half of these went more often than once a week. Those who attended were asked how important attendance was to them and 90 per cent rated it as 'quite' or 'very' important. There was a relationship between frequency of attendance and rating of importance, with two-thirds of those attending more than once a week rating the activity as 'very' important, compared with less than half (44 per cent) of those who attended weekly.

Sixty-one people (20 per cent) attended clubs or organisations which were not specifically for elderly people (this excludes attendance at church). One in four attended less often than weekly, but those who attended weekly, or more often, were slightly *less* likely than those who attended clubs specifically for elderly people to rate such activities as 'very' important. One-third of weekly attenders and half of more frequent attenders rated attendance as 'very' important.

In all, one in three elderly people attended a club or organisation, either specifically for elderly people or a more general organisation, or (sometimes) both. Two-thirds, therefore, did *not* engage in such activity. When asked if there was any particular reason why they did not attend the most frequent response, as might be expected, was that the elderly person did not wish to do so (42 per cent), but one in three of those who did not attend pointed to disability, with consequent restriction of mobility. A small number mentioned that their disability (for instance, deafness) made enjoyment of social events difficult.

Church membership. One in three elderly people attended church, at least occasionally, and half of attenders rated church membership as 'very' important. Middle-class respondents were about twice as likely to be church members as working-class respondents, although since two-thirds of all respondents were working class, this had the consequence that there were about equal numbers of working-class and middle-class among the members.

There were no class differences in attendance at clubs specifically for elderly people, but middle-class people were more likely to attend other kinds of clubs or organisations (33 per cent of middle-class respondents and 14 per cent of working-class respondents did so). This lends some, but not unequivocal, support to the findings of American studies (Shanas and Streib, 1965; Rosow, 1967) that middle-class elderly people are reluctant to take part in activities which would label them as 'elderly', and prefer more general activities.

Voluntary work by elderly people. Eight per cent of elderly people themselves engaged in voluntary work, most often once a week or more. Two-thirds of voluntary workers were middle class. A further 9 per cent had engaged in voluntary work since retirement but had since given this up, most often because of their own or their spouse's poor health. Unsurprisingly, participation in voluntary work decreased with age, with no one over 85 taking part, compared with one in ten of those under 80. This may explain why men were more likely to report such activity than women, to the extent that the elderly volunteer workforce was only just over 50 per cent female.

The significance of other forms of voluntary activity, such as campaigning or lobbying on behalf of, or by, elderly people, cannot be assessed from our data. However, it is clear that there is a greater impact on the lives of elderly people through their membership of clubs or organisations than through any direct provision of services by voluntary organisations. It is also clear that health or disability prevents about one in five of all people aged 75 or more from attending such activities when they might otherwise wish to do so. This underlines the importance of transport, or the lack of it, as regards the opportunities available for social contact for disabled people over 75 (see Chapter 3).

Need and care: case studies

Before concluding this examination of need and care two detailed case studies might help both to underline the diversity of need in advanced old age and, as an introduction to the second half of the book, illustrate contrasting family networks and relationships. The first, an elderly woman with appreciable disability, had no close family and, consequently, a very limited family network. However, there was a wider neighbourhood support which she, in turn, contributed to herself. The second reveals intensive family assistance to a more severely disabled elderly woman.

Mrs Crampton

(Appreciable disability: no regular assistance)

Mrs Crampton was a widow of 90 who lived alone in a privately rented house. She moved to this house to join her mother and sisters when she was widowed 40 years ago. She had no children and had only one sister living, who was aged 96 and in a geriatric hospital. Mrs Crampton did not visit her sister; she said that her sister 'knows no one' and that she did not really want to see her. The only relative with whom Mrs Crampton had any contact was a niece, aged 65, who called in weekly and offered help with shopping, which was rarely accepted.

Mrs Crampton suffered from arthritis in her knees and could be unsteady on her feet. She described her health as very good although she had difficulty with washing herself all over, cutting toenails, heavy shopping and heavy housework. She had a regular medical check-up from her doctor every three months but considered herself to be, in general, 'unimpressed by the medical profession' and treated any minor illness with herbal remedies. Mrs Crampton described herself as an 'awkward devil' when it comes to accepting help, and generally coped with all her own washing, cleaning and shopping. She went out without assistance, although she could not get on a bus, and made regular trips to the local shops where she was well known and readily provided with a chair for a few minutes' rest and a chat before the walk home.

Gardeners from the local park sometimes came over to clip her hedge and cut her front grass but Mrs Crampton attended to all the lighter gardening tasks, as well as caring for a flourishing collection of houseplants. Gardening (primarily grass-cutting) was the only activity with which Mrs Crampton said she would like more help; however, she was at pains to stress she would not ask for any. One neighbour had asked if she might 'try out a new pair of power shears' on Mrs Crampton's hedge, which suggested a sensitive appreciation of her desire for independence. She did feel that she had friends among her neighbours, although she had little contact with her immediate neighbours on either side. She kept in touch with a small group of friends by visits and correspondence and said she was 'never' lonely. Indeed, when asked whether there were any days in the past week on which she saw no-one she replied 'If there were, I was glad'.

Mrs Crampton had no particular wish to remain in her current home, which she felt was too large for her needs, especially as she had difficulty in climbing up and down stairs. However she was anxious to remain in the same neighbourhood where she had easy access to friends and shops and where she was known. She had recently applied for a flat in a local sheltered housing scheme (run by a charitable trust), unfortunately she was told that it was not possible for her application to be considered because she was 'too old'. Since she felt this would be the only acceptable alternative to her present circumstances she anticipated that she would remain where she was. If she became unable to manage alone it would 'not be possible' for her to live with her niece. 'I tell them, if I become incapable, send me off to Lodge Moor [hospital]'.

Mrs Crampton's morale was high and she said that people came to her to be cheered up.

Mrs Crampton did have a limited network of informal support which was sufficiently unobtrusive for her to find it acceptable. Equally, she provided emotional support to other people. There were insufficient resources in the network to provide intensive support in the short or long term. However, it was clearly important to Mrs Crampton to remain in her current locality, even though her immediate environment posed some problems. Her unsuccessful attempt to transfer to sheltered housing demonstrated the limitation of a policy of allocation based on ideas about the relationship between chronological age and dependency which clearly did not apply in this case.

Mrs Williams

(Very severe disability: considerable statutory and informal help)

Mrs Williams was a widow of 80 who lived alone in a council flat which was just across the road from her daughter. She was housebound, severely disabled by arthritis and able to walk short distances only with the assistance of a walking frame. She had lived in her present flat for only a few months, and she moved in order to be nearer her daughter, Mrs Jones. In fact Mrs Jones had provided regular assistance to her mother for four years, but a combination of Mrs Williams' deteriorating condition and Mrs Jones' husband's illness meant that Mrs Williams finally acceded to her daughter's repeated requests to move closer.

> The main thing was when my husband came to be ill, I think she looked at it in a different light ... I think that's what prompted her to come down here, because I've asked her lots of times. I don't think she particularly wanted to when she came, but I think she thought about us as well. (Daughter)

Mrs Williams reported that she never saw any neighbours in her new flat and no longer felt a part of the neighbourhood. She would have liked to see her old friends and neighbours more but could not, now that she had moved. She said that she was 'sometimes' lonely but that there was 'nothing' she could do about it. She did not have a telephone, and an application for assistance with the cost of a phone had been refused. Mrs Williams received supplementary pension and had no savings. She had applied for an attendance allowance but did not know the result as yet.

Set against this diminution in contact with friends and neighbours must be additional contact with family members and a better quality of physical care. All Mrs Williams' meals were provided by her daughter or son-in-law, who also did some housework, laundry and shopping. Previously, meals had been a problem: 'she wasn't getting anything to eat up there. Because she couldn't cook anything, she couldn't hold anything to put in the oven. She had to rely on her sister calling. They said no to meals on wheels.' None the less the daughter recognised her mother's current problem: 'the main thing what my mother needs is company, that's definitely the main thing. The more company she's got the happier she is.'

At the previous house, Mrs Williams had received regular home help and warden service. However, once she had moved, services were reduced: warden service ceased completely and the home help service became irregular. Mrs Jones said: 'Before she came here, she had the home help, she also had a warden every morning. They wouldn't let her have one here because they said I'd have to do it, they knocked that off.' Regular help from a bath nurse was still received.

Mrs Williams said that she would prefer a home help to do some of the tasks which her daughter did but commented: 'if it were possible, but there's no chance'. Mrs Williams considered that her daughter should have more help in doing what she did for her, and also mentioned that her daughter was in need of help financially herself. (When the carer interview was conducted it transpired that the attendance allowance application had been successful.)

Mr Jones, her son-in-law, who regularly provided assistance on the two days a week when his wife was at work, had been made redundant three years ago and had subsequently developed a disabling disease which made it impossible for him to go to work. Two adult grandsons still lived at home with their parents, although Mrs Jones commented at interview that she was 'dying to get rid of them'. They visited their grandmother daily, sometimes taking meals across.

Mrs Jones described a typical day as follows:

About 10.30 a.m.   Go over and give Mrs Williams her break-
                   fast. Stay about half an hour and make sure
                   Mrs Williams begins to get up.

I don't do anything for her more than what I have to because
she's got to move about . . . once I start it she's going to stop
. . . I see that she gets herself up, it takes her a long time, and
she dresses herself, I mean, she's all day, and it doesn't matter
if it takes her all day she's going to do it and that's it.

5.30 p.m.   Go over with evening meal. Stay about half-
            an-hour.
7.30 p.m.   My husband might go over with a glass of
            Guinness.
8.30–10.30 p.m.   May stay and watch television with Mrs
                  Williams for a couple of hours before help-
                  ing her to bed.

In fine weather Mrs Williams was sometimes taken out in a
wheelchair. Once a year she had a day at the races, travelling in
the family car. Mrs Jones commented that they would like to go
on more outings but could not afford the petrol.

In previous years Mrs Williams had gone into short-term
residential care during family holidays, but when she had moved
closer an attempt had been made to keep her at home, putting in
an additional warden service in the morning and with one grandson responsible for evening meals.

I said my eldest son would try to see to her at teatimes, with
her meals, which turned out to be a nightmare. He managed
but . . . well, of course, you've met my mother and she doesn't
mince words. She said this warden wouldn't do anything, she
walked in and she walked out in five minutes, and she asked
her if she would fetch her something and she said no, she
didn't do no shopping, and so it wasn't a success, anyway.

Mrs Jones considered that her biggest help and support was her
husband.

My husband is ever so placid, which is a very good thing. I think if I'd got some blokes it would be finito, and they wouldn't stand for it. He's the mainstay because he's absolutely fabulous, he always has been ... I get depressed, definitely. Sometimes you think 'Oh another day the same' but as I say if it weren't for him I'd just ... oh, you know. Sometimes I say to John, oh you go and take her her breakfast, and he doesn't hesitate.

Mrs Jones considered her own relationship with her mother to be somewhat stormy: 'We row like hell, we always have done. We wouldn't live if we didn't. She tells me and I tell her.' When asked what sort of things did they row about Mrs Jones replied, 'Oh, any little thing, it depends who's in the worst temper but we're very good to one another.'

One area of dispute was Mrs Jones' determination to keep her mother moving and performing small tasks for herself.

I'll say to her, 'you've sat there three hours and you've never moved' and she'll say 'I have, I've been there and I've done this'. I say 'You've never moved mother, I can tell. Why don't you just get up and go to the window with your frame? You've got to keep moving' then, when my husband goes she'll say to him 'Oh, she's been playing hell again'. Her and my husband are great mates. I think sometimes she thinks more of him than she does of me.

If she did [deteriorate] I should still want her keeping at home. I could cope. I'd feel as if I'd want to cope, I should try to cope anyway.

This example raises issues about moving house which also troubled other carers. It was recognised that to move meant the disruption of the elderly person's own informal network of neighbours and friends, and sometimes other relatives. On the other hand this had to be balanced against the difficulties for the carer in providing an adequate level of support over a long distance, and the needs of the elderly person which remained unmet. This instance illustrates that a change in the carer's circumstances (Mr Jones' illness) can be as influential as any changes in the elderly person's circumstances. The provision of regular meals might have alleviated the carer's anxieties but statutory help, though sought, was apparently not available in this instance. Mrs Williams exchanged her council house for a smaller flat but, even so, considerable effort had been expended by the daughter in negotiating with the Housing Department to ensure that a flat nearby, which she knew was becoming vacant, was allocated to Mrs Williams. With a daughter nearby Mrs Williams apparently became a less urgent priority case for domiciliary assistance, especially with the home help coming at irregular intervals to wash the floors and clean the inside of the windows. This help was valued but, although Mrs Williams tried to encourage her daughter to telephone and complain about the period (up to five weeks) when no home help called, Mrs Jones' response was, 'What's the use?'

Mrs Williams' loneliness was acknowledged by her and recognised by her daughter. She did not wish to have a voluntary visitor and was 'not interested' in attending a club or other organisation. What would have helped was more contact with people she used to live near, specifically her sister and other friends, or the development of new relationships. Mrs Jones felt that the home helps, and particularly the wardens, had also performed a useful social function in relation to her mother and regretted that the loss of their practical assistance also meant the loss of some friendly company which her mother had enjoyed.

The provision of a telephone would have given Mrs Williams more opportunity for social interaction, and it would also have given her more control over her own life in some respects: for example, she could have rung the home help organiser herself.

Conclusion

By applying the concept of disability to the assessment of need in old age we have demonstrated that the majority of very elderly people do not require assistance and care, or need only small amounts. Moreover this chapter has also shown that where need exists this is being met predominantly by family carers, and daughters in particular. However, despite the effectiveness of the informal sector, we also uncovered a significant shortfall in the provision of care: a gap that was not being filled by the formal sector.

5

Patterns of Caring

Factors influencing the provision of informal care

We now turn from considering the need for care to examining the primary response to such need which comes from within the informal sector and the family in particular. Considerable attention has been devoted in recent research to the issue of who cares and at what cost, but very little information exists on *why* they care and what factors influence the provision of informal care. These are the main unanswered questions to which this research was addressed and both here and in the following two chapters we begin to provide answers to them.

It may be felt, with regard to the generation of informal care, that factors such as individual social contexts and idiosyncratic personal histories may be more important than normative obligations or structural material conditions. For those holding such a belief, attempts to discover detailed 'rules' determining patterns of care or caring personnel would be doomed to failure precisely because individual experiences are so varied and depend on the balance of affect, trust and reciprocity in a particular relationship. Thus, as P. Abrams (1978a) has speculated,

'Perhaps we should just recognise that we are dealing with relationships so entangled, ramified and minutely varied that they cannot be ordered at all or can be ordered only by an effort quite out of proportion to any conceivable results.'

Abrams described (although he did not endorse) this sense of despair as resulting from the consistent appearance of 'other factors' which intervene in any attempt to isolate particular influences upon informal caring. He considered it an established fact that both affect and reciprocity are important determinants of informal helping. We investigated both of these bases for care: first, in questions about emotional closeness and shared interests between the elderly person and their helper and, second, in questions about past and present help given by the elderly person to the helper. The findings suggest that *neither* affect nor reciprocity are necessary conditions for the provision of practical care or tending. This is particularly clear when the carers are the elderly person's children. Of course the focus of attention of this study is the family care of the elderly, whereas Abrams' discussion was of informal care in general. However, in our community-wide survey of elderly people, over 84 per cent of elderly people receiving practical informal help were receiving it from relatives only (see Chapters 3 and 4). So, in looking at determinants of care by relatives, we are investigating the factors underlying the overwhelming part of informal practical caring or tending activity.

It is not intended to argue that reciprocity and affect are unimportant; indeed, as we explore in the following chapter, the qualitative data from informal helpers indicated that they were extremely important factors in determining the nature of the caring experience. However, our initial concern is with the factors governing the *supply* of practical assistance to those elderly people who are experiencing, in Abrams' words, 'low-level chronic dependency' and who form the bulk of the elderly population receiving informal assistance.

There is some debate in the literature about the relative importance of material as opposed to ideological factors in determining why help is given and by whom. The key area in which this debate has been taking place has been in discussion of the causes and consequences of the consistent finding of empirical studies that the vast bulk of caring activity is performed by women (see Chapter 2). For example, Ungerson (1983a) describes the ways in which ideology and structurally produced material conditions could be mutually reinforcing (see also Land, 1978; Finch and Groves, 1980; Wilson, 1982). Most obviously the unequal positions of men and women in the labour market make it likely that for a married couple the most 'rational' decision would be for the woman to give up work to care for elderly relatives rather than the man. This in turn, as it happens on a larger scale, reinforces the general belief that caring is women's work.

The influence of unemployment on caring

An example of a structural factor that has been suggested as a possible influence concerning changes in caring behaviour is male unemployment. This, it has been suggested, alters the material conditions of individual families in such a way as to make caring by men as well as, or instead of, women a more rational proposition (for a contrary view, see Walker, 1982b, p. 33), but recent work on the effects of unemployment on the division of domestic labour have shown little indication of changes in patterns of behaviour (Morris, 1985). Indeed, there is some indication that unemployed men are even *less* likely to assist with domestic tasks than employed men (Morris, 1985). As we began to show in Chapter 3, our evidence about caring showed a similar pattern. That is, unemployed sons not only had *less* contact with their elderly parents than working sons, they were also *less* likely to be giving them any practical assistance. Nearly two in five working sons compared with one in five of unemployed sons provided assistance to elderly parents.

At present the low status of women in the labour market – the likelihood that they work part time and/or earn low wages – and the operation of financial penalties on the earnings of wives whose husbands claim benefits mean that there is often no financial incentive for a woman to work once her husband is unemployed. Thus a husband's unemployment might well mean the wife having more time to devote to domestic or caring activities. However, the shortage of material resources, in particular reduced income, may render helping more difficult (for example, by limiting a carer's ability to travel).

In addition to these material factors, a number of other explanations for the failure to renegotiate domestic relationships have been suggested, most of which would also apply to a failure to assist in practical caring activities. First, there is the suggestion that most unemployed men believe their situation to be temporary, and so there is 'no point' in taking on regular obligations or acquiring new skills which would have to be abandoned on taking a job. Second, there is another suggestion which is more closely tied to a conception of normative beliefs preventing changes in behaviour. Morris (1985) suggests that the assumption of responsibility for 'female' tasks involves a threat to a man's gender identity which is already damaged by the loss of paid employment. Also, through lack of experience, the quality of the husband's domestic labour is likely to be relatively poor – a situation that men have been known to exploit – and so it is felt to be quicker, less troublesome and more efficient for the wife to continue to perform these tasks.

Among carers interviewed in our study only one male was unemployed (although four were retired). This helper had in fact been performing caring activities when employed full time and thus helping while unemployed involved no change to his self-image. All the retired male helpers said that they had become more likely to engage in 'female' tasks since they had retired (although in two cases this was at least partly a consequence of their wives' disability). However, numbers are too small for this to be anything other than impressionistic evidence that engaging in caring activities when retired may be less threatening to men than to do so when unemployed.

Of course, retirement occupies a completely different status from unemployment, being a permanent end to labour force participation rather than a temporary interruption: a fact reflected in the higher levels of morale and low levels of stigma associated with retirement and early retirement (Shanas *et al.*, 1968, p. 323; Walker, Noble and Westergaard, 1985). In addition, these findings lend support to the idea that acceptance of a degree of permanence regarding a new situation makes for a more adaptive response to it. As one retired married man who was providing assistance to an elderly neighbour put it: 'When I retired my attitude changed . . . When I retired I said to Annie [wife] "Well all right, now I am going to retire, you can retire up to a point." My attitude has changed since I retired.'

This example underlines the fact that normative beliefs influencing an individual's propensity to provide care include not only those which cover appropriate behaviour towards elderly relatives or neighbours in need, but also those concerning appropriate gender roles in relation to employment and the division of domestic labour. In the follow-up survey helpers were asked about normative beliefs in all these areas. Inevitably the problematic relationship between normative belief systems, norms of behaviour and material conditions will be a continuing focus of interest.

Belief systems and structural conditions

There is evidence from previous research that normative belief systems persist and continue to influence behaviour even after the material conditions which originally sustained them have substantially changed. Barrett (1978), for example, argues that ideological factors are of prime importance in determining the sexual division of domestic labour.

One theoretical framework, which assumes that such a normatively-maintained disequilibrium could not persist indefinitely, is that proposed by Anderson (1971) in his study of family structure in nineteenth-century Lancashire. According to Anderson, if material conditions favour the establishment of new behaviour patterns which will better assist the actors involved to achieve their goals, then those who are able to disregard the prevailing normative system without serious sanctions being imposed upon them will do so. Once new behaviour patterns are established, it is argued, new normative beliefs will then emerge to support them.

These models reflect a view of structures of normative belief which operate so as to inhibit actors from engaging in changes of behaviour, even when prevailing material circumstances mean that such changes would help in the achievement of goals. Further developments of Anderson's framework imply that normative requirements can be more specific the more homogeneous the society, and the more connected are the actor's social networks (as this latter increases sanctioning power). Much of the development of Anderson's ideas requires an assumption that the goals of individual actors may be assumed to be similar across the population concerned, and he argues (in relation to contemporary concerns) that now people are able to have a much wider variety of goals, and that there has also been an increase in people's ability to meet life crises and difficulties themselves as a result of increased wages and welfare state benefits. His perspective, derived from exchange theory, leads him to argue that, contrary to conventional wisdom, strongly affective, close-knit working class networks were not, in general, a feature of the nineteenth century but were probably only possible from the 1930s onwards.

He then goes further and discusses normative kinship bonds since the Second World War, arguing that it is only since the advent of the public social services that relationships with kin can become a matter of choice within the working class, because the family is one of a multiplicity of sources of help and people have far less need to be dependent on family members alone.

His final paragraph is worth quoting in full because echoes of it appear in P. Abrams' (1977) argument that traditional informal assistance was based on fast-disappearing conditions of poverty and frequent life crises, and so perhaps there were good reasons why its ending should be greeted with relief.

> Thus the working class have come, at least at present, something of a full circle, from pre-industrial kinship weakened because the problems were so great and the resources so small, through a functional 'traditional' kinship system, to a situation where kinship is again weakened but now, by contrast, because the problems are reduced, resources are so much increased, and ready alternatives are open to all. (Anderson, 1971, p. 179)

The findings of the family care of the elderly survey suggest that this is a rather optimistic view of currently prevailing conditions, especially with regard to the extent to which people feel they have a *choice* between family and other forms of provision. However, the relevance of Anderson's work to the current study stems as much from his use of certain heuristic perspectives to develop methodological ideas as from his substantive findings about kinship structure. Of particular interest is his attempt to develop a structural-level, actor-based perspective, which would integrate knowledge about observed structural level patterns of behaviour with an understanding of the definitions and perceptions of the individual actors involved.

In the present study we collected data about patterns of helping at the structural level, such as knowledge of the characteristics of the population who are engaged in practical helping activities, and also knowledge, from open-ended interviews, of the factors perceived to be important by individual actors, some of which, in turn, may be related back to structural conditions.

The next section of this chapter involves analysis at the structural level using quantitative data. It aims chiefly to describe the structure of the pattern of practical caring activity as it was observed in Sheffield.

The patterns of delivery of practical care

A principal helper was defined as someone who performed the major part, or all, of a weekly task such as shopping or laundry, or who provided within-household assistance with tasks such as light cleaning or cooking at least three times a week. This was a minimum criterion. Many helpers provided much more assistance than this. The range of tasks performed and their frequency were described in the previous chapter; here our concern is to indicate how principal informal helpers were selected from a network of family and other contacts.

To concentrate on practical assistance is not to deny the importance of any expressive, supportive care which might be provided in the form of friendly contact. However, it does serve to concentrate on those aspects of caring which might be thought to be substitutable by persons or agencies other than relatives, and also to restrict our attention to activities which can more reliably be measured. Moreover, as the evidence on social contact has already shown, the principal providers of expressive support, in the form of contact – daughters – are also the principal providers of practical assistance. The analysis proceeds as follows: first, the structural pattern is described in detail, then an attempt is made to develop a general model of decision-making within networks at the individual level which, if applied generally, generates patterns similar to those observed.

Sources of informal care

Just under half (45 per cent) of elderly people in the sample had at least one principal helper and one-fifth had two such helpers (42 per cent of those with an identified principal helper). Principal informal helpers were drawn overwhelmingly from within the elderly person's family: only 9 per cent received regular help from non-relatives. Thus more than four in five elderly people with helpers were receiving help from relatives only. We saw in Chapter 3 how the decline in popularity of joint households did not have much bearing on social contacts between elderly people and their relatives, and the case is similar with regard to the provision of predominantly family-based care: only one in ten of the elderly people surveyed were receiving informal help from within their own households compared with three times as many who were being helped by persons living outside their household. If we focus upon elderly people receiving informal assistance, then three-quarters of them received this assistance from persons outside their immediate household, while just over one-fifth received in-household care only.

The efficiency and effectiveness of the informal sector is rarely called into question compared with the constant scrutiny of the formal sector. This is due primarily to the official concern with a very narrow form of efficiency – cost efficiency – and because the informal sector is cheaper in terms of public expenditure, it is considered to be more 'efficient' (see Walker, 1984c, pp. 57–8). But judged by the criterion of the provision of help to those in greatest need we are able to report that the informal sector appears to operate in a very efficient and effective manner. Thus those elderly people who were receiving informal care were considerably more disabled than those who were not receiving any. Moreover, those who had two helpers were slightly more disabled than those who had only one.

The issue of whether existing levels of informal help were adequate, and the related question of whether there exists an unused pool of potential helpers who are not contributing but might be mobilised, are not covered here but will be discussed later.

Which relative was the one most likely to be providing care? As in all other similar studies, daughters were predominant (see for example, Hunt, 1978; Nissel and Bonnerjea, 1982). Over half (52 per cent) of elderly people receiving help (and just under one-quarter of all elderly people) had at least one daughter helping. One in four people with helpers were being helped by a lone daughter.

The next most common source of help was a spouse. Just over one-fifth of married elderly people (representing 7 per cent of all elderly people and 16 per cent of those with helpers) were receiving personal or practical help from their spouse as a consequence of disability. One difficulty here was that in a number of instances elderly wives fulfilled the criteria for classification as a principal helper simply by carrying out what they regarded as normal domestic duties for their non-disabled husband. These cases are excluded, although it seems likely (and in fact this was borne out by the second stage of our research) that many of these husbands could be viewed as dependent upon their wives and, if widowed, would be unable or unwilling to cope alone. However, to reiterate, a spouse has only been regarded as a principal helper if the division of domestic duties was regarded by the couple as a consequence of one partner's disability rather than as a normal state of affairs. It must be noted that the vast majority of spouse principal carers were men: wives helped by husbands outnumbered husbands helped by wives by more than 2:1. This predominance of men as spouse carers was also reflected in answers to questions about whether our respondents had anyone depending on them. Nine men and seven women said that their spouse depended on them, by virtue of disability, for at least weekly personal or practical help.

Since, it must be said, speculation in the literature on informal care has tended to assume that caring wives would predominate (see, for example, Oliver, 1983), these findings require explanation.

In the first place the special demographic features of our particular population group have to be borne in mind. Even though women of this age outnumber men by 2:1 there are, in absolute numbers, more *married* men over the age of 74 than married women. This may be attributed to differential death rates and to the tendency of men to marry women younger than themselves.

Second, however, there is evidence that elderly women are more likely to be disabled than elderly men. Within our sample, women were significantly more likely to be disabled than men, and national research studies support this finding (M. Abrams, 1978; Hunt, 1978; Townsend, 1979). Thus, despite the distorting effects of the demographic structure of the population, it may well be that there are more elderly husbands caring for disabled wives than vice versa.

The next most frequent source of help was sons (11 per cent of elderly people with helpers and 5 per cent of the total). Fifteen sons were named as principal helpers but a minority of only six were helping alone. The remainder were helping with another person, most often (eight cases) a daughter.

Table 5.1   *Sources of informal care for elderly people*

Principal helper(s)	Number of elderly persons	Percentage of elderly persons	Percentage of elderly persons with helpers
None	165	55.2	—
Spouse	15	5.0	11.2
One daughter	35	11.7	26.1
One daughter-in-law	8	2.7	6.0
One son	6	2.0	4.5
Other relative	8	2.7	6.0
Non-relative	5	1.7	3.7
Daughter and spouse	5	1.7	3.7
Two daughters	11	3.7	8.2
Daughter and son	7	2.3	5.2
Daughter and son-in-law	5	1.7	3.7
Daughter and other relative	3	1.0	2.2
Daughter and other	4	1.3	3.0
Daughter-in-law and spouse	2	0.7	1.5
Daughter-in-law and son	1	0.3	0.7
Daughter-in-law and other relative	2	0.7	1.5
Son and non-relative	1	0.3	0.7
Two other relatives	5	1.7	3.7
Other relative and non-relative	4	1.3	3.0
Two non-relatives	7	2.3	5.2
Total	299	100	100

One in ten elderly people with helpers were receiving care from a daughter-in-law. In contrast to sons the majority (nine) of the 13 daughters-in-law who were helping were doing so alone. All the five sons-in-law who were named as helpers were assisting their wives (the daughters of the elderly people concerned).

If we begin with seven possible categories of helper – spouse, daughter, daughter-in-law, son, son-in-law, other relative and non-relative – there will be a large number of possible combinations (27 possible two-person combinations, and seven single-person possibilities). Not all of these possibilities have been realised in our sample. The full list of combinations of principal helpers is shown in Table 5.1. We have no reason to believe that the combinations not shown in the table provide a significant source of informal care, so what explains the highly selective nature of the caring relationship?

The structural pattern shown in table 5.1 is the result of large numbers of individual decisions about who is to help a particular elderly person in need. Apart from the consistent preference for daughters, some features of the structure may not be immediately apparent. It was obviously important to discover whether or not there was any generally observed order of preference amongst available helpers. Since information about existing relatives was available for each elderly person, it was possible to compare the results of possible theoretical decision-making rules against what actually happened in practice. The analytical process which follows should be distinguished from the quantitative testing of statistical models. The latter is not the intention of this chapter. Instead, a hypothetical model of a hierarchy of carers, which is initially generated from our findings and from the literature, is used as a tool for exploratory analysis of the data. This analysis leads to modifications of the model.

The pattern of decision-making

Stage I: relationship

The most obvious first basis for constructing a hierarchy of preference is relationship. A simple hierarchical decision model was constructed which gave priority to available relatives as follows:

1. spouse;
2. daughter;
3. daughter-in-law;
4. son;
5. other relative;
6. non-relative.

This initial hierarchy reflects what might be described as a traditional Western normative preference structure. The rules are that close relatives are preferred to more distant ones, any relative is preferred to a non-relative, and female relatives are preferred to male relatives.

124

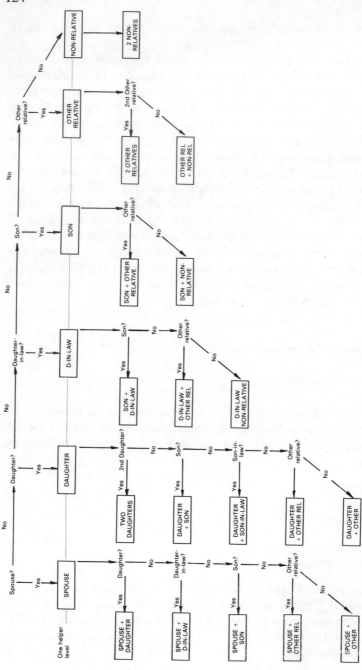

Figure 5.1 *Selection of relative(s) to provide practical assistance: flow chart to show decision-making process*

Since 19 per cent of elderly people had more than one helper it was also necessary to specify rules for the selection of a second helper, should one exist. If the first helper was a spouse then the situation was viewed as equivalent to selecting a single helper for a married couple, and so the same hierarchy was repeated. However, if the first helper was not a spouse, then the second helper might be called upon to perform a complementary role in relation to the first helper, or indeed, be called upon to assist by virtue of obligations to the first helper, rather than direct obligation to the elderly person. Thus the hierarchy for choosing a second helper, once the first is chosen, is slightly different with, for example, sons and sons-in-law replacing daughters-in-law as appropriate co-helpers for daughters.

The detailed flow chart is given in Figure 5.1. This decision-making model was applied to each elderly person to see how well it conformed with decisions taken in practice. In fact carers were chosen in accordance with this hierarchy in 62 per cent of cases.

Stage II: household type

Of course it has to be recognised that normative decision rules are modifiable in practice by circumstances. As Anderson (1971) observed, norms relating to the care of elderly relatives can rarely be specific, and certain factors might render behaviour, apparently contradictory to such norms, acceptable. The initial focus of interest was upon the 38 per cent of cases in which the preferences which we believed accorded with 'traditional' norms were apparently not observed. Would it be possible to detect consistent patterns of explanation for the deviation, or consistent differences which might indicate that either the norms were not as had been surmised, or that there were specific areas in which they were breaking down?

The initial model of the decision-making process had merely taken account of the existence or non-existence of particular relatives; no account had been taken at that stage of the many other factors thought to be important in decision-making about help in the informal sector. In particular, neither proximity nor the state of health of the potential carers had been taken into consideration.

On investigating those cases where decision-making did not

appear to have followed this pattern, it became clear that the hierarchy was overruled if a relative lived in the same household as the elderly person. In a number of joint households the decision *was* in accordance with the model, because the elderly person lived in the same household as their predicted principal carers. Here we must look back to what has already been noted in Chapter 3 about joint households: they were only rarely formed as a result of the increasing dependency of an elderly person. Clearly if a joint household were formed as a consequence of dependency we might expect the hierarchical decision model to be followed in making the decision about which relative would share their home. If the joint household was lifelong, however, this might no longer be the case.

In order to take on board the special influence of these households the second stage in the construction of the decision model added a condition that relatives living in a lifelong joint household would be preferred to those living outside it. Thus the hierarchy for the selection of principal helpers became:

1.   spouse;
2.   relative in lifelong joint household;
3.   daughter;
4.   daughter-in-law;
5.   son;
6.   other relative;
7.   non-relative.

The accuracy of fit for this two-stage decision model rose to 68 per cent of cases.

Stage III: proximity: an independent variable?

Since more than three in four listed relatives lived in Sheffield or South Yorkshire, it seemed unlikely that considerations of comparative proximity would prove overwhelmingly important. Although it was the case that principal helpers were slightly more likely to live within five minutes' journey, this was not a clear or consistent enough pattern to embody it in the decision-making model. In any case the interviews with carers cast considerable doubt on the suggestion that proximity is an independent variable (see, for example, R. Parker, 1981). Over one-third of carers said that the distance to the elderly person's home had been deliberately manipulated by one of the two parties moving house to bring about greater proximity.

The only way in which it proved possible to bring proximity into the model was to exclude those who lived more than two hours' journey away from any obligation to provide regular care. This improved the agreement between the model and the observed decision to 71 per cent of cases.

Stage IV: health of household members

Finally it seemed desirable to take into consideration the health of potential helpers. Unfortunately specific health questions had been asked only in relation to spouses and members of the elderly person's household. Since the model as it stood predicted, for example, that a paralysed stroke victim would be his disabled wife's principal informal helper, it was felt to be more in accordance with traditional, not to mention reasonable, normative expectations to exlude household members in poor health from the obligation to help.

This done, decisions about the correct helper or helpers conformed with the model in 75 per cent of cases (80 per cent of single principal helpers, and 67 per cent of pairs of helpers were in accordance with this revised model).

Our information on the health status of relatives outside the household was insufficient to allow this to be used as a predictor variable. Although we often knew that particular relatives suffered from health problems there was no reliable indication of degree of seriousness. In any case a number of principal helpers did suffer from health problems, and so any attempt to build this in as a mitigating factor would probably not have improved the fit of the model.

The accuracy of the model

It is not sufficient simply to say that 75 per cent of decisions accorded with the final model; clearly the question of where the model fitted best and where it did not must be pursued. Table 5.2 shows the percentage of each category that was predicted correctly.

Clearly the assumption of the model that other local relatives, if they existed, would come forward to assist elderly people who had no local children is not borne out in the majority of cases (six out of eleven). However, it should be noted that one such prediction

Table 5.2   *Capacity of the model to predict principal carers (percentages)*

Principal carer predicted by the model	Prediction		Total
	Incorrect	Correct	(Number)
Spouse alone	18.0	82.0	100 (17)
Lifelong in-household relative	—	100.0	100 (11)
One daughter	14.0	86.0	100 (37)
One daughter-in-law	25.0	75.0	100 (8)
Other relative	54.0	46.0	100 (11)
Daughter and spouse	16.0	84.0	100 (6)
Two daughters	23.0	77.0	100 (13)
Son and daughter	14.0	86.0	100 (7)
Daughter and son-in-law	40.0	60.0	100 (5)
Spouse and daughter-in-law	33.0	67.0	100 (3)
Son and daughter-in-law	80.0	20.0	100 (5)
Two other relatives	50.0	50.0	100 (8)
Other relative + non-relative	50.0	50.0	100 (2)
Two non-relatives	—	100.0	100 (1)
Total	25.0	75.0	100
Number	33	101	(134)

was in fact incorrect because a spouse who was in poor health (and thus excluded by the model) was nevertheless acting as principal helper. In most of the remainder of incorrect predictions under this heading, the elderly people had little contact with local relatives: two lived with friends who provided them with assistance, whilst the remainder received help from neighbours.

The other conspicuous failure of the model was in predicting son and daughter-in-law as a combination. However, the number of cases involved was too small for any general conclusions to be drawn. In all the four cases where the prediction was incorrect, either the son or the daughter-in-law was involved in helping, but not both. In two of these cases, ill health was the reason given. Alternative helpers were either other relatives or neighbours.

Application of the decision-making model to elderly people not receiving informal practical help

Thus far analysis has concentrated only upon elderly people with at least one informal helper who met the criterion for principal helper. However, the majority of elderly people (55 per cent) had no such helper(s). Although elderly people not receiving help were on average susbstantially less disabled than those with informal help, inevitably there were some people who, despite being as disabled as those receiving informal assistance, received no such help. To identify such cases the criterion used was that the elderly person should suffer at least the median level of disability for those receiving informal help: that is, appreciable disability (a score of 7–10 out of 18 on our scale). Twenty-six elderly people were identified with appreciable or more severe disability but who were not receiving informal practical assistance.

The predicted carers, according to the decision-making model, in these 26 cases were:

		Percentage
Spouse	5	19
Daughter	2	8
Daughter-in-law	7	27
Son	1	4
Other relative	6	23
Non-relative	5	19
Total	26	100

The number of spouses largely reflects difficulties in applying the principal carer criterion to married couples. Most did perform some household tasks, but couples were felt to be interdependent in such a way that one could not be identified as a principal helper to the other. In only one case did there seem to be some evidence of a shortfall in assistance to one partner and a degree of marital disharmony. In one other case paid domestic assistance was received.

It is undoubtedly worthy of note that over 40 per cent of elderly people who were disabled but received no informal help had no children living within two hours' journey. In a number of cases the only available local relatives were themselves over 75, and often in poor health. Two people were attempting to move house in order to be nearer to relatives who would then be able to help them, but of the remainder all but one had no realistic hope of receiving any form of family assistance. The one exception was a 90-year-old widow who reported that she regularly received, but generally refused, offers of help from her local niece: 'I'm a bit of an awkward devil,' she explained. It is of interest to note that, of those with no living relatives, none were receiving assistance from other informal helpers. Four of the five people for whom non-relatives were the only potential informal helpers expressed a desire for more practical assistance, even though two were receiving some statutory help.

In comparison with the previous analysis of those who were receiving informal practical assistance, the number of daughters-in-law identified as not assisting seemed to be the most substantial difference. Indeed, if the 26 elderly people without principal helpers were added to the 134 with such helpers, and the overall predictions of the decision-making model were assessed for this population, the major difference in results was that the expectation derived from the model that there would be a daughter-in-law as helper was incorrect in 60 per cent of cases (see Table 5.3). Two-person predictions were not revised because only one predicted carer had been identified for those who in fact had no helpers.

Of course, where the elderly person had no principal carer, there could be no carer interview to shed light on why such assistance was absent. However, where alternative carers existed and were interviewed, discussion of this issue was possible. Such qualitative information in turn may influence the investigation of which structural factors may be related to the provision or non-provision of help. Therefore further investigation as to why some children and, in particular, daughters-in-law did not provide

Table 5.3 *Prediction of one-person principal carers (percentages)*

Principal carer predicted	Prediction		Total (number)
	Incorrect	Correct	
Spouse	36.0	64.0	100 (22)
Daughter	18.0	82.0	100 (39)
One daughter-in-law	60.0	40.0	100 (15)
One son	100.0	0.0	100 (1)
Other relative	71.0	29.0	100 (17)
Non-relative	100.0	0.0	100 (5)

assistance will be deferred until after consideration of relevant qualitative data from the carer study.

Interim summary of the pattern of decision-making

To sum up so far; it can be argued that in making decisions about who provides tending, people very largely behave as if the hierarchical principles described in the model operate in practice, although these may be overruled by the ill health of prospective helpers.

What has not been shown should also be noted: first, that people themselves believe they have followed the principles implicit in the model and, second, that this structure reflects peoples' beliefs about what it is right to do. In order to investigation these questions it is necessary to turn to the qualitative information obtained from interviews with carers. We are thereby restricted to the views of out-of-household carers.

Why people become carers

An attempt was made to discover normative beliefs both directly and indirectly. Carers were invited to discuss directly issues such as children's obligations to parents and whether caring was women's work. In addition, however, normative beliefs were also revealed by comments upon the existing situation. Apparent conflict between what is happening and what is normatively prescribed will often call forth an explanation, or may be an occasion for complaint.

Answers given by individual carers to questions about why they help may centre on factors internal to the relationship with the particular elderly person, such as affect, past history or reciprocity; or, alternatively, they may be network-related, describing why *they* help as opposed to other apparently available helpers. It is this latter type of response which will be the primary focus of interest in the remainder of this chapter.

Carers were asked whether they felt that they were the right person to be helping and if so (or if not) why they felt that was the case. This question occurred (intentionally) in the middle of the section on other informal helpers, and thus tended to elicit network-related replies. That is to say, where helpers did elaborate they were likely to discuss the 'rightness' of their helping in relation to the help, or lack of it, from other members of their, or the elderly person's, informal network. Since it has been argued that behaviour that is in accordance with established norms needs no explaining, it would be predicted that those helpers who perceived their help to be in accordance with such norms would see no need for explanation or elaboration. Thus the exchange between interviewer and helper might take (and sometimes did) the following form:

> *Interviewer*: Do you feel that you are the right person to be helping Mrs X?
> *Carer*: Yes of course.
> *Interviewer*: Why is that?
> *Carer*: What do you mean?

Just under one-third (30 per cent) of helpers could elaborate no further, whilst a further one-fifth pointed to the fact that there was no one else: 'You see, I'm the only one, so there's only me to do it.'

The remaining half of the helpers gave a variety of reasons, of which the most common was a statement of the family relationship such as: 'I'm her daughter.'

Only one helper (a friend) felt that she was not the right person to help, but three out of ten helpers indicated at least one other person whom they felt should give more assistance. Twelve per cent of all carers identified two or more family members who should do more.

There were two possible grounds for complaint: one was that another family member should be performing tasks instead of one or both of the current carers; this would correspond to a mismatch in the hierarchical model. Second, there was a requirement that another family member should provide additional assistance. The major demand was that other relatives should provide more social contact, although carers would also have welcomed practical assistance in about half the cases.

The hierarchy of obligation

The comments of non-family carers make it clear that family, and particularly children, are seen as the first line of assistance for elderly people:

I didn't think I should be doing it, because I think your family should come first ... Mrs Murphy needed somebody, and the family wasn't going regularly enough to see how she is coping day to day, so that was it. I took it on myself more or less. (Friend; daughter-in-law predicted by model)

Some other helpers who were not children stressed that they had, in the absence of other family, taken on family roles:

Well I mean it would obviously be a daughter [the right person to help], but she hasn't got a daughter obviously, and I am like a daughter to her in a lot of ways. She relies on me like grandma relies on me mother. (Niece)

The best way I can describe it, it's almost as though they, sort of, were parents, and all these things seem to have arisen naturally. (Neighbour)

All carers who were children felt that they were the right people to be helping, but a number qualified their answers by indicating that other members of the family *should* do more. If the model reflects people's views about what is right, then people who are helpers when another family member would be predicted should be particularly prone to offer explanations of this deviation, or give accounts of normative conflict:

I used to accept that it was my place to do until father became really bedridden, and then I didn't think it was fair that my husband should do the work, you see. It should have been my brother ... and that's where the problem came ... When we were called out my husband had to clean him up, help me to clean the bed, and to tidy him up and wash him; and it wasn't his father. And my brother refused to do anything – he said it wasn't his place. But yet it was my husband's place to go with me and do it, you know. (Daughter, helped by son-in-law)

I don't mind. I don't mind helping his mother and I don't mind doing it because I know John [husband] can't do it but it annoys me that his sister doesn't do it. (Daughter-in-law who helps where daughter does not)

There's many a time I think 'Well if it was my mother and I
know she was ill as what Vera is . . .' I mean Vera can be all right
one minute and then in an hour can be poorly . . . I think 'Well if
it was my mother I should ring up every week, you know, and
visit at least once a month.' I mean it's only an hour-and-a-half
on the motorway, and I just can't understand why she doesn't
come. But there again, I don't know what's gone off in their life
between them, you know. But I do think, I mean it's her mother
and she ought to do more. (Daughter about care of her
step-mother)

The priority of daughters-in-law over sons is implicitly illustrated in these quotations: 'I've got a brother. My brother's wife is
an ill person so I mean she can't do anything', and 'If my daughter
went with us [on holiday] I should have to ask my brother to call.
Well, what he'd have to do is call from work because his wife's
sister is in hospital, so she hasn't much time, you see.' A caveat
should be entered here to the effect that some carers felt that they
were the right person to help with some tasks but not with others.
While some tasks were appropriate for families others (such as, for
example, providing help with bathing, or long-term financial
assistance) were often seen as specifically not appropriate. However, these perceptions will be discussed in some detail in Chapter
8 because they concern the relationship between family and other
sources of help.

Of direct relevance to the decision-making model, however, is
the perception that there are clear sex differences in task-appropri-
ateness:

I think it depends on circumstances, I think that . . . not
circumstances, I think, like I said, that if it's a daughter, yes [she
is expected to help], and if it's a son, then if the daughter-in-law
helps, then I think that is expected. I think only because the help
is housework, and this sort of thing, and it's more natural for
women than men. (Daughter-in-law)

I would say a woman is better qualified or better able to look
after, whether it be a man or a woman [the elderly person]. I
think it's got to be a rather exceptional man because . . . I'll give
you a for instance of what I mean. If a chap can't do any

cooking, well he's not qualified to look after anybody else . . . I believe I'm right in saying that with the majority of women they can do it but I would say that with the majority of men they can't do it. (Son)

Carers also argued that it was generally easier for a woman to give up work than a man: 'I think for a man who is sort of running a home, it would have been a big thing for him to consider not going out to work again . . . I mean he has a wife to support, whereas a woman . . .'.

Just under half of carers (48 per cent) gave an unqualified 'yes' in response to the question of whether care for the elderly was women's work. A further 12 per cent replied that it was so in practice, if not in theory. Three out of five were convinced that 'other people' thought that care for the elderly was women's work.

However, even those who did argue that male relatives had obligations generally attached more importance to their duty to maintain social contact rather than to perform domestic caring tasks.

Particularly nowadays in this day of equilization sort of thing, I feel that a son should . . . well, if he did nothing else he should visit the parents and take them out if he's got a car, and help with the shopping. (Daughter)

You don't expect men to do [as much] . . . if they don't do owt for them, I think they should go and see them, and spend an hour with them. After all they're their mother and father. (Daughter)

Thus helpers' comments give considerable support to the idea that obligation towards elderly people falls more strongly upon family members, particularly children. But also, given the nature of the tasks required, daughters were expected to discharge obligations to provide domestic assistance directly, whereas sons might be able to discharge such an obligation through their wives' labour. The obligation to provide social contact, however, remained.

As earlier discussion of the accuracy of the model showed,

a substantial proportion of predicted daughters-in-law did not provide assistance and, further, when they did not, neither did other relatives.

It might be the case that the passing of obligation through son to daughter-in-law depends upon the division of labour existing within the household, and the relative importance attached to participation in the labour market by the husband and wife. Alternatively, or perhaps additionally, it might be that daughters-in-law are caught in a web of conflicting obligations. As daughters themselves, they have obligations to their own parents which are reasonably felt to have priority:

> No I don't see her very regularly at all, because my mother also lives down there. So sort of, Jeff [husband] looks after his mother, and I look after mine, more or less. (Comment made by wife of son identified as principal helper)

The existence of other informal obligations could not be formally built into the model, but may go some way towards explaining the fact that a higher proportion of daughters-in-law than daughters failed to assist when it was predicted they would do so. Seventeen per cent of such daughters-in-law were caring for their elderly parents. (This is a minimum estimate because it relied upon the elderly person spontaneously mentioning the care of other elderly dependents when asked about problems experienced by relatives.) Thirteen principal helpers were daughters-in-law and

Table 5.4 *Assistance given by work status (daughters-in-law of disabled elderly people)*

Work Status	Not a principal carer		A principal carer		Total number
	Number	%	Number	%	
Full-time work	8	50	1	8	9
Part-time work	1	6	3	23	4
Retired (ill health)	2	13	0		2
Housewife	5	31	7	54	12
Not ascertained	0		2	15	2
Total	16	100	13	100	29

16 daughters-in-law (representing 13 elderly people) failed to assist when it was predicted they would. These numbers are too small to enable generalisation, but it may perhaps be mentioned that half of the daughters-in-law who did not provide practical help, when the 'traditional' preference model predicted they would, were in full-time work, whilst only one of those who did help was working full time. The full figures are given in Table 5.4.

Reasons for failure to discharge obligations

Of course, not all failures to help give rise to normative conflict. There are a variety of deviations from the norm which are regarded as legitimate.

The alternative informal obligations of some daughters-in-law provide an illustration of one type of reason generally perceived as 'reasonable' for failing to meet obligations to elderly relatives. Three reasons recognised as legitimate were advanced:

1. other normative obligations within the informal sector;
2. personal incapacity of relative;
3. the elderly person breaking the rules of acceptable informal behaviour in a long-term and sustained way.

Of these the last is the most susceptible to differing interpretations by the actors involved and will be discussed at length later.

For any individual in contemporary Western society it is argued that the order of priority among normative obligation is:

1. family of procreation (spouse, children);
2. family of orientation (parents, siblings);
3. affinal family (spouse's family of orientation).

Thus there is an obligation on those fulfilling duties in one sphere to ensure that prior obligations have been fulfilled. Of course the relative weight of the needs of different priority groups have to be assessed, and this can lead to difficult decisions:

We may have moved had it not been for my mother some time ago, but we stayed put. But my husband had a heart attack in

August last year and he was finding the hill ... difficult, and we were seriously considering moving somewhere ... that would be flatter for him, so that he could walk more, and it was a question of who had priority, sort of thing. I thought my husband had in that case.

I had to leave him [father] a little bit when, in the last two or three weeks, when my husband was poorly, I couldn't get down but he managed ... He'd still come up for his dinner and that but I couldn't give him as much ... which was only natural. I had to see to him [husband] you know.

Equally, members of the various groups may make their own demands on the carer:

I think it's too much for one person to take on, particularly when she is working full-time and you've your own to do here. (Husband of carer)

In more than one case the unemployment of the husband was seen as an additional problem for the wife. The following exchange took place in one interview:

Husband: It's half past eleven and quarter to twelve before she comes in house, and if she [mother] wants her again during the day, I say she's got us to see to. 'Well, you're not working' that's all you get.

Wife: You see it's more so when they're not working. If I'm in house on me own I can get done and get out, but I've got these to see to.

The heavier the demands, the more acute such problems become; however, the purpose of specifying the priority of obligations here is to illustrate the nature of the framework within which decisions about the importance of other normative obligations are made.

The second excuse, personal incapacity, requires less definition, although of course all the actors involved might not agree on whether a particular person's difficulties were a 'sufficient' excuse. Often, however there was no dispute: 'I've only got one sister and she's crippled with arthritis. She can only get up to see her and that's all', or 'Her son lives up at . . . He's had two strokes . . . so I go up and see her' (reported by a niece).

Since our interviews were with active carers, rather than relatives who did not help, the discussion of the third reason for not helping – the breaking of informal rules of behaviour by the elderly person – is not directly informed by those said to have taken this decision. None the less, the views of carers were often enlightening, although elaboration on the causes of family disagreements was not always forthcoming: 'I don't really know what happened and we can't find out and I don't want to find out . . . There's some bad blood between them, dear.'

However, one type of event which had led to family arguments and which is of concern because it seems likely to become more prevalent is divorce and remarriage (not necessarily of the carer).

> My sister, well she'd been 7 years without coming to see my dad because she didn't agree with him getting married again. (Daughter)

> Margaret [daughter of elderly person] divorced her husband, eight years ago, and my mother-in-law was a bit upset about that because there was no reason to do it. And then she went off with somebody whom my mother-in-law didn't like and there was a grievance there. So Margaret didn't come for 12 months, didn't come near her mother's for 12 months. But they are all right now, she accepts him. She doesn't like him, but she has to accept him for Margaret's benefit. (Daughter-in-law)

Other responses on this theme mainly concerned a failure of reciprocity. On a general level the assumed basis of the obligation towards parents is reciprocity:

> Let's face it, they've brought you up, haven't they? They struggled to bring you up, so that when they get to that age you should automatically take over. (Daughter)

> I mean they will have gone without to bring their children up . . . It's more or less saying thank you for what they've done for you. (Daughter)

At the same time it was recognised that in individual cases children might not feel that they owed anything to their parents: 'I know some have a hard life with their parents and they just resent them for it, [they say] "they didn't do nothing for me." I couldn't think that.' A very few helpers (three) attributed failure to help by their siblings to this cause: 'He never did anything for any of us. I think that's why my brothers didn't want to know them because they never lifted one finger to do anything for anybody in the family'; but even when they shared this belief, the helpers interviewed had clearly not considered this sufficient excuse to themselves cease helping. The above helper (a daughter) described her own motivation thus:

> I couldn't stand him but yet I knew it was my duty and no matter what it cost me I would have done that for my own conscience . . . and because of what people say, 'Well he's got a daughter and she doesn't do anything for him' . . . I've seen all these articles in the Star. I've seen all these pictures of old people and it's been said 'Got a son who didn't do anything for them', but nothing is said about what the son or daughter had to put up with to cause them to turn that way.

This response illustrates both the strength of internalised values and norms and also resentment of social disapproval directed indiscriminately towards children who do not help; in this instance the disapproval was manifested through the media. This helper was not alone in her resentment of the indiscriminate condemnation of non-helping children. Others felt the weight of what they considered to be unjustified disapproval:

> *Husband:* I blow my top sometimes when you read in the paper, sometimes from social services, or it could be from you people [researchers], I don't know, they seem to condemn people for not looking after the elderly. And it's not true in every case; you try and you just can't. There's many a time I've said to her [wife], 'I should love to write to that paper about them printing this'.

> *Wife:* I agree with you there on that. This is what I mean with my father. As I said to you, some people would appreciate

what you're doing, [but] such as my Dad – 'Oh, leave it' – you're kind of interfering in their life. But not everybody knows that do they? They say, 'Oh, the daughter doesn't do anything', things like that.

Husband: If ever he collapses and neighbours go in, what are they going to think?

The assumed, or actual beliefs of other people, or society in general, clearly did affect carers, who sometimes felt that some elderly people's claims of neglect by relatives received too uncritical a hearing:

I do hear them talk about old people that they go to see and . . . [they say] 'relatives don't go to see them'. And I do think it's wrong because, you know, relatives do go, but they don't always know that they go, and I think this is a wrong attitude that they get because I do think old people . . . some old people say 'Oh I haven't seen so and so, and I haven't seen so and so' and they have, you know, they have been. (Daughter)

Normative values versus individual feelings

P. Blau (1964) has drawn attention to the fact that, in any long-standing relationship in which social exchanges are involved, a set of shared values will have been built up as to what constitutes 'correct' performance of roles. Some values will reflect pre-existing general value beliefs, but others may be unique to that individual relationship and have been mutually evolved by the partners within it. This distinction can be applied to the relationship between individual elderly people and their carers. Although it is recognised that the internal and unique values and obligations pertaining to the particular relationship, as a result of its past history and previous exchanges, are an important part of the influences upon any individual carer, such 'internal' factors have been discussed in this chapter only in so far as they illustrate the pervasiveness of the underlying belief in a generalised obligation of children towards parents. It is argued that this belief influences the behaviour of carers irrespective of the quality of individual relationships.

These beliefs may be supported externally by sanctions such as disapproval, operated through social networks or other means of communication. Additionally, normative beliefs may be internalised, so that carers make reference to conscience, or guilt or mental anguish. Isaacs, Livingstone and Neville (1972) have commented on the phenomenon that even children who had, for example, received little other than abuse from a violent and alcoholic parent still felt an obligation to help, or expressed guilt at their failure to do so.

The following two examples show the powerful influence of normative values in ensuring that care is provided even when feelings and general norms are not mutually reinforcing at the level of the individual:

No matter what anybody does or says to me, I can't say 'right, that's it, I've done, I am going [to stop helping]'. I have to go back, my conscience won't let me. I mean some of the things I used to have said and done to me, some people would never have gone to my mother's again. (Daughter)

I've said if I could think of a few good things my mother had done for me it would make it easy, it would make it a lot easier. You'd do the world, wouldn't you, for anybody that's been really good ... You see it depends how good people's been to you in early life what you're prepared to do for them, but biggest part of people in my circumstances would leave her ... but I couldn't no matter what I had to give or what I had to do, the only thing I would wish for is to be able to keep seeing her, keep doing what I can for her and hoping to get a bit of help with her. (Daughter)

Of course, carers may suffer guilt or pangs of conscience through feeling that they are unable to repay a personalised obligation to their parent or relative, and such 'individual-level' obligation is the subject matter of the next chapter.

Normative and material factors

Finally, we must return to the theme of the interaction between material and normative factors. Most of the analysis and evidence presented in this chapter has concentrated on the influence of normative beliefs, although the opening discussion did question the extent to which such beliefs could be changed, or supported, by changes in material conditions, especially participation in the labour market by men and women.

It seemed that one way to investigate the relative influences of material as opposed to normative factors would be to find instances in which an apparently 'rational' decision in material terms cut across normative beliefs. To this end examples were sought in which families contained *both* daughters who were working fulltime *and* sons who were unemployed, in order to see who provided help. In our sample there were only five such cases, but only one elderly person suffered appreciable disability (the median level of disability for those receiving informal help), one had no disability, and the remaining three suffered minor disability. None of the five had any identified principal helper. This rather inconclusive exercise suggests that in many instances material and normative factors were mutually reinforcing and, in those few instances where they operated in conflicting directions, the consequence was less rather than more help. It might be instructive to repeat such analysis on other data, preferably containing more cases, and perhaps drawn from areas with different social and demographic characteristics from those of Sheffield.

Where the influence of material factors did seem to be more evident was in determining choices at a given level of the decision-making hierarchy; for example, and most frequently, in determining choices *between* daughters.

Analysis based on daughters who were members of families in which there was more than one daughter, and at least one principal carer existed, showed that employment status and marital status did apparently influence the likelihood that a particular daughter would become a principal carer (see Table 5.5).

Numbers are clearly small, but Table 5.5 does give an indication that those not participating in the labour market (unless as a consequence of ill health) were more likely to be giving help, although it must be borne in mind that it might be that involvement in helping mitigated against working, rather than that greater availability led to participation in helping activity.

Table 5.5   *Choices between available daughters: percentage of daughters who were principal helpers by employment status*

Employment status	Total number in category	% who were a helper
Sick or disabled	1	—
Full-time work	25	24
Part-time work	24	42
Housewife	32	56
Retired	3	100
Total	85	44

Marital status is more clearly an independent variable, but the vast majority (85 per cent) of such daughters were married and so comparative percentages are based on very small numbers (see Table 5.6). Although no claims for generalisability can be made for such small numbers, Table 5.6 does illustrate how it can be that although women who are not married are more likely to be giving assistance, nevertheless the vast majority of those who are helping are married.

Table 5.6   *Choices between daughters: percentage of daughters who were principal helpers by marital status*

Marital status	Total number in category	% who were a helper
Married	76	42
Divorced	2	50
Single	5	60
Widowed	4	75

It has been demonstrated that, irrespective of the quality of relationships, decisions about who should provide assistance to elderly people are made in accordance with a consistent hierarchy of preferences among available network members, although there are a variety of reasons regarded as legitimate for failure to conform. The external pressures, particularly upon women, to supply tending form an important part of the context of care-giving in every case.

6

Exchange, Reciprocity and Affect

The previous chapter concentrated upon the substantial minority of elderly people who received at least weekly practical assistance from friends or relatives, and in this context attempted to uncover the general structure of normative beliefs determining upon whom the obligation to provide assistance is assumed to fall. Discussion of individual relationships, and the experience of reciprocity and emotional closeness, were largely eschewed in order to focus upon the practical, instrumental aspects of tending activity, and to investigate the material and ideological structural factors which might be said to influence those who provide such care. However, such specific instrumental activity is, of course, only one element among a range of types of activity and feeling which constitute our idea of what is meant by the term 'care'.

Ungerson (1983a) has drawn attention to the distinction between caring *for* and caring *about* someone: the latter implying only feelings of concern, the former necessarily involving some form of activity. Graham (1983) argues that what is understood by informal care is a specific type of social relationship, based upon both affection and service, and that these two interlocking elements have too often been artificially separated for the purpose of analysis by different disciplines. Earlier studies in the field of psychology, she argues, concentrated upon the emotional meaning of caring whilst neglecting its material basis; but more recent work in social policy has focused upon caring as a political and economic relation, supported by prevailing gender divisions, whilst neglecting the equally important subjective experience of caring and its individual-level meaning to those involved.

145

This analysis perhaps gives insufficient weight to the work of Philip Abrams, who argued most strongly for the importance of understanding the meanings defined by the actors involved in any investigation of informal care. He argued, as Graham does, that only help from the informal sector (of friends, neighbours and relatives) could make people feel *cared for* rather than simply serviced (P. Abrams, 1978a). The special nature of informal care is that it is personally directed: given to people by virtue of their pre-established social relationships, and not therefore equally available to others in similar need. In contrast, formal care is delivered through a bureaucratic structure, with distribution rules laid down in an attempt to ensure equal treatment of equal cases. The personally-directed nature of informal help, it may be argued, means that there is a special quality to informal care which formally-organised care could never hope to provide.

This special quality rests upon the perception that the provision of practical services is only a part of the relationship between giver and recipient, possibly not the most important part. P. Abrams (1978a) described informal care as produced and sustained by a 'productive balance of reciprocity, affect and trust'. In particular, the care given to elderly people is seen as the result of an often long-established relationship in which mutual assistance may have been given and received many times. According to P. Blau (1964) one function of such giving and receiving over time is the establishment of bonds of gratitude and affection which make the exchange – even of apparently identical commodities – more rewarding when carried out with some individuals than others. The existence of such intrinsic rewards from particular relationships is seen by Blau as one of the features of social exchange which most sharply distinguish it from purely economic exchange.

The first part of our investigation of the bonds of reciprocity, affect and trust in this chapter will concern the quality of relationships between elderly people and their relatives, particularly their children, as reported in other studies and as determined in the community-wide sample in Sheffield. This builds on the detailed information contained in Chapter 3 about the extent of contact between elderly people and their children and the importance attached to their families by elderly people. This discussion of family relationships will be followed, in Chapter 7, by a consideration of the reactions to, and effects of, any increase in disability and dependency of the elderly person.

The relationships between elderly people and their families

Large numbers of studies throughout the 1960s demonstrated widespread help patterns among kin, including the exchange of services, gifts, advice and direct and indirect financial assistance. In particular, with reference to elderly people, it was clear that the provision of personal care, shelter, shopping, escorting and household tasks were natural and expected practical roles for children and other kin (see for example, Shanas and Streib, 1965). For some writers this activity was, in itself, evidence of the 'lasting devotion' felt by children towards parents (Shanas *et al.*, 1968), but other investigators, such as Rosenmayer, attempted to investigate the qualitative nature of such relationships more directly. Rosenmayer and Kockeis (1963), as a result of their studies of elderly people and their families in Western Europe, coined the phrase 'intimacy at a distance' to describe the living arrangements preferred by both elderly people and their children. The mutual preference was to live near, but not with, children; to maintain some distance, but not to be isolated. Such a view suggested a high degree of congruence between the degrees of geographical and emotional closeness desired by children and elderly parents. Some later writers, however, have argued that this apparent concord conceals an essentially asymmetrical relationship. One strong expression of this view is found in the work of Zena Blau (1973), who dismissed the idea of intimacy at a distance as a 'myth'. For Blau, although elderly people may wish to pretend that intimacy exists, the preferred living arrangement represents a precarious compromise between the elders' desire for intimacy and the young adults' desire for distance. Rosenmayer (Rosenmayer and Kockeis, 1963) did acknowledge the existence of an emotional disparity in as much as 'aged parents seemed more attached to their children than vice versa', and he suggested that this was overcome by the children's sense of moral obligation.

In Western European society it is often, though not always, the case that parents do not control resources or opportunities that their children need. Anderson (1971) cites literature demonstrating a high association between the degree of respect accorded to the elderly in particular societies and the extent to which elderly people control resources. Any obligation to care in Britain is not currently reinforced by material incentives. A number of studies have suggested that there are factors connected with the process of ageing which should lead us to expect that the relationship between elderly people and their families will become increasingly asymmetrical.

It has been argued that older people's attention will inevitably become more focused upon their children as time passes. Rosow (1967, p. 74) documents this process in convincing detail. He observes that increasing mortality, as well as increasing the likelihood that the elderly person will be widowed, will reduce the number of contemporary friends and kin such as siblings. However, even where friends or relatives are still alive, the combination of low income and increasing physical frailty will reduce mobility and thus cut down opportunities for contact. In addition, compulsory retirement means loss of contact with workmates and an increase in spare time. In a sense these factors – bereavement, the death of contemporaries, increasing disability and the loss of work – are all arguments which imply that children come to represent, almost by default, an increasing proportion of the elderly's social world.

In contrast, the children of elderly people are likely to have many other demands upon their resources and time. Brody (1981), in her series of articles on the theme of 'Women in the middle' described the conflicts affecting middle-aged women, given the competing demands of older and younger generations, as well as any aspirations a woman may have for the development of her own independent activities.

Teeland (1978) comments that in our culture the family of procreation dominates the family of orientation. The focus of individuals is downwards, upon themselves, their spouses and their children. In support of this view he notes that Weiss (1973) found that whilst older people used the term 'family' to refer to their married children, these younger adults tended to refer to their parents as 'relatives'. Teeland emphasises that this reflects a genuine structural difference, and one which assumes a greater importance as ageing progresses.

Teeland's own study, which investigated the relationships between a group of non-disabled elderly people and their children in

Sweden, led to the conclusion that in most cases the form and frequency of contact with elderly parents was dictated by the children. In a few cases the disparity between the generations was such that it seemed that the elderly parent engaged in 'vicarious living' through the activities of their child or children. Where this tendency was extreme, children admitted to experiencing their parents' obsessive interest in the minute details of their activities as oppressive.

Whilst there were examples of genuine changing, affectionate, equal relationships between parents and adult children, Teeland emphasises that this is not given in the structure of the relationship, but has to be achieved. Then it may be grafted on to the normatively required structure of the relationship. In Teeland's study parents and adult children reported few common interests (apart from the family) or common activities of the kind that friends might have. Although a majority of parents and adult children reported consensus on values to exist, there were differences with regard to specific value issues. Where issues were considered private (for example, religion) neither agreement nor disagreement had an effect on relationships; but with a public issue, such as politics, agreement seemed to strengthen family ties, whilst disagreement led to tacit avoidance of the sensitive subject.

How to measure, or to find indicators of, the quality of the relationship between elderly people and their relatives is clearly a difficult and complex area. Since one object of interest is the effect of helping on the quality of the relationship, and vice versa, it clearly is not sufficient to take the existence of helping behaviour as an indicator of a good relationship. Equally the indicators used by Teeland – consensus on values and shared activities – would seem to be relevant, but it is not clear that they are necessarily signs of a warm, close, loving relationship. Of course it is possible to ask directly about emotional closeness within the family generally, or to particular individuals. Responses to a general question on these lines may mask significant within-family variability and, in common with questions in relation to particular individuals, may evoke defensive or socially acceptable replies, especially in the context of a structured interview. Equally there may be forms of emotional closeness which do not appear to involve liking, or warmth and affection, although closeness has usually been seen to be associated with the existence of a confiding relationship between the parties (Brown and Harris, 1978; Taylor and Ford, 1983).

Approach and findings of the current study

In the main-stage interview with the elderly people, respondents were asked a general question on the closeness of their family, and were also asked whether there was currently anyone within their family they felt particularly emotionally close to, anyone they had felt close to in the past and, finally, whether there was anyone outside the family they felt close to.

Two other questions drawn from Teeland's study were included: whether the respondent felt that they saw 'eye to eye' with their children on 'most important things', and whether they had any 'shared interests or hobbies' with their children.

Further questions were designed to deal with the all-important topic of reciprocity. Elderly people were asked whether they themselves gave help to anybody. In addition, a history of helping within the family was sought, particularly in relation to children, and between siblings.

At the second-stage interviews with carers, fewer specific questions were asked, but parallel questions on past exchanges of help were included. Information on the quality of the relationship was more diffuse but richer in quality, and questions of emotional closeness, confiding, areas of annoyance, seeing eye to eye and shared interests were also covered directly. Discussions of data from this part of the survey will be reserved for the next chapter until after the main-stage findings have been reviewed, as the focus of interest will then shift to the effects and consequences of increasing dependency.

As will be clear from previous chapters, the structural features of the situation of elderly people as described by Rosow (1967) were broadly confirmed. Decreasing mobility and increasing disability with age were clearly indicated, with 82 per cent of those under 80 being able to go out without assistance but only 31 per cent of those over 85 able to do so. The majority (59 per cent) of elderly people were widowed, and most of these widows or widowers lived alone. In addition, 45 per cent of elderly people named at least one person within their family to whom they used to feel close, and this loss of intimacy was attributed to the death of the relative in over 90 per cent of such instances. The largest group of lost family intimates (not including spouses) were siblings. One in five elderly people referred to deceased brothers or sisters in response to this question. Older respondents had fewer living relatives on average than younger respondents. Comments from carers made it clear that elderly people also suffered a diminution of contact with friends outside the family.

Then her friends used to visit her but now they're all old, they are all more or less housebound, you see. (Daughter)

He likes to go out a bit in the afternoon to the betting shop, and he sees most of his old friends, but he's lost a lot recently, they've all died. (Daughter)

Three elderly people (1 per cent) were still in employment (these were all owners of the firms in which they worked), but many of the elderly women had not been employed since marriage in any case, and so would not have suffered the loss of workmates. In contrast, 71 per cent of sons and 54 per cent of daughters were in employment and over half of all children had their own dependent children still at home. About one-quarter of daughters had children at home and were also in employment.

Quality of family relationships from the perspective of the elderly person

Perceptions of the family as a whole

A small number of elderly people (7 per cent) did not list any relatives and so could not be asked questions about their family. However, the remainder were asked whether they would describe their family as 'close', 'on good terms but not close' or 'distant'. One per cent considered that relationships were too variable to make such an assessment, but of the remainder (92 per cent of all elderly people in the sample) about two-thirds (68 per cent) considered their family to be 'close', 27 per cent favoured 'on good terms but not close', whilst a small minority (4 per cent) considered their relationships with their family to be 'distant'.

There was a clear relationship between describing one's family in general as 'close' and specifying particular emotional closeness to individual family members. Among the whole sample, 60 per cent of elderly people were able to indicate at least one relative (apart from their spouse, if present) to whom they felt particularly close. Just under half (45 per cent) of those 'on good terms but not close' did *not* specify any family member to whom they felt particularly close, whereas less than one-third (31 per cent) of those who saw their family as 'close' were in this position. Of those elderly people who specified *more* than one individual to whom they felt particularly close, 85 per cent described their family as 'close'.

Not surprisingly, 'close' family networks were significantly more dense in geographical terms than less close ones: on average 63 per cent of relatives lived within half-an-hour's journey, as opposed to an average of 49 per cent of relatives of those 'on good terms'. The degree of face-to-face contact with family (as measured by total hours of contact in the previous week and excluding those who lived with relatives) was almost three times as high for those who were 'close' (15 hours' contact on average, compared with six). Occupational class differences in the perception of closeness were apparent but not substantial. One in three middle-class respondents used 'on good terms' compared with just over one in five working-class respondents (using a simple manual/non-manual split). Working-class respondents were both more likely to feel 'close' and more likely to feel 'distant' than middle-class respondents. Indeed, no middle-class respondents at all described their relationships as 'distant', but 6 per cent of working-class respondents did so.

There were differences along gender lines too: women were slightly more likely than men to describe their family as 'close': 72 per cent of women did so, compared with 62 per cent of men.

Shared interests

If we restrict our attention to elderly people with children, about one-quarter of them reported at least one shared interest with at least one child, but class differences were very apparent here. Just over half (54 per cent) of children in classes I or II, whose parents were also in those classes, were said to have shared interests with their parents. But only 10 per cent of children in classes III, IV or V were reported as having shared interests (other than family matters) with their parents. Should this be seen as evidence that relationships among middle-class families are often based on extrinsic factors and, therefore, should properly be regarded as more similar to friendship than the traditional intrinsic basis of working-class family ties? This has been suggested in some of the American literature. It may be simply that middle-class people are more likely to see themselves as having 'interests'; certainly specific interests mentioned often had class associations: 'antiques', 'theatre' and 'music', for example.

When it came to questions on emotional closeness, class differences were much less apparent. Elderly people indicated particular closeness to about 20 per cent of their children, irrespective of class. Daughters were equally likely to be reported as being close whatever the sex of the elderly person, but sons were more likely to be thought of as close by fathers than mothers. Overall sons were less likely to be regarded as close than daughters. Only 15 per cent of elderly people with children were prepared to admit to any failure to see eye to eye with their children over most important things, and so this did not prove very useful as a discriminator.

Among the whole sample three out of five elderly people were able to indicate at least one relative (apart from their spouse, if present) to whom they felt particularly emotionally close, and among those with children this rose to just over two in every three (67 per cent). One-third of elderly people said they were unable to see enough of the person they felt particularly close to, and the most common reason cited for insufficient contact (54 per cent) was the elderly person's own poor state of health. The relative was said to be too busy in a further 16 per cent of cases.

Elderly people were also asked whether there was anyone outside the family to whom they felt close. Responses to this question did not seem to indicate that close relationships outside the family were likely to be compensating for lack of close relationships within it. Moreover, they cast doubt on the extent to which informal helpers outside the family can fully substitute for the caring relationship within the family. Table 6.1 summarises the results.

As Table 6.1 shows, in common with other studies of male and

Table 6.1   *Percentage of elderly men and women expressing particular closeness to people inside and outside their families*

Expressions of closeness to individuals	Women	Men
Within family only	39	40
Both inside and outside family	26	9
Outside family only	7	2
None specified as close	28	47
Total number	202	97

female friendship patterns (see, for example, Weiss, 1973) women were more likely than men to have close relationships with someone outside their family, and less likely to be unable to specify anyone (apart from their spouse) to whom they felt close. About half of all men said they felt close to someone in their family, compared with just under two-thirds of women.

We found, not surprisingly perhaps, that there was a tendency for elderly people's descriptions of their families as 'close' to be associated with receiving assistance. For example, among elderly people who were widowed, those with 'close' families were twice as likely to report receiving family help at the time of widowhood as those who were only 'on good terms'. (The comparative proportions who reported receiving help were 91 per cent and 45 per cent.) Of course, with cross-sectional rather than longitudinal data it is not possible to determine whether such an association is observed because feelings of closeness encourage the giving of help, or because the receipt of help enhances feelings of closeness. It seems entirely possible that both of these processes operate; certainly, those who were widowed were more likely than the single and slightly more likely than those who were married to describe their families as 'close', but the difference between the married and widowed was not substantial. (The relative proportions describing themselves as close were single: 58 per cent; married: 66 per cent; widowed: 73 per cent.)

Relationships with individuals

Elderly people were asked why they felt close to the particular person or people they had named. Just over half of them gave a reason for closeness, although in 12 per cent of these responses they felt unable to elaborate and the 'reason' amounted to an affirmation of the existence of closeness. There was a wide variety of answers, as might be expected, not all of which could be classified; but one in five of those who gave a reason referred to help received from the relative, and this was the most common reason given. Other commonly cited reasons were having a similar temperament (19 per cent), shared activities (12 per cent) and the affection shown by the relative (10 per cent). Finally, a smaller number (7 per cent) referred to help which they themselves had given to the relative.

Quality of relationships: carer's perspective

It was possible to investigate the question of emotional closeness in greater depth in the less structured interviews with carers. Comments by carers about the quality of family relationships certainly covered a broad range, including the obviously negative:

> He leaned on me a lot and depended on me a lot but he didn't like me. He didn't like anybody ... I didn't like him either. In fact, one bit of me life I hated me father. (Daughter)

> It's difficult if you haven't the same wavelength, it's very difficult, I must admit. My mother and I aren't on the same wavelength, and I think she gets better company from other people than she does from me. It's as simple as that. (Daughter)

> With my mother and I there's usually been a bit of conflict. For instance she'll cause trouble, or she'll try to cause trouble, between my brother and myself by playing one off against the other, so there is an element in my mother's character that I know I could not live with. (Daughter)

However, the range also covered some very positive responses:

> My relationship with my father has never changed since I were born. We've just been good friends all us life kind of thing, you know. It's no use me telling you it changes because it doesn't. (Daughter)

I took to my mother-in-law when I first met her, well before I
was married. I took to her straightaway. She was a person you
could take to, you know, straightaway. (Daughter-in-law)

If you were to have a party with your friends you wouldn't have
to like [say] 'Oh we wouldn't want her there', you just don't
think like that with her because she can make conversation, talk
about anything, and everybody will say . . . everybody asks after
my mum. Boys who I used to go dancing with, if I see them now
it's the first person they ask after, she's that sort of person.
(Daughter)

Results from the carers' study tended to confirm those from the
survey of elderly people, particularly with regard to the close ties
between children and parents and the failure of non-family
relationships to rival the depth of family ones. When asked
directly about emotional closeness children were much more likely
than other relatives or non-relatives to say that they were
emotionally close to the elderly person being helped. In fact a
large majority, 73 per cent of children, said that they were
emotionally close to their parent, while 18 per cent said they were
not and 10 per cent gave answers which it was considered could not
be unambiguously classified, such as:

No, not one little bit I don't think. If I was all emotional over my
mother she would think she were ready for her box. We have to
keep swords drawn all the time, but if she dies I shall die.
(Daughter)

This quotation testifies to an intense emotional involvement,
expressed not through conventional expressions of warmth and
affection but through verbal conflict.
   Of those carers who were not children only 44 per cent
considered themselves to be 'emotionally close' to the elderly
person; usually these were relatives or friends with whom the
relationship was long-standing and who often considered themselves as 'like' children:

I suppose it's like a grandma really, because John's [husband's]
Mum and Dad being dead, and I don't get on with my mother,

you know, and my Dad being dead, its always been Auntie. (Niece)

When they'e talked to anybody about us they, well me and my sister-in-law, they've talked of us more as daughters than daughters-in-law. They've always said we've taken the place of daughters that they didn't have, you see. (Daughter-in-law)

Neighbours were less likely to consider themselves 'emotionally close' but preferred more circumspect terms such as 'neighbourly friendliness'. Non-child relatives who were not close did not refer to 'friendship' ties but biological ones:

Not specifically [emotionally close] no, not really. Except that she's my father's sister, and you have that relationship that you are blood relations , . . I mean now, she's the only remaining half of my family, you see (Nephew)

Two out of five carers who were not children said that they were not emotionally close to the elderly person. The comparison between carers who were children and those who were not is summarised in Table 6.2.

Table 6.2 *Percentage of carers who regarded themselves as emotionally close to the elderly person being cared for*

Emotionally close to elderly person	Children	Not children	Total
Yes	72.5	44.4	63.3
No	17.5	38.9	24.1
Other answer	10.0	16.7	12.0
Total number	40	18	58

Factors associated with feeling 'close'

What were the factors associated with feelings of closeness? Certainly the mutual exchange of confidences was not a necessary condition. Three-quarters of carers said that the elderly person confided in them, but only half would themselves confide in the elderly person. Occasionally the failure to confide in the elderly person might reflect a lack of trust, as in the case of the daughter who said:

> I don't think it would be any use [confiding in mother]. For one thing she wouldn't be able to help, and for another thing it would be broadcast everywhere. Whatever one tells mother, she's been like that for years, father always used to say the same. (Daughter)

However, other helpers said that they would no longer fully reveal their problems to their elderly relatives because it would be too upsetting for them,

> We wouldn't worry her with anything, you know what I mean. (Neighbour)

> Now I try to keep a lot of things from her because she does get more upset with her not being very well herself. I do keep things away but I never used to do. I never kept anything away from her, I've always told her. Now I'm careful what I say to her because she worries. (Daughter)

Others, felt that they had alternative confidantes who could more satisfactorily answer their own needs:

> I think the age difference is such that I would consider him too old or too woolly about my problems. I am at the stage when husband and wife would talk together. (Daughter)

> I would perhaps tell her about things after they had happened and it's all over and sorted out. I don't know if I would go and confide in her and ask her how to deal with things, because she gives very short, sharp answers and expected them to be obeyed instantly, and it's not quite the sort of advice you need, you know. (Daughter)

None the less in a substantial number of instances carers did report being able to confide in the elderly person:

> If I've any worries with Michael [husband] I can discuss them with her more than I could discuss them with my daughter. I

mean, she's [daughter] got a family of her own, I wouldn't put it onto her, I'd ask Mum's advice, I'd draw her into it and if anything erupts between Michael and I, I can talk it over with Mum quite easily. In fact she's the first one I'd go to. (Daughter-in-law)

The majority of carers who felt close to their elderly person named at least one shared interest, whereas none of those who did not feel close named any.

Reciprocity from the elderly person's perspective

While mutual exchange of confidences was not a necessary condition for the provision of informal help, reciprocity was clearly one of the main foundations of the caring relationship. Thus we found a relationship between the help given by relatives currently and the reported help given by the elderly person in the past. For example, just over one-quarter of those children identified as principal helpers were said by the elderly person to have received regular help from them in the past, compared with only 7 per cent of children not so identified. Of course it may be that elderly people in receipt of help are more likely to recall past occasions on which they have given help. However, we were able to take this enquiry a stage further: where carer interviews were obtained it was possible to compare the perceptions of elderly people and their children of past exchanges of help.

A comparison of the replies of elderly people and their carers (children or daughters-in-law only) about regular help given by the elderly person in the past showed that carers were more likely to recall having received regular help than elderly people were to recall having given it. Although there was agreement in the majority of instances, in the 44 per cent of cases where the two parties disagreed the vast majority of discrepancies (84 per cent) were found to be situations in which the carer recalled receiving help which the elderly person had omitted to mention. These findings would seem to militate strongly against any suggestion that elderly people in receipt of help might overinflate their perceptions of their past level of assistance to the carer.

Reciprocity from the carer's perspective

The majority of carers (two-thirds of children and 56 per cent of other carers) considered that there was currently nothing that the elderly person did for them, although just over half of all children and over one-third of other carers reported receiving regular help in the past (for children this meant help after leaving home). Moreover, 29 per cent of carers reported receiving help in a past crisis.

Carers were asked whether they felt that the relationship was more one-sided now than it had been in the past. A few carers could give no answer because the start of the relationship had been the point at which help began (these were mostly, but not all, neighbours) and so there was no previous relationship with which meaningful comparison could be made; but 49 helpers did answer, although six of these did not feel able to analyse the overall relationship in these terms. The responses of those who did answer in the terms expected are given in Table 6.3.

Table 6.3 *Comparison of past and present relationship by carers (percentages)*

Whether one-sided or not	Children	Others
More so now	38	43
Always has been	17	14
Never has been	45	43
Total number	29	14

As can be seen, slightly under half of those carers who replied felt that the relationship was not, and never had been, one-sided, whilst just over half felt that the relationship was now one-sided, although the majority of these considered that this was a change from the past. Carers who felt that the relationship was not one-sided stressed the contribution that the elderly person still made, or the relative unimportance of the practical assistance which they gave in the context of the relationship as a whole:

> She always just seems to be there. If the kids have been ill she'll come and sit with them while I go out and do the shopping and that, and she's very good with them. All the grandchildren are the same with my Mum, she's very patient. (Daughter)

I feel in a way I suppose I owe it to her in some ways, you know. I mean she's always been a good friend to me and I'll help her as long as I can and in any way I can, although, as I say, she's not a person that is easy to help except in little practical things and visits. (Niece)

Indeed, two carers expressed surprise at being identified as 'carers' at all. One emphasised that although she did perform tasks for her mother-in-law this was part of a continuing reciprocal arrangement:

If she's going into town ... she's just nipped into town now to pay her rates ... just come to see if I wanted anything, I didn't, but if I wanted anything from Marks' she would get it for me. (Daughter)

Another reported that the assistance received from her mother in caring for her mentally handicapped daughter outweighed any assistance that was given: 'I think she helps me more than I help her at the moment.' Carers who felt that the relationship had become more one-sided explained that their elderly relative or friend could no longer perform reciprocal services:

My mother isn't capable of living on her own. She has arthritis so badly some days she can't turn her taps on, she couldn't lift a teapot up, she couldn't open a milk bottle. Simple things like these. (Daughter)

She used to do ironing and this sort of thing, and she used to wash up ... she still helps a little bit but she doesn't do as much. One thing – her eyes aren't very good, you see. (Daughter-in-law)

What of those few who considered that the relationship had always been one-sided? Responses illustrating this position would be:

I've been helping them since I was 8 years old ... I remember going to the shop for my Mum, she's always been ill, every time we came home from school she was laid on the settee with a cold cloth on her head. Mum had got 5 younger than me, well I brought them kids up. Every time I got home my Mum had got this, she said she had bilious bouts, ... I remember getting the kids ready for school, taking them to school, coming home at dinner time and giving my Mum a meal, cleaning up, going shopping. I mean, the others were too young, I got it all. And that's gone on all my life. (Daughter)

She's never been a mother as mothers should be, love ... She was out every day of her life and she didn't want anyone, any kids, any daughter's troubles, coming to her house to upset her routine, because at half past six, no matter if the King and Queen was in her house at the time, she'd be down that path to the Working Men's Club. (Son-in-law)

Such responses illustrate the feelings of those few children and families who felt no obligation based on individual-level reciprocity. There was a clear association between the perception that the relationship had always been one-sided and a lack of emotional closeness. Of course, the number of people involved is too small for any statistical generalisability, but there was a consistent pattern of responses given by the 18 per cent of helpers who did not feel close to their parents. Such carers recalled neither past nor present help from their parents, and the majority of them saw the relationship as always one-sided. Four out of the five children who saw the relationship as always one-sided did not feel close to their parent.

It should perhaps be emphasised at this point that only children who were helping would be included in this study. Thus it might be that other children with such perceptions of their parents were not engaged in helping them. However, as Chapter 5 makes clear, there were not a great many cases in which obviously available relatives were refraining from giving assistance where it was needed.

However, by far the majority of children did make comments which illustrated that they felt they personally 'owed' their parents a debt for past assistance. For example,

Any time I needed her, well she'd come at the drop of a hat, so I feel I owe it back, you see, when she needs it. It works both ways, doesn't it? (Daughter)

and they [parents] were always good to us so I think well we
should be good to them, shouldn't we, they've looked after us.
(Daughter)

A few helpers felt quite unequal to the task of repayment:

As I say, she struggled to bring me up and that's it. It's always
there. As I say, I never think I do enough. (Daughter)

Indeed it seemed that such a strong sense of obligation could cause
children to refrain from seeking assistance from other sources,
even when they recognised the strain on their own resources:

he's so dependent now. It's a strange thing . . . I really should get
some help but I would rather do it for him myself and then feel
as if I looked after him like he looked after me when I were
young. (Daughter)

This has major implications for policies aimed at reducing the burdens falling on individual carers by sharing care more equally within
the informal sector and between the formal and informal sectors.
  Of course, not all recognitions of obligations were simply dutiful:

It's not a duty, love comes into this doesn't it? If you love your
parents and they love their children then you do it out of love
not duty. I mean there again that depends on the individual
doesn't it? I mean Ray is adopted but he loves . . . and he
couldn't have had two better parents, they've showered everything onto him . . . I suppose it's his way of giving back what
they've given up for him. (Daughter-in-law)

However, it must be emphasised that few children specifically
mentioned love as a reason for helping; they were much more
likely to mention duty or obligation. This is not necessarily to
imply that love was absent but simply that it was not regarded as
the most overtly relevant factor in the decision to help:

I'll not say it was a labour of love, because that's too . . . silly I
think, talking like that. But I just thought it was a responsibility
of mine. (Son)

I, sort of, faced the fact that they'd helped me all my life. Now was the time that I'd got to look forward to doing everything I could because I didn't want any regrets. (Daughter)

Affect between elderly person and carer

While reciprocity and duty, rather than love, were the most commonly used reasons for caring for elderly relatives, our research also suggests that emotion too lies at the heart of the caring relationship. So, for example, nine out of ten carers who reported receiving regular assistance from their parent in the past said they felt close to them, whereas less than half (47 per cent) of those who did not report receiving such help felt close to their parent.

Did the elderly people, in turn, feel emotionally close to their carers? We were able to examine the responses of the elderly people whose carers we had interviewed to the question about any feelings of particular emotional closeness to anyone in their family. Of the 49 elderly people whose relatives were interviewed, 31 (64 per cent) either specified the carer as someone to whom they felt close, or said that they felt close to all their relatives. Since, among the sample of elderly people as a whole, particular closeness was indicated with only 30 per cent of children, this would seem to provide evidence of at least some association between the giving of help and closeness.

Information derived from all the main-stage interviews tended to reinforce this suggested connection between helping and feelings of closeness. Elderly people reported giving regular help in the past to 21 per cent of their children, and special intimacy was reported with 41 per cent of those who had received such help, compared with only 27 per cent of other children. A similar pattern was observed with regard to the current or recent provision by the elderly person of financial or material assistance. Elderly people reported emotional closeness to half of those children receiving such assistance compared with only a quarter of those to whom such assistance was not given. In contrast, help given in a crisis (such as divorce or illness) was not related to feelings of closeness. Elderly people were equally likely to feel close to those who had and had not received their help in a crisis.

This suggests, reasonably, that the significance of affect is reduced in cases of family crisis. However, in the case of general non-crisis situations, even if elderly people were more likely to feel close to those with whom help was exchanged rather than others, this begs the question of the direction of causality. Does a particular quality of relationship make help more likely, or is it that emotional closeness increases as a consequence of helping or being helped?

The effects of helping on closeness

Both elderly people and their carers were directly asked about the effects of helping on closeness. The form of the question gave three possible answers: first, that helping had made them feel closer; second, that it had made them feel more distant in some ways; or that it had made no difference to their feelings. Table 6.4 shows the answers given by carers and by elderly people to this question.

In 10 cases (17 per cent of the total) one or other of the two parties to the caring relationship did not answer the question. Therefore comparative responses have been obtained in over 80 per cent of instances. It should be borne in mind that different interview techniques were used in the two surveys, although the particular question was identical. The less structured nature of the carer interviews is evident in the fact that a number of carers felt free to give responses which could not be categorised in the ways which were suggested to them.

Table 6.4 *Comparison of views of elderly people and their carers about the impact of helping on closeness*

	Carers					
	N/A*	Closer	More Distant	No Difference	Other Response	Total number	%
Elderly people							
N/A*		3	2	2		7	12
Closer	2	6		8	2	18	31
No difference	1	12	3	17		33	57
Total Number	3	21	5	27	2	58	
Percentage	5	36	9	47	3		

*N/A = No answer available, e.g. because the elderly person interview was a proxy interview.

For both carers and elderly people, the most common response was to say that helping had made no difference to their feelings towards each other. However, it was significant that both parties were actually in agreement that there was no difference in less than one-third (29 per cent) of instances. In the remaining two-thirds of cases either the elderly person or the carer, or both, considered that their feelings had changed as a consequence of giving or receiving help. There were no elderly people who said that they felt more distant in some ways from their helper, but 17 per cent of carers felt more distant from the elderly person. The reluctance among elderly people to comment negatively on their relationship with helpers has been noted in previous studies (M. L. Johnson, 1972) but, additionally, the in-depth interview techniques employed in the carer interviews may have encouraged more open responses from carers than from elderly people. However, even if elderly people were not willing to report negative changes, this merely suggests that our estimate of the extent of change is an underestimate.

The most common change reported was in the direction of greater closeness as a consequence of helping, although *both* people involved reported feeling closer in only 10 per cent of cases: one niece said, 'We've got closer to each other especially with her relying on me for a few little things, we've got closer that way.' Elderly people who said they felt closer to their carers usually explained this as a consequence of gratitude for help received, or for a sense of security derived from knowing there was someone to rely on.

Elderly people did see practical assistance by their children as a concrete demonstration that their children cared *about* them, and to receive such an assurance in itself promoted warmth of feeling. As one elderly woman said, 'I always knew they would help me if I needed it, but now that they do help me I feel closer to them.'

Carers found additional closeness more difficult to explain: they felt *for* their elderly relatives or friends in their difficulties or, less often, they had simply got to know them better by seeing them more often (more likely for those who were not children).

The most important factors identified in bringing about changes in carers' feelings were alterations in the elderly person's personality and behaviour. Of particular importance were reactions to disability and dependency. This latter subject will be discussed in detail in the next chapter, after the carers' general views of changes in the elderly person as ageing progressed have been covered. One carer pointed out the difference between her parents in this respect:

> Yes it [helping] could have made us less close. I mean depending on what type they are. As I say, my Mum and Dad – Dad's very, very thoughtful. My Mum tends to think I'm her daughter and I've got nothing else to do. 'You should be with me . . .' My Dad will say 'you do your best for us love, and we'll be grateful for what you do.' Well my Mum will say 'you could come a bit more often'. (Daughter)

Carers' perceptions of changes in the elderly person

How many people felt that either the elderly person or the relationship had changed as ageing progressed?

The majority of carers (57 per cent) did not feel that the elderly person had changed as a person as a result of ageing: one daughter replied, 'She's quite stable. She hasn't changed, she's always been more or less the same. In personality she's pretty much as she always has been.' However, one-third of carers felt that definite change had taken place in the elderly person's personality (or the way they related to other people). Half of those who felt that change had taken place judged this to be change for the worse, while 20 per cent considered the change to be for the better, and the remaining 30 per cent indicated that they could make no overall judgement about the changes which had occurred.

Carers who were not children were more likely to consider that the elderly person had changed for the worse as ageing progressed (28 per cent of them thought so compared with 13 per cent of children).

The positive changes were generally instances in which the elderly person was said to have 'mellowed' with age:

> She's mellowed. She's mellowed a lot. Beforehand she was dynamic. She was, what can I say, one who rules the roost as you might say, and me Father just let her get on with it. (Daughter)

Some families had found that the need for, and receipt of, assistance had brought about a new appreciation from their elderly relative who had previously seemed uncaring:

> He used to be nasty at times, he had a drink. Before he was ill he could be nasty, we've had our differences, but now, since he has been like this, he is not a bit of trouble really. (Daughter)

However, such a change was not always regarded without cynicism by all relatives:

> She's more considerate now than ever, love. (Daughter)

> But why she's concerned now – she knows she's depending on Betty. (Son-in-law)

In three instances where changes were thought to be for the worse carers referred to the elderly person's deteriorating mental state; indeed, two were no longer sure that the elderly person recognised them:

> I don't think it registers all that much how often we go ... I don't know what it means to her. (Daughter)

> She knows, I think, that we go. (Sister)

> She's gradually getting worse now in her head ... she's getting worse, her memory is going, well it's gone you can say. She goes to the phone and speaks to somebody, by the time she has gone away, and in less time, she's forgotten what they've said. (Friend)

In such instances, of course, changes in the relationship were not a consequence of helping but rather of perceived change in the elderly person. One-third of carers felt that the elderly person had changed with advancing age; half of these reported changes were seen as changes for the worse, one-third seen as neither better nor worse and the remainder as changes for the better.

Negative changes were varied in degree and type:

> She is getting different, she is getting a bit crotchety, when she never used to be ... she always had a full-time job ... and now

all she has to do is see what the neighbours are doing and moan about them, and I get this day in and day out. (Daughter-in-law)

She's getting more dependent, she says 'I can't make my brain work' and she gets herself into awful muddles, so I have to sort her out and pay her bills etc. (Daughter)

The last six months of Father's life I got so I couldn't go by myself because he was violent . . . he used to be hitting me. Oh, he started hitting me a lot. (Daughter)

Other carers referred to a range of changes, most commonly connected with an apparently excessive desire for dependency, or an increasing reluctance to engage in activities outside the home, or forgetfulness and a tendency to engage in repetitious conversation. It should be clear that the emphasis has been on changes in personality or behaviour, not in the elderly person's physical condition.

Thus in terms of changes in the personality of the elderly person as ageing progressed, a substantial minority of helpers did report some change, with about half of these being definitely considered changes for the worse. There is no doubt that these adverse personality changes proved the most difficult for carers to cope with and presented the most severe challenge to the caring relationship, a finding confirmed by research among the carers of confused elderly people (Levin, Sinclair and Gorbach, 1983). However, it must be emphasised that in this general survey of people aged 75 and over, the most common picture was one of stability in personality.

Changes in relationships

In contrast to this, carers were more likely than not to feel that their relationship with the elderly person had changed. Only 36 per cent declared the relationship to be unchanged, although a further 9 per cent did not feel that the relationship had lasted long enough to make a comparison. Among children, 43 per cent said that their relationship was unchanged, whilst 20 per cent considered that it had improved, and 13 per cent that it had become worse. Overall about one-third of carers reported neither changes in the elderly person nor in their relationship with them. In general, the perceived direction of change in the elderly person did accord with changes in the relationship, and it was clear that the relationship changes were seen as a consequence of changes in the elderly person, although there were one or two carers who commented that perhaps they too had changed:

> I don't know whether it's her that's changed or we have, I feel a bit guilty about all this but I do think that over the past two or three years there's been a big change in my feelings towards my mother you know . . . I feel very hurt at her attitude towards me, but, as I say, maybe my attitude has changed as well. (Daughter)

For those who had experienced close relationships in the past, changes for the worse were particularly painful:

> She was so different from my mother because she worked, you see . . . I always used to think that Mum [in-law] was younger . . . and we really did get on like a house on fire . . . I used to go and really enjoy it, and this worries me because the relationship isn't like it used to be. I am sure she does feel that, we never discuss this, but I am sure she must feel this and my family criticise me about this, they can see it too. (Daughter-in-law)

> She has deteriorated so much in this last three or four years, I mean, I just never thought it would happen to Mum because she was so young and sprightly. (Daughter)

The reaction to disability and attitude towards dependency play an important part in explaining changes in relationships, and the analysis of these topics is reported in the following chapter which continues to build on the above discussion of exchange, reciprocity and affect.

7
Disability and Dependency

This chapter extends the analysis of the caring relationships in the previous two chapters – and particularly the causes of changes in relationships discussed in Chapter 6 – by focusing on the impact of disability and dependency. We commence with a general discussion to give an overview of common feelings and experiences and then go on to concentrate upon particularly problematic and difficult responses to disability and dependency.

It is commonplace, particularly among economists and national policy makers, to lump together children and elderly people as the 'dependent population'. This is often followed by the calculation of a dependency ratio between this 'dependent' group and those of 'working-age'. Such oversimplifications are misleading in two important respects. First, there is no straightforward connection between old age (as defined by retirement ages) and dependency, whether we mean economic, psychological, political or physical dependency (Walker, 1982c). Thus, as was shown in Chapter 4, the vast majority of those aged 75 and over in our sample were neither disabled nor dependent (for a national comparison see Walker, 1985c).

Second, the nature of dependency in old age is different from that among children, although both may be regarded to a large extent as social constructions (Walker, 1980). As Hazan (1980) has pointed out, the position of elderly people with regard to their children cannot be viewed as merely a sort of role reversal from an earlier phase when the children were dependant. Elderly people have past life histories of relatively independent living, and for them the experience of dependency may be accompanied by a sense of humiliation, shame and disgrace. There is certainly evidence (see for example, M. L. Johnson, 1981) that many elderly people

171

attach a great deal of importance to independence. There was a suggestion in work by Mark Abrams (1978) that some older men were inclined to cling to this value even more fiercely than older women, and indeed that this might lead them to reject visits from relatives offering help. Abrams reported that only one-sixth of those over 75 who needed help with bathing actually received such help, and most surveys of need have reported large areas of unmet need, as judged by those conducting the survey, but a much lower amount of expressed demand for assistance (Townsend and Wedderburn, 1965; Harris, 1968; Hunt, 1978). As we saw in Chapter 4 the elderly people in our study were no exception. In his discussion of 'shared care' R. Parker (1981) points out that it may be difficult for people to accept help, however willingly offered, when they have cared for themselves all their lives.

In contrast, the other side of the coin is an all too willing acceptance of dependence. Goldfarb (1965) suggests that individuals who have been heavily dependent upon their spouse may attempt, after the death of the spouse, to transfer their dependency to others. Kalish (1969), in his discussion of the dependencies of old age, speculates as to which earlier experiences, values and behaviour patterns enable some persons to accept a dependent role, whilst others are extremely concerned to avoid it. As Norman (1980) points out, potential helpers may encourage dependence by underestimating the person's capacities, or by being unwilling to suffer the inconvenience, or anxiety, of allowing them to act independently. Of course this can apply to agents of the state as well as relatives (Walker, 1982c), but it is the latter which has been largely neglected in studies of ageing.

The impact of disability on the caring relationship: the general consensus

What then are the effects of increasing disability upon relationships, and in particular how, if at all, does being involved in helping affect the quality of relationships? It has often been assumed that helping is, in itself, evidence of a good relationship, and widespread help has been assumed to be evidence of strong family ties. This assumption has been questioned in Chapter 5, in which it was clear that neither the existence nor the absence of helping behaviour could be taken as evidence of a particular quality of relationship. It was possible, though not usual, for the factors compelling relatives to help to be almost entirely external to the particular individual-level relationship which they had with the elderly person concerned. The remainder of this chapter will concentrate on discussing the experiences of, and reaction to, the need (or perceived need) to depend on other people for assistance, which for a substantial *minority* of elderly people was a concomitant of advancing age.

Perhaps this is an appropriate point to re-emphasise that the majority of people over 74 did not depend upon practical assistance from their family, friends or neighbours. Most, including many of those receiving some help, lived fully independent, or at best interdependent, lives as participating members of their family and the local community.

None the less physical disability was a problem for many: only 17 per cent of elderly people were reported as having no disability at all and 37 per cent suffered appreciable, severe or very severe disability.

Reactions to disability

It should not be supposed that elderly people merely passively accept increasing disability as an inevitable accompaniment of advancing age. Indeed our survey provides firm evidence against the pessimistic caricature of old age as being an inevitably decremental phase of life in which older people are the passive subjects of increasing physiological and mental problems (for a critique of this view see Estes, 1979; Walker, 1985a). The 190 people who suffered from some functional disability were asked whether it ever 'annoyed or upset' them to experience difficulties in performing the activities of daily living. Nearly two-thirds (64 per cent) of them replied 'yes'. People who replied 'yes' were then asked to give an example of an incident or event which annoyed or upset them, and 90 per cent of them were able to do so. The examples were categorised into two main groups: first, a sense of frustration at one's own limitations and, second, frustration at having to depend on other people. The first was by far the most common response; four out of five (82 per cent) were of this form.

When I can't go to the shops or go out.

I can't read or sew, it's frustrating.

Everything I want to do is an effort, even to get a plate out of the cupboard.

I've always had good hearing until now, and that annoys me.

Of course, the need to depend on others is often implicit in such examples: 'I'd like to be able to do my own cleaning and washing, and I just can't do it – it's very frustrating.' But one in ten people specifically referred to the frustration of depending on others: 'If a fuse, or plug, or bulb needs attention, I have to wait for a neighbour – very frustrating'; 'When I have wanted to do something in my own way, and somebody has done it not to my liking'; 'If I needed a couple of buttons on a shirt and my wife wasn't available, I'd try to do it myself, get in a mess and then throw the shirt about' (this last from a married man, registered blind).

A small number of people (10) gave other responses: in particular, two mentioned the problem of being unable to provide services for others: 'I wonder what will happen to my husband. I do a lot for him', and 'If I am cooking, I can't see if it is done. I get upset if someone is coming to a meal.'

Unsurprisingly, the likelihood of feeling annoyed or upset increased with the level of disability. Eighteen per cent suffered from severe or very severe disability and 40, nearly three-quarters of them (73 per cent), admitted to currently feeling 'annoyed or upset' that they could not do things. A further 11 per cent had felt like this in the past: 'It's a long time since, I've forgotten.'

Gender differences in reactions to disability

Overall women were twice as likely as men to express annoyance or frustration at their current limitations, but this pattern was the result of pronounced gender differences at lower levels of disability (some disability or less), whereas at higher disability levels, gender differences in this respect were small. If we restrict our attention to the 46 per cent of the sample (139 people) who were suffering minor or some disability, then only 16 per cent of men, as opposed to 42 per cent of women, reported annoyance or upset. Why should these differences occur at lower levels of disability? The most likely explanation seems to lie in the different past experiences of the two sexes in relation to dependency upon others for the performance of routine household tasks. Married or widowed men over the age of 74, as most men in the sample were, had usually been accustomed all their lives to depending upon others (usually women) to perform these tasks. Indeed, a small number of men (5 per cent) who were *not* disabled expressed annoyance at their difficulties in performing the tasks of everyday living, while no non-disabled women did so. Thus to depend on others for help with some of the routine activities of daily living is experienced as a loss of independence by elderly women, but much less so by elderly men.

Cross-generational differences in gender role expectations

It was clear from the comments of many of the carers interviewed that they felt the division of domestic labour maintained by the older generation had been a more rigid one than that which they themselves followed. Of course, 16 per cent of helpers were themselves over 65, but three-quarters of the remaining helpers considered that there was such a cross-generational difference, although there were a few dissenting voices: 'I go out to work, therefore my husband helps me, I prepare tea, he cooks it, you know, and that's how it used to be with my parents, me Mum used to have a little job, she didn't used to go out to work until me Dad was at home.' In contrast to the above, most of those who felt there was no difference in attitudes themselves favoured the 'traditional' view:

> I think Mum (mother-in-law) . . . I don't think she'd accept the equality. There's certain jobs that men do and certain jobs that women do; no, I'm really not into this equal rights, I mean I'm essentially a woman . . . I'm more of a feminine kind. I mean I don't think I would want to do a man's job. I'm sort of in between if you know what I mean, I don't particularly want to be on level terms with men so in that way I'm afraid I'm with Mum. (Daughter-in-law, aged 62)

However, the general, if not universal, view was that there was a change in both attitudes and behaviour:

> My father's generation – there was a dividing line and that was women's work and that was men's work, but with my generation I think it's become a little bit blurred. I mean, speaking personally, I get up and hoover round, well my father wouldn't. Same as washing, my father wouldn't. Well, I mean, I chuck washing in, and hang it out in t'garden, but there is some people think it's below 'em, to even hang washing out. (Son)

> At one time it would be a crime for a man to wash a pot up. Once they'd been out to work, then that was them done when they came home. (Daughter-in-law)

> My husband will do anything, he'll do anything, but, I mean, when I was at home my father did nothing, my mother ... he used to work in the pit, granted, and my mother used to say 'no, when he's finished work, it's finished, he shouldn't do anything else', I wouldn't like to think my husband wouldn't do anything for me. (Daughter)

These differing expectations could, and sometimes did, cause conflict within families: three different examples are given below.

> Well my mother did, she used to wait on him hand and foot. Clean his shoes and everything, and he thought I were going to be able to do all t'same, but I told him I can't, you know. (Daughter)

> My mother used to mollycoddle him, if you have heard that term ... I just accept it, I mean I've known him so long that I know this is him. I did try and teach him how to cook bacon, he's never done it. He will boil an egg, that's about his limit, you know ... Obviously my husband does a lot more in the home than my father has ever done, you see, and I think it irks him slightly to see me having to get his [father's] supper ready and that sort of thing ... This is a bit of a bone of contention with the rest of the family – that he never does anything when he comes. (Daughter)

I think this is a general moan actually. When Mum [mother-in-law] comes here my husband just gets on with his work, you know, I mean he doesn't ignore her, sort of thing, but I mean she might not be here for what hindrance it is, but with me, I have to give her some time . . . She spoilt him so much when he was at home, she wouldn't expect him to do it anyway. You know, an example is that if he gets up from a meal and starts washing dishes . . . 'don't do that, I'll do it.' She worries about him doing anything . . . I'll say 'let him do it, it will do him good.' He does help now, you see, he does do this for me but I'm sure she wouldn't expect anything. (Daughter-in-law)

These examples illustrate the various ways in which cross-generational differences in assumptions about appropriate gender roles could be a cause of conflict. Elderly men might expect a level of servicing which their daughters, or daughters-in-law, were not accustomed to provide even within their own household. Even if the woman concerned were prepared to conform to such expectations then her performance of the tasks might be resented by her spouse, or other family members. Also, elderly women and men might discourage help which crossed traditional gender boundaries.

Discussion of difficulties with family members

Elderly people who did feel annoyed or upset at their inability to carry out activities of daily living were subsequently asked whether they had told other members of their families how they felt. Just over two-fifths (43 per cent) said that they did so, while the remainder did not.

Sometimes the reluctance to tell their families sprang from a desire not to impose a further burden on relatives: 'Gladys [daughter] has enough problems of her own, with her husband's health.' Others did not need to tell their family: 'My son knows but I don't say anything', or 'They know. They tell me not to expect too much.'

However, those who did discuss their feelings reported a range of reactions: 'My son says "you ought to be ashamed of yourself. There is plenty not so well off as you",' 'Yes I do [tell them] when they come, we have a good laugh', and 'My wife tells me to smile.

Table 7.1   *To whom elderly people turned if they felt low or if they had good news (percentages)*

Person turned to	Feeling low	Good news
Spouse	22	21
Other relative	32	62
Neighbour or friend	22	10
Other	24	6
Total number	299	299

She's not the most patient person if I'm sorry for myself.' Just over 11 per cent of those who were annoyed or upset at their difficulties were prepared to admit that this might make them difficult to get on with at times.

Where relatives are involved in providing assistance there is then a problem for elderly people in that discussion of their frustrations and difficulties may be interpreted as a demand for further assistance, or an expression of dissatisfaction with present help. It was noticeable that people were much more likely to call upon a neighbour or friend if they were 'feeling low and wanted someone to talk to' than if they 'had some good news they wanted to share', as Table 7.1 shows.

Table 7.1 shows that, although elderly people turned most frequently to relatives in either situation, they were almost twice as likely to turn to a relative when they had good news to share than when they were feeling low. Of course, where a spouse was present most people turned to their spouse in either situation.

It may be asked whether substantial numbers of elderly people who are receiving help feel that they are already in debt to their children, and so should not impose upon them further, or is it rather that they are less likely to feel it a proper part of the parental role to discuss their difficulties and feelings with their children, although such discussion is clearly more acceptable between husband and wife?

Impact of disability: the perceptions of carers

Did carers perceive the feelings of their elderly relatives about the onset of disability? Just under a quarter (24 per cent) of helpers spontaneously drew attention to the elderly person's difficulties in coming to terms with disability. Many carers expressed awareness of elderly people's frustrations, and several commented on the consequences of this for the elderly person's mental state, giving examples of depression or resentment:

> She doesn't like being absolutely helpless, she's used to knocking about more, I mean walking out, going out. But now she's not able, she's confined really, in her home. She gets fed up. (Daughter)

> She's always been one of those who had to do everything for herself. I think she was just resentful because she couldn't do it herself, she doesn't like to think that she can't do things. (Daughter)

> She keeps saying 'Shan't I be glad when I can walk about and do shopping and all that.' So you see it's a sore point. (Friend)

'I never thought I'd come to this'

Particularly where the relationship between carer and elderly person was long established, carers often showed a sensitive appreciation of the difficulties faced by elderly people in coming to terms with the necessity of giving up much-prized former roles:

> She'll often say 'I never thought I'd come to this' as though she's totally dependent on everybody, which I mean, she's far from at the moment. Yes, it agitates her to watch the home help physically doing the washing ... at first, although she never mentioned it to the woman, she (a) puts too much powder in or (b) doesn't put enough powder in, or she doesn't give them long enough, or she's a funny way of hanging them out ... all that sort of thing that a woman would say after doing it herself for years. Mrs Robson has the kind of nature and temperament that she likes to be the giver, and the doer, if possible. She's had a life of working for others. (Neighbour)

> It's not that she feels embarrassed if you have to do that [bathing], she knows she'd not be able to do it but it's ... she

feels as though she's putting on you. She says 'Oh I never thought it would ever come to this', you know ... so we say, 'that's what we're here for'. (Daughter-in-law)

Some described struggling to persuade their parent to be accepting:

She went to the doctor's a fortnight ago ... He turned round and said her bones were turning to chalk and if she does fall she will really hurt herself you know. Well we tried to get this through to her but she does not like the idea of having to have a stick. To my mother, it's degrading, kind of thing ... I've said, 'Now look, if you fall ...' 'I shall have to pick my bloody se'n up, shan't I?' Now that's my mother, she makes a joke of everything, but it's no joking matter. (Daughter)

In some instances carers were annoyed at the refusal of the elderly person to use aids which they felt would improve functioning:

Even though my Mum has got a hearing aid she doesn't like to wear it, and that gets me annoyed and I could fall out with her and might be a bit sharp with her sometimes. It annoys me if she doesn't put her hearing aid in, particularly when we are on the bus. I don't want everyone else to hear on the bus. (Daughter)

A number of carers commented that their elderly relative was not particularly disposed to accept advice from them, and therefore they welcomed the intervention of a third party, usually health service personnel, whose opinion in the matter would be accepted by the elderly person as authoritative.

In discussion of the forms of help which carers themselves were willing or able to provide, the difficulty of deciding how to offer or give help when it was needed, while at the same time not threatening independence, was a recurring theme:

I could do all the cleaning up, but you know I don't want to take too much out of her hands because she is very independent, and she would soon feel that she was being a burden and that she was a nuisance, so you have to be very careful. (Daughter)

I'd like to help Auntie more than I can now but it's just a matter of that she's independent and she likes to do it herself, you know. When she thinks it's time that I should help her, that she can't do it herself, then I think she'll let me, but until then I'll be offering. (Niece)

She worries because she says 'now I can't do anything for you that I used to'. This is what I say, she is a very independent person, and she wouldn't take to help because of this, you see. (Daughter-in-law)

The appropriate balance between help and respect for independence was a difficult one to strike, particularly if the elderly person's condition was gradually deteriorating. One in ten of elderly people felt that members of their family did things for them which they could manage to do themselves: 'They come and do things and don't say anything – washing curtains, hoovering, washing up and so on.'

Such household tasks were overwhelmingly the most common tasks specified when elderly people were asked what things were done for them which they could do for themselves. It is clear, though, in consequence of this, that the majority of people who received family help with such tasks did feel that they needed such help. Even those who could manage alone were not necessarily unwilling to accept the help received: 'I let her. I think "she's younger than me".' Others, however, were concerned to maintain at least some independence: 'Cooking. I can do a few things and I don't want to become a cabbage.' There was general approval and understanding amongst carers for the desire for independence: as one carer put it, when considering her own feelings about her children, 'I wouldn't like it. I'd sooner do for them than they have to do for me, put it that way. I'd fight every inch of the way.'

However, a number of carers commented that the desire for independence could be carried too far, and reported occasions on which they felt the determined refusal to accept help crossed the borderline into unacceptable stubbornness:

She wouldn't accept it [more help], she is a very independent lady. Sometimes it is bordering on stubbornness, really. I mean you can take independence too far. (Neighbour)

> She's so independent that (for example) she had a fall at
> [shopping centre] about three years ago and the ambulance was
> called and they took her into hospital, she didn't give my name,
> she wouldn't give me as next of kin . . . she said 'I didn't want
> you calling out, I was in the right place, I didn't want you
> fetching you've enough to do' . . . I was most cross with her, you
> know, of course. (Niece)

In general, although there *were* elderly parents who were fiercely
independent, this phenomenon was more commonly reported by
those caring for elderly people who were *not* their parents. As we
saw in Chapter 5, assistance from other relatives is by no means as
readily secured as assistance from children, and perhaps it is the
case that many elderly parents do feel that their children 'owe'
them assistance even though they may hope never to have to draw
upon this potential resource. Indeed, in the same way as the desire
for independence could be carried too far, there were a few
reports (more commonly from children) that their help was too
much taken for granted:

> The main thing is she expects me to be there when I'm wanted.
> And I suppse it's a natural thing, that. I only hope I never get
> like that. But I think that's it. Taken for granted I think, you
> know, and that you must drop everything and you don't have a
> life. You get that you've not made any plans so you know
> nothing can be put off. (Daughter)

> If she gets anything into her head you've got to do it there and
> then, they get a bit selfish, you know. She never thinks to ask if
> your husband is all right, does it matter about your coming to
> look after me, or anything like that. You are taken for granted
> that you go and that's it. (Daughter)

It was clear that children, as well as being regarded as having
more responsibility, were seen as having more 'right' to take
decisions on behalf of elderly people. The demarcation lines
concerning the proper responsibilities and roles of children, as
opposed to other informal carers, were clearly drawn by actors
within the informal sector. For example, one neighbour, who felt
that the elderly confused lady whom he assisted should go to see

her doctor, recalled how other neighbours had expressed the view that he should not take her because no one would accept his word in the matter, and that he should wait for the next visit of the son. Equally, although he himself had been providing much routine domestic assistance (with aid from another neighbour), he had felt it to be proper for the son and not him to secure assistance from the home-help service. Other neighbours who looked after a confused elderly widow's money took care to explain to the interviewer that they kept detailed accounts 'just in case', and pointed out that there were no available relatives who might otherwise have discharged this function.

From the point of view of an elderly person it may be that the expectation of help from other relatives or non-relatives is not so great as the expectation of help from children, and consequently the receipt of assistance from those who are not children places the elderly person in a sense 'in debt' to their caring relative or neighbour. Certainly, when elderly people were asked for reasons why their carer was the right person to help them, a statement of the family relationship (such as 'She is my daughter') was overwhelmingly the most common response, the only other common response being the statement that there were no alternatives. Those whose carers were not related were more likely to stress that they got on well together. Thus elderly people did seem to see the obligation to provide help as a concomitant of a family relationship, and were much more likely to refer to the emotional quality of the relationship itself as a reason for helping when the carer was not related.

Thus, when assistance is received from non-relatives, or relatives who are not seen as 'like' children, then all but essential help is refused; but, equally, gratitude is expressed for help received. Neighbours and relatives who were not children were more likely to report difficulties in persuading elderly people to accept help, and some of these carers did express the view that not being children restricted their right to 'insist' on giving help.

Really with an aunt it's not like your own mother, I mean, when it was our mothers, we'd just go and do it but you can't with . . . you find you can't with an aunt, you know what I mean. With your own parents you could have a joke and say 'You sit there, I'm going to do this' but you find that with relations you haven't got that persuasion really. (Nephew and wife)

The practical cumulative outcome of these individual and social expectations about the respective roles, responsibilities and rights of children compared with other, particularly non-family, carers is that the obligations on the latter are much less than on the former. It is not surprising, then, as we showed in Chapter 4 and as has been revealed by other research (Wenger, 1984), that neighbours and friends play such a small role in the provision of care to disabled elderly people compared with that of children and spouses.

From consensus to conflict in the caring relationship

The foregoing discussion describes the general picture, of a process of mutual adaptation by carers and cared for to changes in the elderly person's circumstances and capabilities. These adaptations were not accomplished without difficulty: the problem of persuading elderly people to acknowledge their disability publicly by using aids, and the potential difficulties of differing gender-role expectations have been explored. Consideration has also been given to the carers' problems in deciding what help might be offered without giving offence or causing upset, and difficulties for elderly people in coming to terms with a decline in their capacity for independence and the frustration of depending on others. The twin problems of rejection of help and, alternatively, of taking it too much for granted, have been touched upon. But most of these difficulties occurred in the context of a general acceptance by the parties involved of the legitimacy of both the elderly person's need for assistance and the carer's performance of the needed tasks. However, there were variations from this overall consensus, and it is to these particularly problematic areas that we now turn.

Conflicts over ageing and dependency

Of course, where elderly people refused to accept all help, there were no carers to interview and thus the carer study cannot be used to estimate the prevalence of persons resolutely refusing help. However, it was occasionally possible to obtain a carer's (or potential carer's) view of such a situation:

If we went up there [and said] 'Look we're going to give this house a good clean up' he's followed her round – 'Why don't you leave us alone, house is right enough for us. Why don't you leave it?' Now you can't work like that. (Son-in-law)

He won't always accept help if he would get it. You know 'What do they want to come for – noseying round.' That's me Dad. (Daughter, same interview)

Somewhat more often reported, but extreme in only a few cases (about one in ten of children), was the opposite pole of the overeager assumption of unnecessary dependence:

This was one of the things that put my hackles up. My father was alive when I first moved in here and when she first came to inspect the property she said, 'Oh yes, I shall be alright here when your father goes.' I couldn't believe my ears. She'd not only planned that my father was going to go first but that she was coming here . . I thought 'Please Dad, don't go'. (Daughter)

Usually, any expectation of dependency by elderly women after widowhood was not seen as legitimate, if they were in good physical health, and a minority of carers experienced considerable difficulties in coping with what they felt were their parents' illegitimate demands.

Occasionally conflict arose, when carers resisted straightforward attempts to control their activities by parents assuming a position of parental authority:

You see she'd got into her own routine and her own way of thinking, her own way of dishing the orders out, she's not the easiest person to get on with. We had our moments. Anyway I think I've finally got her adjusted to my way of thinking. She would have had me in the asylum – 'Get me this' and 'Bring me that.' If you went out you were late . . . I've finished with that. (Daughter)

More often reported, however, were more subtle attempts at control through dependency.

She used to try things on really, she wanted a lot of attention. Like we do a lot of work for the scouts . . . and when we're sort of busy and involved with them she'd suddenly be ill to get my attention and go up there; like the time we moved in here I got a frantic 'phone message to say she was ill and I had to go dashing over to the other side of Sheffield and when I got there, there was nothing wrong with her. (Daughter)

For some carers this experience was often repeated, with consequent destructive effects on the relationship:

I used to be very upset when she used to ring and she wasn't very well, and we used to go over, but now I get a bit . . . I don't dash straight out of the house. I go, because you can't afford not to go, you know, but the attitude is that when I used to go I used to panic kind of . . . after 2 years you get a bit, I suppose a bit, blasé about it, in a way . . . Of course this is I suppose where I feel guilty that I don't get panicky and I don't rush straight away, you know. (Daughter)

The above carer had often been summoned urgently to her mothr's at two and three o'clock in the morning, sometimes several times a week, yet still, as can be seen, felt that she could not 'afford' to refuse such demands. As another daughter commented: 'It's very difficult, you know, with old people, because you've got to decide whether they're kidding, in other words, or whether it's the real thing.'

Relatives recognised the legitimacy of a demand for ugent help in an emergency, and it was clear that there were a few people who it seemed were prepared to take advantage of this to control their children's activities. Some relatives were not able to accept the 'risk' that would be involved in refusing: presumably the risk that this emergency would prove to be a genuine, possibly fatal, illness and they would be seen (by themselves and by others) to have failed in discharging their duty.

Resisting dependency demands

Some carers felt that they had successfully resolved such difficulties, and resisted their relatives' attempts to become unnecessarily dependent. Our daughter did find support from a professional worker: 'She frightened me to death and I fetched the doctor, and the doctor took me in the kitchen and said there was nothing wrong, it was just sympathy she wanted because we couldn't spare the time to go there, you know.'

This acknowledgement was of some assistance in enabling the daughter to resist future demands, because it enabled an appeal to the views of an authoritative third party in any later disagreements about whether the elderly person was or was not 'really' ill. This carer recalled what she felt were her mother's attempts to transfer dependency after the death of her father:

> My father carried my mother about for years and years and my mother thought I was going to take over where he left off but her doctor told me not to ... to make her do things for herself, 'cos me father used to do everything. It was difficult at first but I've won because she's proved it in herself that she can do things. She was trying to convince me that she couldn't and I knew that she could. [What sort of things?] Well, doing everything. My father did the housework, cooked her meals and everything and she never did anything at all. (Daughter)

However, the daughter's strategy had not endeared her to her mother's neighbour, who was now the subject of frequent visits and requests for assistance from the elderly person (some of which she suspected were unjustified). The neighbour expressed the view that 'her own should see to her more than they do', while the daughter regretted that a 'kind neighbour' had become involved and reduced her mother's enforced independence.

Not all attempts at control through dependency were as overt as the recurring threat of serious illness. A few carers mentioned the development of minor illnesses or depression in their elderly relatives just before they were about to take a holiday break:

> When we're going on holiday, and she knows I'm going to be away for a couple of weeks she starts having these little ailments, you know, and she's not very well. And I think it's just the fear that I'm not there. (Daughter)

> Even if we just go to my son's for a couple of days ... I had a talk with her about it because she was so miserable it used to spoil my break. She said, well, she felt completely lost when I'm not just there to ring up, or to know that I'm there in case she needs me, you see. (Daughter)

Effects on the relationship with carers

The feeling of being manipulated was experienced as debilitating. Indeed, one carer explicitly said that it was less depressing to provide even large quantities of help when it was obviously needed, than to feel that one was being manipulated into helping:

> The last time mother was ill, ... the doctor said [to her] 'keep your leg up as much as possible'. That was when I was going early morning, dinner time, tea time and bed time, and yet then I was desperately tired but yet I wasn't depressed because I knew she was ill ... well physically ill ... I knew she needed help, and she was so sweet about it, you see. But, when I rather feel that what I'm doing the running for is not a physical thing, but because she's depressed then I get very agitated and I do tend to get a little bit down. (Step-daughter)

Emotional dependency could be, for some carers, quite as wearing as the need to provide practical assistance:

> I feel as though I'm smothered in a way. I can't go out and just do. If she rings up and I'm not here she gets quite upset ... I said, 'Now Mum, come off it, this is getting a bit much, surely I can pop down to Tesco's without you getting worried and upset'. And that made her cross. (Daughter)

The more carers became convinced that their parents' fears, or demands, were not legitimate (that is, genuinely based on physical disability), the more damaging were such experiences to the overall relationship.

> She's pulled an awful lot of strokes on us ... I think it was a cry for attention. She was complaining about a pain in her back about three years ago, and she said she couldn't move ... I mean she said she couldn't do anything, she couldn't sit up in bed ... [elderly person was admitted to hospital] ... on the ward they wheeled the lunch trolley in and she came up from a lying down position, she heard the lunch and she got right up ... I thought 'You monkey! My brother and I have been lifting you.' Now when somebody does this to you it hardens you and makes you think 'Now she's not going to do that to me again.' (Daughter)

Of course it is too simplistic to suggest all such elderly people were consciously manipulating their carers. Emotional dependency could well have physical effects, and it cannot be supposed that all would be well if carers were able to ignore the signals and press on with their activities:

> About two or three years back, I think, we went for two weeks . . . and she was really bad then . . . she really got very, very depressed. Then . . . somehow she let herself go, she stopped eating, that's the worst thing, she stopped eating. Anyway gradually, when I came back, I got the doctor in and got some vitamin tablets and she pulled round. I know it depresses her. (Daughter)

When carers recognised mental illness to exist then they were less likely to feel manipulated by an apparently fit person's failure to care for him or herself. However, the difficulties of such a situation should not be underestimated, because the fear that a failure or refusal to provide care might lead to the elderly person's decline or death might well be soundly based:

> She won't go out, you know; like we went on holiday last year, but I got all the food in for her, she just . . . well, if I didn't get all the food in for her she'd starve, I'm pretty certain she would . . . and she doesn't wash, very very little, I have to do that for her. Actually she wears clothes and throws them away, and buys new ones. She changes, you know, very rarely. I really have to ask her and pray for her to change her clothes, you know, it's as bad as that. (Son)

As the need for care increases then the carer's travelling time and level of anxiety when away from the elderly person will increase. Of course, in the majority of cases a decision whether to remove the elderly person from home will never have to be faced. However, attitudes towards this possible eventuality are very revealing of family relationships and responsibilities, and will therefore form the final topic of discussion in this chapter.

Anticipated increases in dependency

Elderly people were asked what they thought about the idea of residential care, and also whether they would mind the idea of going to live with relatives. Of course, given the range of disability levels existing among the elderly population, such considerations were for some respondents safely hypothetical, while for others they represented areas of current concern.

Carers were asked to anticipate what would happen if the elderly person became unable to cope alone. They were specifically asked about the possibility of the formation of a joint household with the elderly person and about the idea of residential care.

Joint living

Only about a quarter of those elderly people living independently regarded the prospect of joint living with relatives with equanimity, and one in three of these said that they would not wish to do so now but would only do so if it became necessary in the future. The majority (58 per cent) of elderly people (excluding those already living with relatives and those with no relatives) said that they *would* mind the idea of living with relatives, and a minority gave mixed or other responses.

Among carers, children felt more responsibility for coping with an extreme situation than did non-relatives or other relatives. No non-relative would have considered a joint household with the elderly person, whereas 10 per cent of children currently wanted their parent to move in with them (although the parent refused to do so), and a further 40 per cent of children said that they would have their parent to live with them if this became necessary.

> If she was ill or anything like that I'd have her here. I promised her that she will not go anywhere, I will look after her, you know. (Daughter)

> I suppose if she gets ill or anything, you know, then we'd do more, or I'd have her up here. I've always said she can live here and she will. (Daughter)

However, just over one-quarter of children definitely rejected the idea of joint living:

> It's just a view that I have that a family is a family and I think when you've got children I don't think they really want old

people living with them all the time, it's all right for a few days, or a few weeks, but not for a life time. (Daughter)

We don't get on at long stages, it's all right for a short period of time, it's all right when she comes to stay with us at Christmas but she is glad to go home and I am glad for her to go home. (Daughter)

One relative had already rejected her father's suggestion of joint living:

He said something once ... he said 'I wondered if I would give my home up and come and live with you'. Well, I said 'I don't think it's a very good idea because Tracey [daughter] is growing up a bit and you know how you are at loggerheads sometimes with the television and that ...' I said 'Young and old don't mix.' (Daughter)

However, in this case the elderly person was not disabled and the daughter indicated that if he became physically incapable of living alone then she might feel compelled to modify her attitude.

Inevitably, not all children gave an answer which could easily be classified as to whether they would, or would not, be willing to form a joint household. About one in five children gave a more ambivalent response, indicating that they would feel that they should take in the elderly person but that they anticipated considerable problems if they did so. Even those who considered themselves to be definitely willing anticipated some difficulties.

One-third of carers mentioned that their accommodation was unsuitable:

I've only two bedrooms, you see I have my own family to think about, I couldn't have her to live with me. (Daughter)

It would be difficult because of the toilet here you see, ours is upstairs. (Daughter)

However, there were a minority of these carers, with access to greater resources, who felt that such difficulties could be overcome if necessary, such as the daughter who replied: 'If he had to come and live with us we would prefer him with his own sitting room or bed-sitter . . we've got to discuss the fact that he would need his own accommodation.'

Three out of four children were convinced that currently their elderly parent did not wish to live with them, whilst the majority of others said they did not know what their parents' wishes were, and only three said that they believed their parent would like to live with them.

One in three carers considered that the elderly person themselves would always resist joint living:

> I should envisage having her here but whether she'd come is another question, you know. (Daughter)

> I can't really see her coming to me, even if it was the last thing ever. I really think she would have to be carried out of that home. (Niece)

> I don't think that's up to me. He's a strong-willed man and if he says no, then it's no. (Daughter)

Another group of carers anticipated problems with other members of their household. Disputes with teenage children were one cause of concern, but other carers (15 per cent of children) envisaged difficulties with their spouse:

> Obviously if there was no other way mum would have to come to us. I wouldn't be too happy because I think really it would cause problems between myself and my husband, but I'm an absolute sucker where she's concerned. (Daughter)

> If it had come to the point of having to bring her here and living with us, like, it would have been quite an upheaval in my life. I'm not going to say it might have been the cause of a split-up of my marriage, but it could have been a very serious setback to my marriage. (Son)

It seemed that the degree of felt emotional closeness to the parent was a factor influencing carers' decisions about joint households. Only 17 per cent of those carers who had said that they felt close to their parent also said that they would definitely *not* be willing to share a house with them, whereas over 70 per cent of those who did not feel close gave this response. (Those who did not feel close were also less likely to reject the idea of residential care.) Thus, although it has been argued that lack of emotional closeness does not preclude the provision of routine practical assistance, sometimes at quite a high degree of intensity, ultimately the quality of the relationship does seem to limit the extent to which relatives are personally prepared to provide care. Almost all carers perceived the idea of a joint household as problematic, but there was a clear difference between an appreciation of likely difficulties and an absolute statement of intent. For instance, one daughter said, 'I have to be honest and say I don't want her to come and live here because I mean, obviously it disrupts the whole household, but I'd rather her be here, than worrying about her down there' (at the elderly person's home). Whereas another daughter said, 'I would never have her to live with me, ever. You can write that down', and a son replied, 'No, it wouldn't work at all. Definitely not.'

In discussing joint households, children were often not speaking in ignorance of the reality. Half of all children had had their elderly parent to live with them for short periods, say for convalescence or following widowhood, but only two had made attempts to form a long-term joint household in the past. Both of these had proved unsuccessful (carers living with the elderly person were not interviewed and so inevitably only instances where such experiments had failed would be included in the study).

It was too much for me to go there every day, you see, so I had to ... sell the house and get him here, but it didn't work. I had him here 13 weeks and he wanted to go and actually I must say I wanted him to go ... So we got him down there [new flat] through the Council. (Daughter)

Clearly, once an experiment in joint living had failed there was a corresponding reluctance to try again. Problems mentioned by those who had tried and failed included: the refusal of the elderly people to make a financial contribution towards their keep, complaints by the elderly person of boredom because the carer worked, and arguments with spouses or cohabitees which directly or indirectly resulted from the presence of the elderly person. In one of these instances, the elderly person had been admitted to residential care by the time of the carer interview, and in the other attempts were being made to secure such admission at the time of the elderly person's death.

Residential care

The elderly people interviewed were slightly less likely to reject the idea of residential care than the idea of sharing a home with relatives. Nevertheless a substantial minority (40 per cent) did reject the idea of residential care, some most strongly, and a further 30 per cent commented that they would only be prepared to accept admission if it were absolutely necessary and as a last resort. About one in ten of elderly people had spent some time in residential care in the past, usually in consequence of illness and, less often, to give relatives a break. Possibly the fact that illness was the most common factor precipitating admission explains the combination of views most commonly expressed by those with experience of residential care, which was that the stay had been enjoyable but the elderly person would prefer not to go again, or would only go if they had to.

It should be mentioned that 3 per cent of elderly people expressed a positive desire to be admitted to residential care, while a further 18 per cent expressed willingness to go if necessary, demonstrating that opposition to such a course of action should not always be assumed. Equally, we would argue that such experiences of willingness cannot be taken as a straightforward vote of confidence in a formal residential solution: they may reflect a perceived and actual lack of alternatives (Walker, 1987a). A few people, possibly those with past experience of residential care, gave conditional responses, such as an expression of willingness to enter such care only if there were not too many people suffering from dementia as fellow residents.

In view of the reputation of residential homes it was not surprising that attitudes towards residential care were associated with the degree of importance attached to independence. Over 70 per cent of those who rejected residential care had said that independence was 'very important' to them, compared with just over 59 per cent of those who were willing to accept residential care as a last resort, and 50 per cent of those who were completely willing to enter such care. For some elderly people, the desire, or willingness, to enter residential care *was*, in one sense, an expression of independence in that they would rather enter such care than become dependent upon their children.

Carers' views of residential care

It was interesting that non-relatives were often unwilling to express a view on the subject of residential care. This, they felt was the business of the elderly person and their family if they had one, and not a proper concern of theirs. Responses to the question on residential care are summarised in Table 7.2. As can be seen, most

Table 7.2 *Carers' attitudes to residential care*

Attitude to residential care	Number	Percentage
Not carer's concern	7	12
Expected when necessary	6	10
Ambivalent	12	21
Rejection of idea	33	57
Total	58	100

carers reacted negatively to the idea of residential care for their elderly person. What was at the root of the widespread resistance to such care? It has to be borne in mind that an increase in disability, sufficient to necessitate admission, is in itself seen as undesirable and so it is highly unlikely that anyone would look forward to such a prospect. However, there was a clear variation in attitudes: from matter-of-fact acceptance of such a course if necessary, to outright rejection of the possibility, come what may.

Underlining this differential response was a stark structural reality: the socially divided access to resources in old age. Matter-of-fact acceptance of eventual admission was most often found in those instances where the elderly person had sufficient resources to afford private care:

> We don't know how infirm she's going to be and she might need a lot of help; she might need to go into a nursing home and that

could use her money, and we would never let her give us any money because we feel she might need it. (Daughter)

About one in ten of carers took this point of view although this did not necessarily mean that the possibility of a joint household was ruled out. Instead there was sometimes a view of a progression in which increasing dependency might at first mean a joint household:

I don't relish the thought but if that did arise then we would move to a house slightly bigger where there was enough room for everybody to get out of each other's way. (Daughter)

Secondly, with increasing disability, this might mean a transfer to private care:

If we got to the stage that my mother-in-law was in, I mean none of us could cope with her in a wheelchair because she can't get upstairs, so that's a different matter altogether. (Daughter)

However, private care was considered to be beyond the resources of the elderly person and their family in 85 per cent of instances, and the discussion which follows largely reflects the majority view of those who believed they could not afford private care (although changes in the board and lodging regulations opened the door to private care for those elderly people receiving supplementary pension in 1981).

Three carers currently wished for their elderly parent to be admitted, and one daughter said: 'I wish, I really do, that she was in a home because she needs round-the-clock attention, love, that's why I wish she were in one.' In one of these instances the elderly person had been admitted but, in the other two, the carers did not feel that they could overrule the wishes of the elderly person:

A home or a hospital – it'd kill her, definitely kill her. No that'd be the finish of her, love, and I wouldn't like to go as far as that with her. (Daughter)

you'd sign her death warrant, if you did that, straight away. We've tried . . . she's been in [private residential home], once or twice, never saw such a change in a person. She's just not that type at all. (Sister)

A few other carers perhaps cherished hopes that their elderly parent might be brought to consider the prospect of residential care more favourably, but either felt that they dare not raise the subject, or were disappointed at the response obtained:

The reaction I got to a [wheel]chair was enough, [let alone] talking about a home. Michael and I have talked about it and said 'Dare we ask her if she is willing . . .' Up to now neither of us have had the audacity or the nerve to ask her. (Daughter-in-law)

My brother once suggested it, he says 'Why don't you try and get me dad in that home'. I says 'you try and get me dad in that home'. I says 'I don't want that on my conscience'. I wouldn't like to think that my dad said [would say] 'They shoved me in here, I didn't want to come in'. Any road, I says, you ask me Dad what he thinks, I'm not asking him. Anyway my sister was in one day and says 'Would you like to go in home at end of street?' and he says 'Why would I go in a home when I've got our Mary [carer]?' (Daughter)

The above two reactions illustrate the two main sources of resistance to the idea of residential care: first, the sense that such care was unacceptable to the elderly person and, second, the influence of normative beliefs that children should themselves provide care if possible.

Seven out of ten carers mentioned that the elderly people themselves were strongly resistant to the idea of residential care.

It's one thing she is definite about. She doesn't want to go in a home, so that's out. I don't think I'd ever do that, she's always said it – 'Never put me in a home.' (Daughter)

No, they wouldn't go. No way, I don't think they'd go. I don't think my mother-in-law would give her home up, no way. She's always said, 'There's nothing like your own home.' (Daughter-in-law)

Residential care and joint households were not necessarily

viewed as alternatives. A few elderly people were seen as strongly resistant to both possibilities:

> I really think that she would have to be carried out of that home: I think we'd have to pull out all the stops for every resource there was to keep her in her own home. She would never go in a home, it would kill her. (Niece)

When an elderly person is dependent on the service of a relative to avoid admission, then this, of course, means that the relatives have a source of power over the elderly person. Occasionally the possibility of admission was reported to have been used as a threat or a weapon in argument:

> I've said many a time 'you'll be in a Home, I can never get on with you'. (Daughter)

> 'Mother, you're going in a Home.' [You say that to her do you?] Oh yes. [What does she say?] Nothing, I think my mother has had enough of going in homes. (Daughter)

However, such reports were rare, not least because not all the resistance to residential care stemmed from the elderly people. One-half of carers felt that they themselves would not be able to accept such a possibility:

> I said to her 'I would never expect you to go in a home.' She said 'I hope it never comes [that] I'd have to live with you' because she had two brothers living with her, you know, years ago, and she says 'I never had any privacy for a long, long time.' But no, I just couldn't see her going into a home, and she knows this. (Daughter-in-law)

Indeed, five carers (9 per cent) felt that they were more resistant to the idea of residential care than was their elderly relative: one daughter replied, 'It were my mother that said it to me, said that she'd want to go in a Home. I said, "Well you're not going in a home while I can look after you".' In general, carers' resistance to admission was not based on any sense that homes for elderly people were in themselves terrible places (a sentiment that *was* expressed by a few elderly people). Carers pointed to possible disadvantages like lack of privacy, or other features of institution- alisation, but were also aware of advantages such as the company of a peer group and round-the-clock attention. Rather, there was a sense of failure, summed up by one daughter who said:

> She's always said that, more or less 'Don't be afraid to put me in a old folks' home if I get to be . . . don't let me be any trouble' but I wouldn't like that. [Why not?] I don't know really, I suppose you must feel you are letting them down in some way.

Or, as the carer previously quoted, said: 'I don't want that on my conscience.'

However, there was one feature of residential homes and especially geriatric hospitals which did cause carers concern, particularly when they had first-hand experience of such institu- tions, and this was the mental state of other residents. One carer commented, on a visit to a geriatric ward:

> When I saw the people – there was a man walking about wetting himself and a woman sort of [wailing noise] all the time – my father wasn't like that and I couldn't have left him. I would have had to have brought him here, no matter what it cost me. (Daughter).

> That's the thing with my mum, her mind is perfect, she's not confused at all, in fact you find so many at her age have gone confused and just don't know what day it is. Well I would hate her to go into somewhere and be in a little room for two weeks [carer was considering short-term care] with somebody that is, and there is such a lot like that.

> She couldn't afford to go into one, to pay for herself and I think the Council ones [homes] – they are so feeble, the ones that are there, that I don't think she would be happy. A lot of them, I think are mentally disabled and I think this would upset her. (Daughter)

Experiences of geriatric wards were usually more negative than those of homes for elderly people; indeed, one carer explicitly pointed to differences in the reactions to the experience of these two environments:

> She went to visit a neighbour of her's in Rowantrees [old people's home] and she did say 'Oh well it's quite nice there, if it came to the push I wouldn't mind somewhere like that' but we used to go and see my Auntie who was in [psychiatric hospital] in the geriatric ward and, 'Oh, don't ever let me come in a place like this, shoot me first, don't ever let me come here.' (Daughter)

There has in fact been considerable investigation (see, for example Wilkin 1986) into the proportion of confused residents who can be tolerated by other residents in old peoples' homes.

There is no doubt that such questions do exercise the minds of people considering the possibility of residential care, although this is not to suggest that such fears explain all, or even most, of the resistance to residential care.

> I wouldn't put her in a Home, she is so much against going anywhere. I know there are Homes and Homes, I know there are some nice ones, but I think they are all Homes, and this is what she's got this aversion to. Oh, I would do anything else rather than that. (Daughter)

Given the fears about the mental state of other residents it is perhaps ironic, although understandable, that quite a number of carers identified the appropriate point at which they would consider admission to residential care for their elderly person as being 'if her mind went'.

> I wouldn't like her to go in a home, not as long as she knew what was happening to her. (Daughter)

> I mean, if her mind went as well, well that's another matter. I mean, her mind is all right and I wouldn't want her in a home like that. (Daughter)

> When she gets to that stage that she wouldn't recognise us then she's all right to go in a mental place. But I don't want ... as long as she can recognise us I wouldn't want her shut away with nobody she knows. (Neighbour, male)

In a recent public opinion survey, (West, Ilsley and Kelman, 1984), two-thirds of those surveyed considered that residential care was the most appropriate form of assistance for confused elderly people, whereas less than 10 per cent considered this as best for elderly people suffering only from physical handicap.

When an elderly person is unable to distinguish between sources of supply of help, then clearly the distinctive role of family members – the uniqueness of their particular relationship with the elderly person which makes them personally irreplaceable – is at an end. This does not mean, however, that all carers necessarily regard their responsibility towards their elderly relative to have finished.

Conclusion

This chapter and the previous one have demonstrated the importance of understanding affect and reciprocity as dynamic processes. Liking and helping do not remain constant over time, but are interrelated within particular relationships in complex ways. In Chapter 5 it was demonstrated that choices about who should help elderly people were based on rules which derived from stereotyped beliefs about the debts owed by children to their parents, and expectations about appropriate gender roles which may be subject to change.

Even though, in most instances where help was given, it was clear that people did feel a personalised sense of obligation towards their parents for past help, it was equally clear that a significant minority did not share these feelings and felt compelled to help by pressures external to the particular relationship. Indeed, in some instances it was evident that relationships between family members could be far more difficult and emotionally damaging than many other relationships. Of course, as has been shown, a failure by family members to help elderly relatives does not necessarily reflect a poor relationship. The physical incapacity or other obligations of family members may well provide an explanation. However, it should not be regarded as controversial to argue that some relatives should *not* be expected to help, even if they apparently have the capacity to do so. In a recent collection of papers on intra-family violence (Finkelhor, *et al*, 1983), one author observed: 'Publicly at least, we think of the family as a loving, tranquil, peaceful social institution to which one flees *from* stress and danger. Privately, the family is perhaps society's most violent institution' (Gelles, 1983, p. 157).

The papers in the above collection concentrated on violence within the nuclear family: between spouses, and from parents to children. It should not require a great imaginative leap on the part of policy makers, and professionals working with elderly people, to consider at least the possibility that not all relationships at the end of the life cycle will be characterised by love, affection or even a sense of obligation.

The problem of so-called 'granny-battering' is, we would argue, only one minor facet of the variation of family relationships in old age, and such variation should be more openly recognised and acted upon in the construction and implementation of policy towards elderly people and their families. People who wish to help should be assisted to do so without too great a personal sacrifice, and in particular more help should be available to those coping with mental disorder; but perhaps the main principle that policy makers and society in general must recognise is that not all families should be expected to care.

8

Formal and Informal Sources of Care

Britain, like most other industrial societies, has a pluralistic system of welfare provision. Indeed the term 'welfare pluralism' means nothing more than a diversity of sources of welfare provision and service delivery (Gladstone, 1979; Rea Price *et al.*, 1987; N. Johnson, 1987). It is generally recognised that services are organised and delivered by a variety of sources, usually identified (by Wolfenden, 1978, for example) as the statutory, voluntary, commercial and informal sectors.

The existence of pluralism in personal social care has led to the suggestion that such provision can be discussed in terms of a 'mixed economy of welfare' (Webb and Wistow, 1982). However, as we pointed out in Chapter 2, there are considerable reasons for caution in the use of such a framework for the analysis of social welfare. To take a narrowly economic view of the commodities and services provided by each sector is to neglect the key issue of the *subjective* meaning of care. But this dimension has to be taken into account because it means that normal economic assumptions about substitutability of products from different sectors cannot be made. In a strictly economic exchange the benefits exchanged are extrinsic (that is, detachable in principle from the source which supplies them). By contrast, in social exchange it is often the case that benefits are intrinsic because their significance depends on the person who supplies them (P. M. Blau, 1968). This point has particular relevance in any attempt at discussing a consumer's view of welfare services. Although there may be no obvious difference in the extrinsic benefits supplied in a particular caring exchange – commodities such as meals, shopping, cooking, cleaning and so on

203

– it is likely that those who receive services will have preferences among the suppliers of such commodities which will depend on the intrinsic benefits – such as emotional warmth, affection and interest – which are expected from potential suppliers. Thus a visit from a daughter may have a different value to an elderly person compared with a visit from a volunteer friendly visitor, even though the two events may seem, externally, to be identical in form. Even where intrinsic benefits are less obvious, preferences may be influenced by the source of supply. For example, a sum of money from a charitable organisation may be less acceptable than the state's Christmas bonus for pensioners, because even an apparently identical sum of money has a different *meaning* to the recipient according to perceived rights to receive.

Differences between the formal and informal sectors

Family care is undoubtedly part of the informal sector of care and there are important respects in which this sector differs from the other three sectors which, for ease of analysis, collectively will be termed the formal sector. At the beginning of Chapter 6 were outlined some of the arguments about the special nature, the alleged qualitative superiority, of informal care, which was said to be rooted in its origins in pre-existing social and/or biological relationships between helper and helped. Of course, the subsequent evidence demonstrated that the superiority of family care should not be accepted without question. In fact, it was clear that some of the most damaging and emotionally destructive relationships may exist within families, with negative consequences for all concerned. None the less, the claim that informal care is *prima facie* preferable to recipients must be taken seriously.

Of course, the fact that informal care is personally directed may be seen as a disadvantage from the point of view of its overall distribution. Indeed, as we argued in Chapter 2, the world of informal care does not secure equal provision for all cases (in particular defined categories of need) and neither can it adequately meet the needs of all those who do receive its services. However, if it is argued that it is impossible for the formal sector to be an adequate substitute for informal care (because the latter is experienced as qualitatively different) then such a view has the implication that *replacement* of informal care by care from the other (formal) sectors would have the undesirable consequence of lowering quality.

The previous two chapters dealt at length with processes and meanings in the informal sector, with particular focus on family care. This chapter will look outwards from the point of view of elderly people and their families towards the other sectors from which assistance may be obtained, and will discuss the expectations of, and interactions with, formal service providers.

This will lead, in turn, to a discussion of alternative policies in the following chapter. The formal/informal distinction used by Abrams, and outlined in the previous chapter, is drawn from sociological literature on bureaucracies, and differs from that used by some other writers (for example, Pinker 1979) who have identified formal provision with statutory provision and thus defined provision by voluntary organisations as 'informal' (unless covered by statute). It is argued that the current usage enables the sharp distrinctions between the principles of organisation of formal and informal care to be clearly delineated, and that such a theoretical distinction is helpful in discussing examples of welfare provision even if, in practice, the lines are sometimes blurred.

It has been argued (Seyd, Tennant and Bayley, 1983) that a voluntary visitor may become friendly with the person visited to the extent that the formal origin of the relationship is forgotten and that the activities of the visitor then become part of the informal sector. This is, of course, correct but it serves to illustrate, rather than cast doubt on, the usefulness of the distinctions made in theory to provide a suitable language to describe what happens in practice. It shows that, whilst voluntary organisations are part of the formal sector in terms of their objectives and principles of organisation, this essentially static distinction between systems of service delivery has most relevance for the consumer only at the moment of the initial delivery of service. From then on a dynamic perspective is necessary in order to understand the development of informal elements in the relationship between the two people specifically involved. If we do not have clear conceptions of the differences between formal and informal care then we cannot describe the evolution of one into the other.

One of the distinguishing characteristics of bureaucracies

(formal organisations) is held to be the use and development of professional expertise. In his discussion of professions and professionals P. M. Blau (1968) makes the point that an essential element of professional detachment is the absence of direct exchange relationships with clients. Officials who are obligated because of, or dependent on, rewards from particular clients are open to the charge that their decisions may be subject to improper influence. Rewards to officials are collectively provided not simply in the form of a salary, but also by the approval of professional colleagues, thus providing compensation for the rewards forgone by treating clients impersonally. Equal treatment of equal cases is the requirement and this, of course, is in stark contrast to the mode of operation of the informal sector.

Informal care, as has been described, is directed towards a particular person by virtue of their social relationships with others: care for a mother, a sister or a friend, for example. In contrast, formal statutory or voluntary care is organised to be delivered to all people in particular defined categories of need: the disabled, children at risk, and so on. The criterion for eligibility for commercial care is, of course, the ability to pay; considerations of need or merit are not relevant.

Apart from their differing criteria for eligibility, the sectors also differ in the degree to which acceptable forms of intervention and outcome are prescribed. As we demonstrated in Chapter 5, there are undoubtedly 'rules' operating in the informal sector of care which are 'understood' by most participants. However, it is characteristics of the rules of such social exchange that they are not well specified. Indeed, with reference to social benefits such as warmth, affection and interest, the 'rules' of social exchange dictate that such social commodities cannot be explicitly exchanged or bargained about lest this compromise their genuineness as expressions of true feeling (P. Blau, 1964). Warmth and affection from those suspected of ulterior motives (being 'remembered in the will' perhaps) are inevitably suspect. The degree of certainty of return in social exchange depends upon the level of trust existing between the parties to the exchange, and so to bargain about return is to express mistrust.

With respect to the meaning of care there are related arguments about how the basis upon which a particular commodity is exchanged can affect its meaning, and therefore its value. This was perhaps most clearly spelled out by Hirsch (1977) in his discussion of the 'commercialisation effect', in which he demonstrated that some commodities essentially change their meaning when exchanged on a commercial basis. Hirsch used the illustrative example of sexual relationships, but the argument can be extended to make the general point that the expressive aspects of a caring relationship have to be freely and spontaneously offered to be experienced as genuine; to the extent that they are felt to be coerced, or induced, their value to the recipient is diminished. It is conceptions such as these which, perhaps, underlie resistance to the idea of paid 'good neighbours', or the 'colonisation' or 'professionalisation' of lay help (Caplan, 1974; Bayley, 1982): the sense that as informal care becomes more like formal care it will change its *meaning*, so its value to recipients will be inevitably lessened and its quality diminished. However, this argument also has the consequence that informal care, if unwillingly given, or perceived as imposed upon helpers, is unlikely to possess those superior qualities which can make it so uniquely valuable to recipients.

Advantages of formal sector provision

There are some recognised advantages in the services provided by bureaucracies. From the point of view of the individual, there is the availability of greater resources than the family is likely to possess (the capacity to provide long-term income, for example), as well as the availability of professional expertise, such as medical care. In addition there may be occasions when impersonal services are preferred because, for example, agents of the formal organisation will not be involved in family disputes or be acting in the hope of unspecified personal recompense from the client. Finally, there is more commitment towards coverage of all members of the population in need, and an obligation to provide equal services for similar cases; which obligation, unlike informal sector obligations, can still be discharged in the event of illness or incapacity of particular individuals. It has also been argued, taking a dynamic perspective on services, that agents of the state, such as home helps, can and do develop informal relationships with at least some elderly clients (Hunt, 1978; Seyd, Tennant and Bayley, 1983), and also that state services can serve a symbolic function in making elderly people feel that they are cared *about* as well as cared for (M. L. Johnson, 1981).

Interactions between the sectors

As we argued in Chapter 1, a continuing concern of those responsible for service provision has been the belief that publicly provided services may in some way supplant informally-provided help. This concern is based upon two main factors: first, fears about the escalating costs which would have to be borne because family members who had the capacity and resources to care would choose not to do so if public alternatives were available; and second, a more generalised belief that 'family ties' would be weakened if bonds were not strengthened by the need to provide practical assistance for family members. This latter belief seems to see a loss of expressive benefits as inevitable if the need to provide instrumental assistance is removed from the informal sector.

The relationship between practical help and family ties

Against this view it might be argued that removal of the necessity to provide practical help would enable the informal sector, particularly kin, to concentrate on providing those expressive rewards which it is so difficult for formal organisations to deliver.

From a historical perspective Anderson (1977) shows that such considerations exercised the minds of those concerned with administering the Poor Law in the nineteenth century, some of whom certainly believed that help thus given would lead to the extinction of family ties. However, in this case Anderson argues that the evidence tends to suggest that compulsory cash support for elderly relatives induced tension within families, whilst the take-over of such functions by the state enabled an improvement in family relationships.

Appropriate roles for the different sectors

There have been two main theoretical responses to these percep-tions of the differences between the worlds of formal and informal welfare provision. On the one hand, it can be argued (as P. Abrams, 1978a did) that the two worlds have antithetical

atmospheres, and considerable difficulties are therefore anticipated in attempting to integrate the two. In particular, Abrams
implied that there was a danger that formal care would somehow
overwhelm and subsume informal care. On the other hand, has
been the development of a theory of shared functions between
bureaucratic and other groups (Litwak and Meyer, 1966; Litwak
and Szelenyi, 1969). This is based on the premise that bureaucracies are best equipped to cope with large-scale, routine, tech-
nical problems requiring professional expertise, whilst primary
groups are best suited to handling non-uniform tasks, unantici-
pated events which require no more than everyday socialisation to
master, and those requiring intimate personal knowledge of
individual members of the group. The latter theory has been
further developed to differentiate among elements of the informal
sector of care and to suggest that each can most efficiently perform
specific tasks (Dono *et al.*, 1977).

However, at least some empirical evidence from an American
study (Cantor, 1979) implies that the task-specific model, whilst
perhaps suggesting what would ideally be the most efficient model,
bears no relation to the subjective perceptions of older people
seeking help. Cantor argues that elderly people in the USA have
an overriding preference for help from kin in all circumstances
and, according to this 'hierarchical-compensatory' model, support
is sought from other groups only when the initially preferred
element (kin) is absent. Similar results might not be obtained in a
British context since, for example, it may be that such preferences
reflect the absence of alternative non-stigmatising sources of help
in the USA. Cross-cultural comparison of Western countries
shows the proportion of elderly people receiving family help to be
highest in the USA, less high in the UK and much less high in
Scandinavia (Shanas *et al.*, 1968). Teeland (1978) suggests that the
Scandinavian pattern is a consequence of a wealthy economy and a
comprehensive welfare system. In the USA relatives compensate
for the lack of the latter, in Britain for the former.

The actor-based perspective on preferences

At its most abstract, dependency may perhaps be defined as a state
in which actions by others are a necessary condition for an actor to

achieve his or her goals. If a range of 'others' are available in relation to a particular goal then (following Anderson, 1971) it may be that the actor will choose the option which will cause him or her to bear the least costs. However, this statement must be modified to take account of the fact that an actor may wish to save others from bearing a particular set of costs, either for reasons of altruism or to save a limited resource for other purposes for which it is more suited.

Discussions in the previous chapter should reinforce the assumption that, at least in capitalist society, physical and material independence is the preferred state except in a few exceptional cases. But, it is important to note that the independent attainment of social rewards, such as affection, warmth or respect, is impossible. Their achievement requires interaction with others. However, even if people acknowledge themselves to be dependent in the sense defined above, the recognition of failure to reach a goal may lead to the modification or abandonment of that goal rather than any help-seeking behaviour. Some elderly people who were unable to bath unaided preferred to strip-wash rather than to seek assistance with bathing. Others, who could no longer reach distant shops, modified their diet to include only items available locally rather than accept assistance (which had sometimes been offered) with shopping. One elderly widow, for example, no longer ate fresh meat because there was no local butcher.

Naturally, in any particular situation, it may be that a failure to obtain help, even though it *has* been sought, has led to the abandonment of goals, so no assumption should be made that a person's current state is their preferred state. How then are we to infer the preferred state? A number of problems may be identified in trying to obtain meaningful statements about preferences among different sources of help in a research interview.

Problems in discussing preferences

First there is the problem that expressed preferences are constrained by what is perceived to be possible. Willcocks (1984) reported that elderly people in a residential home responded to questions about whether they would like a television by explaining that televisions were not allowed. In the Sheffield study elderly people who received practical help from family members were asked whether they would prefer paid help. The initial reaction of many was that they could not afford paid help.

However, when people were then asked whether they would prefer paid help if they could afford it, one prominent response was that if the elderly person could afford paid help they would prefer to give the money to their existing informal helpers.

Of course, such a transaction would not convert informal assistance into paid (commercial) help because it would be clear that the practical help was not given only on condition that the money was paid (as definitely *is* the case in a purely economic exchange); rather, the elderly people were expressing a desire actively to share any extra resources they might possess with family members on whom they depended.

Here we may perhaps usefully extend and modify the illustration which P. Blau (1964) gives to demonstrate the difference between social and altruistic exchange. If A gives money to B on condition that B return it with interest, this is economic exchange; if A gives money to B in return for B's expressions of gratitude and esteem, and/or to obtain the approval of others, then this is social exchange; but if A gives money to B because A derives pleasure from improving the welfare of B, then this is altruistic exchange. The main practical differences between the latter two exchanges are found in determining under what conditions the giving would cease.

The importance, already outlined, of not bargaining explicitly about social benefits illustrates the second difficulty in discovering preferences: that the expression of such preferences is constrained by the rules of social exchange. It is acceptable to express a preference for informal help, once received, but it should not be necessary to demand such help since it should be freely and spontaneously given. When carers were asked whether it was an obligation for children to provide friendship or company for their parents the general tone of answers was that one would hope that they would *want* to do so, and some of the elderly people interviewed did comment that they preferred help from their family as long as 'they want to do it'. In the light of our previous discussion about the nature of informal care this seems a reasonable reaction: if informal care is unwillingly given then its quality is diminished, because its meaning is changed. The majority of carers interviewed did argue that they had taken the initiative in offering assistance, although there were exceptions.

Difficulties in generalising about preferences

One problem in interpreting and using information about the expressed preferences of individuals in order to assist in the formation of judgements about the appropriate roles of different sectors of welfare provision is that the abstract category 'informal help' represents a completely different concrete reality for each individual person in need of help. Some people will be able to call upon a well-resourced network (in human and material terms) in which long-standing obligations have been generated and are recognised; whilst others may face a network whose members, if any, are themselves experiencing considerable difficulties in achieving goals and are in need of additional resources. Even in relation to statutory and voluntary care it may be that, for individual users of services, differences within sectors are as important as those between them. An elderly person might happily accept a food parcel from a pensioners' club or church which they had attended for 20 years, but be less pleased with one from another voluntary body more clearly identified by them as 'charitable'.

Abstract or hypothetical questions posed in public opinion surveys may uncover normative beliefs about which source of help is considered to be appropriate, in most cases, for various dependency groups. However, such questions alone are unlikely to discover the many 'allowable exceptions' which are observed and accepted in practice. For example, people may willingly endorse a general belief that children have a responsibility to help parent in need, but would nevertheless be prepared to accept many exceptions to this if particular circumstances are spelled out which render helping difficult (see Chapter 5). It may be argued that those cases which come to the attention of statutory services are precisely the instances in which people feel there are good reasons why the generally appropriate form of help – family care – cannot be secured, or is inadequate.

It is questionable to what extent the ideological differences between the political left and right about the appropriate roles of state and family influence the attitudes, beliefs and behaviour of individuals faced with choices about providing or securing assistance. West (1984) described an extremely interesting study designed to elicit the views of members of the public (in Scotland) about the family and the welfare state as appropriate sources of support for various groups of dependent people. He concluded: 'The results suggest that with the exception of certain groups of ideologues there is only a faint echo of the rhetoric of the two main political parties in the attitudes of people towards these issues and the more concrete the issues are the fainter it gets' (West, 1984, p. 418).

Far from seeing the family and the state as ideological opposites, West argues that there is a general level of support for the family and qualified approval of the welfare state, although some differences in attitudes towards the welfare state were found between Labour and Conservative voters. He also finds that there is only a slight relationship between traditional views about the family and support for family care, and goes on to demonstrate that other factors (such as social class, age and religion) are associated with traditional views about the family but are not related in any way to support for family care. Significantly, gender was related to support for family care, with women less frequently in favour, a result which is (plausibly) attributed to the greater likelihood that they will be called upon to provide such help. Brody (1981), in her study of three generations of women, found the middle generation least likely to express support for family care for elderly people, and the youngest generation (least likely to be immediately affected) most likely to endorse it.

It is clear that there will be a whole network of factors affecting expressed preferences. Perhaps it will prove possible to specify the general factors upon which preferences depend; likely candidates might be the nature, intensity, complexity and duration of the tasks required (R. Parker, 1981), but the actual or perceived quality of the service available is also a factor. For domestic assistance an elderly person might prefer a reliable home help to family assistance, but if the home help service was considered to be unreliable then relatives might be preferred.

Whilst fully recognising the diversity of individual circumstances and preferences there are none the less some findings about services received by elderly people which consistently appear. For example, the failure of many elderly people to seek statutory services, and in particular to claim their full entitlement of financial assistance, is well documented (Cole and Utting, 1962; Supplementary Benefits Commission, 1978; Townsend, 1979;

Walker, 1986b). A number of reasons have been advanced for this failure to claim, some of which (such as lack of knowledge about entitlement and a desire for independence) might also apply to other groups of people in need, but others of which are felt to apply specifically to elderly people because of their common past experiences. The elderly respondents in the Sheffield study had passed over half of their lives before the main elements of the Welfare State came into existence, and so the subjective framework within which they make their decisions as help-seekers cannot be fully comprehended without some understanding of their history. Of course, statements by politicians and others may act to reinforce certain elements within this subjective framework, such as the stigma associated with claiming social security (Walker, 1987a).

The reluctance of elderly people to seek statutory help

It has been argued that the reluctance currently observed will diminish as the present 'young elderly' (those curently under 75) become older, because such reluctance has been based upon a number of factors which will eventually cease to apply. First, it is argued that many elderly people are experiencing relative affluence, compared with their younger days, and are therefore content to survive on very little. Second, they have personal memories of past formal welfare provision as particularly stigmatising to recipients and, because of this and because of the timing and short duration of their education, they have a less well-developed sense of the right to receive services than elderly people of later generations will possess (Moen, 1978; Tinker, 1981, p. 179).

For at least some elderly respondents there was no doubt that their present material circumstances compared well with those experienced in the past:

> It's wonderful when you've lived a life without any real static money, you know, and could never depend on money. It's a lot that, because even when we worked we never could depend on it. Never knew from Saturday to Monday if you were going to work on Monday or not ... there's all this grumbling and 'how poor they are' but yet you never see them poorly dressed or poorly shod, you don't see 'em with holes under their shoes like we used to have. (Elderly widow)

However, the experience of relative affluence cannot be assumed across the board. There were exceptions to the rule of a rising standard of living among people born into middle-class families: although most had remained consistently comfortable financially, a few, through the failure of their business in the 1930s or through personal ill health, were now relatively badly off. Among the whole sample of elderly people, three in ten respondents reported some degree of worry about money, and so contentment with their current financial situation clearly does not prevail for substantial numbers of elderly people.

Comparisons with the past and formal services

The vast majority of elderly people (four out of five) definitely considered that it was better to be old now then it had been 50 years ago. This was overwhelmingly seen as a consequence of the availability of state benefits such as pensions, housing and, to a lesser extent, personal social services: 'You needn't go without. It's your own stupidity if you do.'

There were accounts of stigmatising experiences of past welfare provision: 'It was "cold charity", that was' commented one respondent of the institution in which she was brought up, whilst another elderly widow recalled, 'I can remember my grandma going to the "Parish" and getting a cob to eat.'

A few respondents spontaneously mentioned the workhouse as a memory which had reality for them: 'Yes, they had nothing years ago, it had to be the workhouse then', or 'Yes, better now. You don't have to go into the workhouse now which you had to then.'

Most examples of such difficulties in the past were given to illustrate how much better things were today, but when people gave comments as to how they came to receive supplementary pension or benefit, it was clear that there was still a reluctance on the part of many elderly people to put themselves forward as claimants for help.

If it had been left to me I don't think I would have applied off my own bat . . . having to bring myself up I've always tried to be independent and I wouldn't ask for anything.

I did at one time but I don't now [mind about receiving supplementary pension]. I were glad of it but it used to upset me, but it doesn't bother me now because, as I say, I never ask for anything. If they give me anything that's up to them, I accept it with thanks. (Elderly widow)

Only one-third of claimants (excluding those who could not remember) said that claiming was their idea, implemented by them. Another third reported the involvement of statutory workers, usually 'council officials'. It seemed that people who were rehoused (and likely to face substantially higher rents) had received routine visits from 'someone from the DHSS' to assess their eligibility. One in ten of those claiming said that the initiative had come from relatives. Some carers interviewed did comment on their elderly relatives' reluctance to apply for statutory help and the different perceptions of rights between generations:

She still feels embarrassed, and yet I know my husband certainly said at the time 'well look you have paid and Dad has paid all these years and it is your entitlement, and that's it' but she is not very ... she doesn't like people to know she is on supplementary. (Daughter-in-law)

Let's face it, in my mother's day there were none of this social help. I mean they get more now – people – [in the way of help] than ever they used to do, and I think my mother wonders why she can have these things when they didn't used to in her younger days. (Daughter)

People not in receipt of supplementary pension were asked if they 'would mind' claiming if they were eligible. One in eight non-claimants said that they would mind or that they were not sure. About half of these people put their reluctance down to the fact that it would be 'too much trouble' or 'not necessary' to claim, but the remainder mentioned pride or said that 'it seems like charity'. Of course, to some elderly people the question was purely hypothetical. One telling comment made by a middle-class respondent was that whilst he would not mind claiming if he were eligible, he certainly would mind being eligible!

Material exchanges within families

Since the primary focus of the study was family relationships, the financial data collected was insufficient to assess exact benefit entitlements in each case. Few elderly people reported receiving any financial help from their families, although one in five did receive regular material help from family members, most often in the form of goods, such as food or clothing. In contrast, material help from elderly people to their families (reported in one in five instances) usually took the form of monetary gifts or (more rarely) loans.

There is very little comparative data available about material exchanges within families, especially when parents and children live in separate households. Few carers considered that financial support for elderly parents was part of filial obligation unless the disparity in material circumstances was very great. The key factor determining material exchanges seemed, not surprisingly, to be the relative degree of affluence of the two parties. Half of all elderly people with savings of over £5 000 reported giving gifts or loans of money to other family members.

Of course, even where elderly people received a supplementary pension their families were not necessarily better off materially than they were. A number of carers (for example, two whose husbands were unemployed and one who was widowed) commented that their parents' material circumstances were more comfortable than their own:

old people as regards the money they get, quite honestly I don't think they are badly off, it's only if anything goes wrong, anything big, but I think the basic day-to-day living ... I think other people are worse off that aren't working today, the unemployed. (Daughter, husband unemployed)

I don't think he's too bad off really [father]. You see he's probably a bit better off than some of the others. I mean he gets his allowance for that coke from the pit [ex-miner] to keep his fire going ... Well he doesn't have great big gas and electric bills, not like I have. (Daughter, widow)

Only 8 per cent of elderly people, when asked whether there was anyone for whom they wished to buy things but could not, mentioned other members of their family they wished they could afford to help financially (such as unemployed sons, or single-parent daughters). Unemployment did mean that families found themselves unable to provide material help to their elderly relations which they had provided in the past.

> While I was working and he was working we never asked anybody for anything. Me and him paid for everything ... Last winter ... the gentleman upstairs [from mother] had a burst [pipe] ... It came through my mother's pantry, ruined the food ... the decorations, the curtains and of course the carpet that was on the floor ... I could not afford it with him not working. (Daughter)

One in four elderly people said they had 'no' savings, although it became evident in the course of pilot interviews, that some people with a few hundred pounds for 'burial money' were inclined to report, at least initially, that they had no savings at all.

> *Wife:* No, we don't have any savings, we just carry on weekly what we can. We manage all right.
> *Husband:* We just nicely cover it [bills]. We guess what it's likely to be and try to cover it.
> *Wife:* We never owe for anything.
> *Husband:* We put something away each week so that when the bills comes we can pay it ... [discussion of finance continues]
> *Wife:* Well, I'll tell you what we've got in the bank; we've £700 towards a funeral, that's all. That's what we've got to bury us and I don't think that will cover us . . not for two.

This couple had no children but those with children still worried about the cost of a funeral, and several were saving out of their supplementary pensions against this eventuality, despite family opposition.

> They laugh at me because I try to save a bit each week. And they say 'what are you saving it for?' and I say, 'I'm saving it to bury me' and of course they think I'm being crackers, because they say 'Oh, you'll get buried all right, mother.' I know I won't *know*. I don't want to feel they've had to help. I suppose that's at the heart of it. (Elderly widow – pilot interview)

Statutory care

Statutory assistance comes in a variety of forms and from a wide variety of sources. Over half of the elderly people surveyed lived in council accommodation, and two in five were in receipt of supplementary pension. Just under one in five had the services of a home help, one in ten the assistance of a bath nurse, and one in twenty help from a home warden. About one in twenty attended a day centre, usually once a week.

Home helps and home wardens

Domiciliary assistance from personal social services did not seem to be concentrated on people without children. Indeed, controlling for disability, people with sons only were more likely to be receiving assistance than those without children. Those with one daughter were as likely to be receiving help as those without children. However, those with more than one daughter were less likely than any other group to be helped by a home help or warden. Did this reflect the wishes of individuals or policies followed by service providers? Sheffield City Council has currently no formal policy that people with daughters should not receive home help; however, a number of elderly people and caring relatives certainly believed that such a policy existed, and some gave examples of the operation of such a policy in the past. Others claimed that their parents had suffered a reduction in services because of the availability of relatives:

if they know that they've got a daughter or anything like that, it's very unlikely that you can get one [home help]. (Daughter – former home help)

I was told that by Mrs A. [home help organiser], that there's been a cut back on all social services and – 'only when it's absolutely necessary' – so that threw the onus back on to me. Apparently in their way of thinking it wasn't necessary because I was there. (Daughter)

Before Betty used to go over there regular she used to have it [home help] twice a week . . . One day the woman of the social service ... came up, found Betty there and said 'I didn't know she had a daughter.' Oh yes – because she had a daughter she's [down to] four hours a week now. (Son-in-law)

They rely on me, you know, wardens. Don't think that I don't want to do my share, with me saying that, but a lot of old ones have them at weekends, but I mean if they have any family, it's left to the family. (Daughter, in poor health)

Only one of the elderly people who shared a household with relatives received any assistance from a home help or home warden (this household consisted of two disabled elderly sisters). Few had applied, but sons who shared a household seemed as likely to be refused as daughters. One daughter said: 'They said that because my brother lived there he could do it, according to what me dad told me.'

Evidence from other studies, including national data (OPCS, 1981; Rossiter and Wicks, 1982, p. 56), shows that the allocation of home-help services seems to follow similar lines elsewhere. Nationally, as in Sheffield, people living alone are most likely to get home help, followed by married couples and, last of all, those living with others (see Table 8.1). The overall proportion receiving home help (18 per cent) is exactly the same as the proportion found nationally (OPCS, 1981, p. 213).

In interpreting Table 8.1 it should be noted that people living alone are more likely to be disabled (both because of their greater age, and because they are more likely to be women) than people living with their spouses.

Although nationally women over 74 are twice as likely as men to get a home help (OPCS, 1981), in Sheffield the chances are about equal, even though women are more likely than men to be living alone and disabled. On closer investigation of differences in

Table 8.1 *Receipt of services by household type (percentages)*

Household type	Receiving home help (OPCS)		Receiving home warden	Social work help	Total number
Single person	26	(31)	9	6	156
Married couple	13	(4)	9	9	94
With others	4	(7)	–	12	49

disability levels, it seems that differences in home-help allocation are more evident at lower levels of disability: men suffering minor, some or appreciable disability are twice as likely as equally disabled women to get home help (22 per cent do so compared with 12 per cent of women). Hunt (1978) found similar differences in mobility levels among home-help recipients of different sexes.

Among home-help recipients in the Sheffield study (55 people), 59 per cent of men could go out without assistance compared with only 32 per cent of women. It may be that this allocation of domiciliary help reflects the prevailing sexual division of domestic labour among elderly people. The comments of carers, reported in the previous chapter, made it clear that many men of the older generation had never taken part in domestic work, and a substantial number were unable (or unwilling) to do so in later life. It seems that the process of home-help allocation was based on the principle of assisting more severely disabled women to retain independence, but for men the emphasis was on replacing women on whom they had been dependent. The few women who experienced low levels of disability but received home help most often reported that this had been given during a period of ill health or convalescence, and never subsequently reviewed.

It is interesting to note that Table 8.1 shows that social work help is not distributed in the same way as domiciliary help. This corroborates other evidence (Sinclair *et al.*, 1984) that social work help and domiciliary assistance go to quite different groups of clients. General comments on social work help are given later.

Ideas about eligibility among non-recipients

The majority (56 per cent) of those who did not get home help considered that they would not be eligible. Although this was usually felt to be because they were too fit, a substantial minority (just under one in three) considered that the availability of relatives would render them ineligible for such help. Three-quarters of those who took this view lived in the same household as their relative(s). One in five non-recipients felt that they could get a home help if they wished to on grounds of disability or age, whilst the remaining one in four did not know whether they were eligible or not. Almost all knew that the home-help service existed.

Of all those people *not* receiving statutory domiciliary assist-ance, one in six said they would choose to have such help if it were available, but only a few had applied. How did those in receipt of the service come to be in this position? This question will be followed up in the next section.

The process of referral

Elderly people hardly ever claimed to have thought of the idea of applying for home help themselves, and neither did they report having been involved in making initial contact with the relevant agency. GPs or health visitors and (to a lesser extent) relatives and friends most frequently suggested the service and 'set the wheels in motion'. Goldberg and Warburton (1979) reported only 20 per cent of referrals (to a social work team), where the problem was ageing or physical disability, were made by the prospective client.

Suggestion of original idea	Number
Respondent's own	3
Relative	10
Friend	2
GP or health visitor	32
Social worker	4
Other or don't know	4
Total	55

Overwhelmingly the problem specified as causing the need for such help was a deterioration in the respondent's own health (62 per cent), or in the health of the respondent's spouse (16 per cent).

In the majority of instances both home helps and wardens took over tasks which had previously been performed by the respon-dent. Only a small minority (16 per cent) of home helps took over tasks from relatives, and wardens were even less likely to have done so.

Of course, even if relatives are not explicitly consulted, it is probable that their likely activities (in terms of the provision of practical help) are to some extent known, or are reported by the elderly person, to the doctor or the home help organiser. Even though people with local relatives were sometimes refused help, it seemed that elderly people with children were more likely than those without children to be in receipt of help if the deterioration in their condition was gradual. A sudden event such as a stroke, heart attack or fall apparently led to the involvement of health service personnel; indeed, there were no instances in which relatives initiated requests for services after sudden health-related events. However, most people who experienced a deterioration in their capacity for self-care (in the previous year) described this as gradual. Only one in five experienced sudden deterioration. In the majority of cases where deterioration was gradual the most common source of referral was still the GP or health visitor, but one in four referrals in such cases were made by relatives, compared with none in instances of sudden deterioration. This ties in with other evidence (Challis and Davies, 1986; Levin, Sinclair and Gorbach, 1986) that the presence rather than absence of informal supporters can mean that more help is likely to be secured from formal sources. This suggests that relatives and (occasionally) friends sometimes act as advocates in securing services for elderly people, and has the corollary that those without such support, if they suffer gradual deterioration, may be less likely to receive statutory help. This situation is obviously reinforced by the reluctance of elderly people to refer themselves for help.

Experience of relatives in obtaining statutory help

In the case of domiciliary services, the Sheffield Family and Community Services department operated a policy that the initial assessment visit should be made within 48 hours of receiving a referral, and there is no evidence to suggest that this policy was not observed. However, an initial response to other queries, especially if made by letter or telephone, seemed to be subject to much longer delays. In most cases, some delay between assessment and delivery of services would inevitably occur, but perhaps the most common impression given by carers who had sought help from various statutory services (with the possible exception of urgent medical attention from GPs) was of the extremely slow response. The interviews gave an overwhelming sense that a tremendous amount of time, patience and persistence had to be invested in securing assistance. The fact that people frequently only sought help when they felt that their problems were urgent could only add to their sense of frustration. Of course, this was less likely to be the case if the referral was made by a GP or health visitor, when relatives might not know about it at all, but those carers who had made attempts to secure help from social services directly experienced considerable delays:

> I wrote a letter [re phone for disabled father] to Redvers House and I never heard anything. I didn't get a reply or anything. [six weeks] ... Then I phoned up and she said 'Oh it's not our region it's Darnall', so I phoned down there ... I filled in a form and sent it back [four weeks] ... I phoned yesterday and she said 'they'll be coming sometime' so that's been left. (Daughter)

> We're going away 23rd September. Now I started [application for holiday relief residential care] at the beginning of February this year, and we are still none the wiser what will happen to my mother [July]. This Mr B. [social worker] said 'Well, next year, make early arrangements and we'll get her in wherever she wants to go.' So I started in February as I know they're busy. She said 'Well you know it might be a few months before the social worker gets round to seeing you.' (Daughter)

Not all carers resented delays. A few accepted them as an inevitable part of the process. One son said: 'it was only, probably a couple or three months before she passed away that we started about getting it [home help] for her, like ... by the time we'd got the wheels in motion she unfortunately passed away. I've no doubt that she would have got it.' However, on some occasions, where it was believed that services had been refused to apparently physically able elderly people who were suffering from confusion or depression, the refusal was resented by relatives:

> They said, '... he's not incapacitated in any way, he's not crippled, he's not bedfast, he's not incontinent and therefore you can deal with it' which is very unfair. (Daughter)

> The nurse that came [about bathing service] said 'you know, there are thousands a lot worse off than your mother', which is no great help to me, but I realise that there are [those] that just can't help themselves, you know, but it's no good to me when I ... well, I can smell me mother, I put it as blunt as that.' (Son)

Reasons for refusal are investigated more closely in the next section.

People who had applied for domiciliary help but were not currently receiving it

Thirty-three people not currently receiving domiciliary services had applied for home-help or warden services in the past. About half of these had received the service but no longer did so; two had received an offer which they had refused; one claimed to have had no response to the enquiry; and the remaining 13 people had been refused the service.

The majority of those people who were refused felt that their rejection was unfair. All except one could recall a reason for refusal being given, and it seems that refusal was more often made on the grounds that alternative sources of help were available (usually relatives) than that the elderly person did not need such help. Two people had been told that their refusal was a consequence of 'government cuts'. People once refused were unlikely to appeal or try again at a later date: 'They've already told us "No".'

Of course, the reluctance to make a second attempt to secure assistance applies across the board to a whole variety of services: Sinclair *et al.* (1984) comment on the reluctance of people once refused social services to reapply. Given our previous discussion of the failure to apply for assistance, it may well be imagined that once the initial resistance is overcome a refusal is experienced as humiliating, and the elderly person feels that after all they were correct in thinking that a right to receive help is not recognised.

> I've got a thyroid, I've got pernicious anaemia, I've got angina. I've got all these things and I live on me own and I still can't get a free phone. I don't want it all, but if they could have helped me with it, but they wouldn't, and I've no money so I can't get one . . . I shan't ask 'em again . . . I never ask 'em for anything, that's only thing I've ever asked 'em for and they refused me so I said I wouldn't ask again. (Elderly widow)

People who had received services in the past

Where people had received the service in the past but were no longer doing so (17 people) it seemed that the initiative to stop services came about as often from the elderly people as from the department. Most elderly people who had stopped the service did so because their condition had improved and they felt they could manage without. Two were dissatisfied with the service.

In the majority of other cases the department had stopped the service in the light of changes in the elderly person's health or circumstances, although there were two people who did not know why, and one who claimed that the alleged availability of help from relatives was the reason.

Once the service had been withdrawn, who took over? In by far the majority of instances (65 per cent) the respondents themselves took over the tasks that the home help had performed. One person said that no one had taken over the tasks, and three people had employed paid help. There was no instance in which tasks were taken over by a relative.

Opinions about fair distribution of services

Most elderly people and carers expressed agreement with the idea that people without families should have priority for services. Thus one elderly woman in the pilot survey, who received regular help from two of her daughters, said: 'I don't think that I would get it [home help], not with having two daughters. But, you see, I don't really need it, not with them coming and doing the necessary.' Carers too, often considered that their availability ruled out the need for home help: the wife of a grandson said, 'She doesn't need a home help because if his mother [mother-in-law] couldn't do it, I would do it. If there was anything she couldn't do I would do it.'

Preferences

Only one in ten of those elderly people who were in receipt of informal practical help said that they would prefer to have such tasks performed by a home help. The most common reason given for preferring a home help was to relieve strain on the carer.

Carers who wanted home helps for their elderly person usually indicated either their own already intensive commitment to helping or their own health problems:

She's quite happy at having home help, she's sorry if they don't go. If they don't go, it's left with me, and that upsets her – if I have to do it, if I've got to set to and hoover. My mother would rather have a home help knowing that I'm not really well. (Daughter)

Those whose capacity to help was limited because they were working were more likely to express some ambivalence. One daughter said, 'I always felt that if ever I went to my mother's and the home help was there, I always felt a slight sense of shame, thinking "that woman is doing what I should be doing".' However, sons who were working and helping were less likely to express such a view.

Those factors which have already been mentioned as constituting 'sufficient' excuse for a failure to meet informal obligations are the factors which underlie requests for statutory assistance: namely, other obligations in the informal sector, personal incapacity, or a poor relationship with the elderly person. With regard to other commitments such as work, this is seen as part of one's informal obligations if one is male, but is less likely to be thought so if the potential carer is female.

Carers who themselves suffered problems were, unsurprisingly, less likely to give a blanket endorsement to the idea that services should be concentrated on those without families. They were more likely to give qualified agreement, arguing that the circumstances of families should be taken into account in making decisions.

Overall distribution of domiciliary services

Some carers argued that the current distribution of statutory services was unjust because they knew of elderly people with low levels of disability receiving home helps whilst those in greater need had been refused. Our data suggest that there were a few such cases and discussion with both elderly people and the Department of Family and Community Services indicates three linked reasons for this.

1. Changes in allocation criteria over time. Thus people who were allocated a home help in the past might not be judged eligible were they to apply now. Even where review could identify such cases it was difficult to withdraw services already provided.
2. Failure to adjust to changes in circumstances. One elderly

woman with no disability had received home help and warden services when caring for her severely disabled husband. She had continued to receive these services since his death two years previously. One elderly man had received home help when convalescing after a knee operation. He still received the service although he complained to the interviewer that it was rather annoying having to wait in one morning a week for the home help when he would rather be out playing bowls.

Of course, not all such failures were in the direction of overprovision. One elderly man, who cared for an ailing wife, asked the home help not to call while his wife was in hospital (for two weeks). One year later no one from the department had ever called again.

It should be emphasised that the failure to reassess and review cases adequately is not a strictly local problem, but a reflection of difficulties which have been widely acknowledged to exist in the delivery of domiciliary assistance in many areas (Hurley and Wolstenholme, 1979; Carpenter and Paley, 1984).

3. A further reason for apparently inconsistent allocation policies was that the distribution of home helps and wardens was uneven throughout the city. It was, apparently, more difficult to recruit suitable workers in the more prosperous areas of the city. People in these areas were more likely to be assessed as having to pay full fees but, in at least two cases irrespective of this, the amount of help offered was perceived as so totally inadequate as to be not worth having. One neighbour remarked, 'When she came out, this lady in charge of the home help came out and saw her; all she offered her was an hour, or was it half an hour, a week. Well, that was useless.'

Although this neighbour's perception might have been inaccurate, since home help was not normally allocated for a period as short as one hour, it was the case that 30 per cent of recipients of the service felt that they currently needed more of such help. There was some resentment at what appeared to some to be a discrimination against those living in particular districts:

Having a bit of money, that was it. You can't get anything if you've got a bit these days. Or if you live in a decent district. (Sister)

When my father first came out of hospital ... they came to the door ... they didn't even go inside the house. I don't know whether they saw the property and thought 'they've got plenty of money' or what was the reason. (Daughter)

Two elderly people had refused home help becuse they would have had to pay full charges. One of these had subsequently employed private help. At the time of writing, charging recipients for home help services in Sheffield has been discontinued.

Paid help

About 10 per cent of elderly people received domestic assistance for which they paid privately. Although those who were disabled were slightly more likely to be receiving paid help than those without disability, this was not the most important factor governing the receipt of paid help. As might be expected there were substantial class differences, with one in three middle-class elderly people receiving paid assistance compared with less than one in 20 working-class people. Sometimes the paid help had been received for years, commencing long before the onset of disability, and the elderly person considered their relationship with their 'help' to be more like friendship.

Opinions of those receiving statutory domiciliary help

Two-thirds of elderly people receiving home help considered that a good home help was one who did the required work, while just under half mentioned friendliness as desirable. There was considerable overlap between these two groups because by far the majority (82 per cent) of people who wished their home helps to show friendliness *also* wished the required work to be done.

At the time of the survey the home help system in Sheffield was organised on a rota basis, so that the home help allocated to a particular client changed every fortnight. In contrast, wardens were allocated to particular elderly people. The rota system was not very popular with the elderly people. Only one in eight said that they preferred such a system to having the same person. The remainder of recipients were split equally between those who reported that they were not bothered, and a substantial minority (41 per cent) who said that they would prefer to have the same person all the time.

A rota system seems designed to prevent the development of any informal elements in the relationship between home help and elderly person; indeed, the arguments put forward to A. I. Harris (1968) in justification of this form of service delivery in Sheffield – that it protected home helps from unjustified extra demands by clients, and protected clients from home helps who might 'take advantage' – precisely concentrated upon the possible negative consequences of the development of informal or quasi-informal relationships.

Given this form of service delivery it was not really possible to investigate the extent to which home helps took on roles and activities beyond those which they were contracted to do, or the extent to which relationships became personalised. However, some attempt was made to do this in the 14 instances where home warden services were received. The majority of recipients of warden services said that the warden had met other members of their family and when this had occurred it was more likely to be 'often' rather than 'at least once'. Most knew something about the warden's own family, although only one had met any members of their warden's family. Two-thirds of recipients felt that they knew the warden 'as a person' and three-quarters that their relationship with the warden was more than just a 'working relationship'. In half of the cases the elderly person said that they would be 'quite' or 'very' upset if their warden were changed for another person, although one person would have been 'quite pleased' with a change. The remainder would not have minded either way.

Thus this impressionistic evidence seems to imply that continuity in personnel has encouraged the development of a more personalised relationship in quite a large number of instances. Of course, the advantage of a greater emotional attachment to service providers has the corresponding disadvantage that such elements would be lost by a change of person and so substitutes would be less satisfactory. Also, in at least one case, the relationship developed was not one of liking, which indicates that fears about possible negative consequences of the development of relationships cannot be entirely disregarded. To complete the picture it would be necessary to have the views of individual formal service providers and these were not a part of this study. However, it is perhaps worth mentioning that, since the study period, changes in the pattern of service delivery in Sheffield have meant that the rota system has been largely replaced.

There is considerable evidence (see, for example, Hunt, 1978; Sinclair *et al.*, 1984) that home helps in many areas do develop personalised relationships with some clients, and this may include extra visiting and even taking the elderly person to the worker's own home.

However, it is clear that such extra commitment has to be freely given; it cannot be coerced, or required as 'part of the job', without losing much of its meaning to the participants in the relationship. It is likely that such help is only given to those with whom the worker experiences a rewarding relationship of some kind. Alternatively, extra help may be given where caring relatives are perceived as particularly deserving of assistance.

Carers' views on the home-help service

Just under one-third of the elderly people whose carers were interviewed were in receipt of home help. This reflects their higher levels of disability compared with those prevailing within the sample as a whole, where just under one in five persons received home help. Not all carers knew how the service had been initiated but slightly fewer than half recalled taking the initiative themselves, whilst most of the remainder who knew referred to the GP.

Where the service *was* received, day-to-day negotiations were generally conducted by the elderly person, although one in three of those carers who helped in conjunction with a home help had engaged in some direct negotiations with agents of the service.

Taking the sample of informal out-of-household carers as a whole, two out of three helped without assistance from statutory domiciliary services and one in eight had taken the initiative to seek statutory help. Such contact as existed with home helps was largely contingent; regular two-way contact was reported in only three instances (this represents one in six of carers who helped where a home help was also present). The general impression of the home help service was 'mixed' or 'poor' in the majority of cases (61 per cent) where home help was received:

Sometimes they don't go on a Monday, they should go for three hours, I do think they shouldn't drop that off, but I can appreciate the problem that there aren't many of them, and they are short staffed. (Daughter)

I've seen them leaving it as long as three weeks, and when I've rung up to see what's happened 'Oh, we're short' or 'Somebody is on their holidays' and this and that and the other. (Daughter)

Such responses soon led to low expectations and sense of helplessness:

It's supposed to be about four hours . . . but they never come for four hours. They come for two hours and this is the first time they've come in five weeks. She hasn't been for five weeks. [Did she give any reason why?] She said that it's the holidays. My mother said to me, 'Why don't you phone them up?', but I said 'what's the good?' (Daughter)

The failure of home helps to turn up regularly at the promised time or to work the full hours were the most frequent complaints, although mention was also made of the restrictions placed upon home helps' activities:

I think you want them to come and clean, and they are not allowed to do windows and can't climb. Well, that's it, when people are older they want things like that doing, don't they? (Daughter)

Home help services seemed to be given in general on only one· or two days a week, for a specified number of hours. As it stood this was not much relief to carers if it could not be relied upon, but also this was often the time when relief help was least needed (except by carers who worked, and then it was insufficient). The times when carers felt that such help would help them were at weekends and during holidays. These were, of course, the times that home help and warden services found it most difficult to cover, and during which families were most likely to be expected to 'do their share'. When carers were unable to have free weekends or holidays for such 'frivolous' purposes as visiting their own children or giving regular care to grandchildren, this was a cause of some distress and, of course, such failures to discharge informal obligations could undermine the whole structure of mutual assistance and reciprocity between the generations which forms the basis of the system of informal care. The diminution of contact with other family members could be a cause of considerable distress:

> you feel a bit depressed, some days . . . it's probably because I'm not getting out at all. I used to really enjoy going to see my daughter, that is one thing I really miss going to see . . . I have two grandchildren, I used to always go and see them on Thursdays and have the day there, and all that's gone now. (Daughter)

Carers' view of the home warden services

One in six carers interviewed were helping an elderly person who also received home warden service. Just under half of these carers had had no contact with the warden, but all those who had described their impression of the service as 'good': one daughter said, 'She used to look forward to the warden, she thought they were very good, better than the home help, she got particularly friendly with them.'

However, one carer, whose mother had received warden service in the past, recalled an incident in which a warden had narrowed her definition of responsibilities to include only direct service to the elderly person, and to exclude activity which would have enabled the elderly person to participate as a giver in her own informal network:

> She was a bit nasty with my mum. She used to come Saturday morning before I got there, but apparently my mum put some jelly babies or something down [on shopping list], and she [warden] played pop. She says, they're not for you. She knew she had a little girl, a little granddaughter. She said 'I am not shopping for your grandchildren'. That upset my mum, you know. (Daughter)

In general, however, satisfaction with the warden service was high.

Social work services

Stevenson and Parsloe (1978) found that social workers were preoccupied with the needs of families and young children, and disinterested in work with elderly people, which was often left to unqualified social workers and social work assistants (see also Bowl, 1986).

Only 8 per cent of elderly people (24 people) reported seeing a social worker in the previous year, but only one in four of these had been seen by a social worker more than four times in the previous year. Of course, this might imply that social workers came in response to one-off problems that were quickly solved. However, just under half of those who had been seen infrequently wanted more contact. Over half of those who had seen a social worker had been referred by health service personnel, most frequently as a result of hospitalisation, and in these cases the role of the social worker was usually concerned with hospital discharge. Carers did feel that it was proper to consult them on such occasions and inadequate consultation, or failure to take account of carers' views after seeking them, were both mentioned as annoyances:

> When they've been in hospital they send them out, and they don't know whether they're having people visiting them, or if they can manage, and different things like that. They don't seem to be bothered. (Neighbour)

> the social worker [at the hospital], you see, I had never seen her, they never had a visit. She [the social worker] had spoken to my father in hospital and he was drugged after he had his operation, he didn't know what he was doing or saying ... How did she know how we were coping? When they said he had got to come home, my mother is 79, I could see what was going to happen. (Daughter)

When asked why their social worker kept in touch with them, one in four of those elderly people who had seen a social worker replied that the social worker did not keep in touch. About half of the remainder said that their social worker was engaged in monitoring or periodic checking of their condition. Only two people mentioned specific objectives, such as obtaining short-term residential care, and of those whose social worker *did* keep in touch, about one in four did not know why. One in three social work clients said that they did have a specific query that they would like to put to their social worker should he or she call again. Two of those elderly people receiving regular social work visits had their mentally handicapped adult children living at home with them.

Carers' views of social work

Only three carers interviewed reported that their elderly person received social work help. Carers who had long experience of difficulties in dealing with their parents were not on the whole inclined to complain if social workers could not do any better:

> A social worker came to see her, you know, three or four times. He was very, very nice but he said he just couldn't get through to her, she just ... she didn't want to talk to him, you know. (Son)

> She has been in a holiday home once or twice when we've gone on holiday but, you see, a few times she's given back word at the last minute and not gone. So I can't blame the social workers if they get fed up of this. (Daughter)

However, other carers had sought help from the Department of Family and Community Services on behalf of the elderly person whom they were helping. Carers usually wanted practical assistance, such as the installation of a telephone or relief care, either in the form of day care or short-term residential care.

Requests by carers for assistance

Facilitating contact

About half of all carers interviewed had no direct contact route with the elderly person; some even had to rely on their elderly relatives' neighbours to phone neighbours of theirs in order to make contact. There is no doubt that the lack of a direct contact route was a cause of anxiety to carers, even though in some cases (such as when the elderly person was deaf) a telephone would obviously not solve the problem. One carer pointed out that a telephone would have many advantages for her parents over and above the possibility of contacting help in an emergency: it would allow them to keep in contact with other members of the family who perhaps could not visit often, and enable the elderly people, although housebound, to continue to play an active role in their network of family and friends. However, no carers reported a successful application for help in this area, even if the application was on health grounds:

> Not unless you've got a bad heart, that's what we were told, unless you are likely to collapse. I think she desperately needs one but it's very expensive to put in. (Daughter)

> She's collapsed twice in the street, weather was cold and we were really worried about her. We'd no way of contacting her and she'd no way of contacting me if she couldn't get out ... I applied for some help for her, by the way, for a telephone and didn't get any ... I just wrote and asked them, filled the form in, and they just wrote back and said 'No', even though she'd got really bad blood pressure, couldn't get out ... and she's on social security. (Daughter)

Relief care

Both short-term holiday care and day care were experienced as helpful when received, although the long delays and uncertainties surrounding such applications have already been mentioned:

> I think the fact that she's had two visits over the last three or four years to the council home at Matlock, I think this has been a great help, just the break of getting away and being looked after. (Daughter)

> My husband said he'd like to go [on holiday] this year, so she's going to Matlock for a fortnight. I thought it'd be a good idea while I'm away and I've nothing to worry about you know, I know she's being taken care of. (Daughter)

However, although a holiday booked well in advance could probably be achieved once a year, carers who, for example, had retired and had looked forward to spontaneous weekend trips or other holidays, found themselves unable to do so.

> I'm not unhappy about doing what I do for mum, but I would just like to feel we could . . . you know . . . we've both been out at work, I've worked most of my married life and I feel we'd love to just drop tools and go away for a week. (Daughter)

Equally, as has already been mentioned, trips to visit distant children might have to be forgone.

Housing

Just over half of all elderly people interviewed lived in council accommodation. Among the main categories of tenure accommodation provided by the council, or (in a few cases) by housing associations, was *least* likely to be perceived as unsuitable by respondents. Half of those living in private rented accommodation, and two out of five owner-occupiers, specified some aspect of their accommodation which was unsuitable, but just under one in four council tenants did so. This perhaps should sound a note of caution in relation to beliefs that all elderly people suffer intense desires to remain 'in their own homes'. Certainly, previous evidence implies that many (but not all) elderly people do not wish to enter institutional care; however, a move to alternative accommodation might well enable the postponement of that eventuality by providing a more suitable environment for independent living.

The problem most frequently mentioned was that the accommodation had stairs or steps which could not be managed, and this affected one in ten of all elderly people interviewed. The other, slightly less frequent, difficulty was that the accommodation was felt to be too big, although owner-occupiers and private tenants were considerably more likely to say this than council tenants. Dampness and inadequate, or expensive, heating were also mentioned as problems by a few respondents, as was a location on a steep hill.

Moving house

Three-fifths of respondents had moved house in the previous 20 years. It might be expected that moving house could affect family relationships, but also that people may move house for family reasons. One in six movers had moved specifically to be nearer relatives, and about the same proportion indicated that a deterioration in their own health or the health of their spouse was the cause of the move. Working-class and middle-class respondents were equally likely to have moved at least once, but whilst in general middle-class elderly people had moved for health reasons, or to go into smaller property, working-class people were more likely to have had to move in consequence of the demolition of their previous home. This was the result of large-scale slum clearance operations in Sheffield, which affected 22 per cent of all working-class respondents, or just over one in three of all those working-class respondents who had moved house. In contrast, 7 per cent of all middle-class respondents had been so affected, or just under one in eight middle-class movers.

To summarise family influences: one in ten of all elderly people had specifically moved house in the past 20 years to be nearer relatives. The majority of those who had moved for this reason reported that they had thereby achieved greater contact with relatives, although a minority (one in six) reported less contact than before. A majority of those who had been compulsorily moved reported no effects on their distance from, or level of contact with, relatives, although one in ten reported more contact and one in four considered that they now had less contact.

As might be expected, the effects on contact with neighbours were more pronounced. Although two-thirds of all those who had moved reported unchanged levels of contact with relatives, only 39 per cent reported unchanged levels of contact with neighbours. Over half of all those who had been moved compulsorily reported reduced levels of contact with neighbours.

Carers' views of the housing department

Among carers interviewed just over half (31 people) were assisting an elderly person who lived in council housing, and two were giving help to someone on the housing waiting list. Thirteen carers had themselves had some dealings with the Housing Department on behalf of their elderly relative or friend. This was most frequently in an attempt to obtain a housing transfer so that the elderly person would be nearer to the carer, or in more suitable accommodation. The other reason for contact was an attempt to secure repairs. Success in transfer seemed to depend on a variety of factors including the elderly person's state of health, the relative desirability of the area into which they wished to move, and the size of accommodation which would be vacated by the move.

Carers found that a great deal of time and effort had to be invested in ensuring that their wishes were taken into account, and found the slowness of response frustrating.

I had a bit of a job, you know, going up and down to the Housing . . . Well it was two bus rides and I used to go two or three times a week, it got you down . . . I knew this flat here was coming empty and so I kept going up nearly every day for a month, but I kept pushing it and eventually when these people went I got it. (Daughter)

It must have been last May [12 months] when we first put in for the transfer and they've only just been to see her about it . . . so they really do take their time about it. I mean I expected, actually, with it being an old person who always pays her rent, never been in arrears, no debt . . . I expected 'they'll come and see you in a few weeks, perhaps a month at the outside', but it just drags on . . . A young man came [he said] 'it could be another 10 or 20 years before you get over [to a flat near daughter]'. She says 'Oh, I'll be bloody dead and buried by then' and, you know, he upset her. (Daughter)

Conclusion

Of course there are many ways in which government policies affect the capacity of families to provide care, as well as the capacity of elderly people to care for themselves. Policies on health, housing and social security affect far larger numbers of people over 74 than do personal social services. Equally, policies which may enhance or inhibit families' capacity to care would include, at a structural level, those affecting public transport, safety of the streets and ease of housing transfer, as well as employment policies which will affect the material resources available to be devoted to caring, and the need for geographical mobility.

Our findings can only reinforce the view that many elderly people are reluctant to express needs or to demand services. There was evidence that, in some circumstances, families did act as advocates in securing formal services for elderly people, and that therefore those without informal support might receive less formal support. The reluctance of some families to accept assistance despite great hardship has been identified as an obstacle to providing shared care (R. Parker, 1981). Although it has to be accepted that careful and sensitive initial involvement may be necessary when people have been coping alone with difficulties for a considerable time, the prevalence of resistance to appropriate formal assistance can be overstated: Challis and Davies (1987, p. 24) report that, of 493 referrals of potential cases of elderly people on the margin of need for residential care, only five were excluded from the experimental or control groups because they received substantial informal support from carers 'who despite difficulty were unwilling to cede part of this caring activity to others'.

With regard to the most appropriate sources from which care should come, there is a degree of acceptance that families are not expected to be able to provide services which require professional expertise or very high material resources (such as regular income). As we have illustrated, people's informal networks can be sources of support, conflict or, in some cases, a drain on the individual's resources. In general, where there were no material, physical or emotional factors inhibiting the provision of support by families, such support was given. There were no massive untapped sources of support within family networks. People who themselves approached statutory services for assistance were in the best position to have already evaluated, and presumably rejected, the possibility of using family support. Are there untapped sources among friends, neighbours or 'the community'? In our experience those few neighbours or friends engaged in regular helping had usually become involved on the basis of a good prior relationship not based on disability or, less often, the transfer of the obligations of such a relationship to a relative (for example, a retired husband taking over his disabled wife's helping activity for a neighbour);

or, very rarely, chance possession of a relevant formal skill (a neighbour being a retired GP and therefore able to assist an elderly person with medical needs). The basis of care embodied in a long-established good relationship cannot be artificially created. We do not see much hope for generating more care *by* the community without resources to compensate helpers for the work involved, and to provide a reliable back-up of statutory services. We do see scope for assisting families who are already caring, and for improving services for elderly people.

It is not necessary to restate at length here the many criticisms which have been levelled at the bulk of social work activity with elderly people. The case has already been made in a number of studies that elderly people are a low-priority client group, frequently allocated to unqualified social workers or welfare assistants, and their needs are rarely comprehensively assessed but rather considered only in relation to specific services such as home help or day care, whilst their social and emotional needs are neglected (see Goldberg and Warburton, 1979; Goldberg and Connolly, 1982; Bowl, 1986). As we have seen, agents of statutory services may convey stereotyped expectations about family obligations and family relationships, and have been accused of perceiving informal networks only as potential sources of additional support without regard to the diversity of family relationships and circumstances (Rowlings, 1981). Social work intervention, in our study, was most likely to occur when people were being discharged from hospital, or were applying for long-term or short-term residential care, reflecting the often-voiced criticism that services are crisis-orientated to the detriment of long-term or preventative work.

The necessity for a flexible response, designed around an individual's recognised needs and in the knowledge of their particular social circumstances, implies a need for well-trained workers with access to resources which can be readily deployed in a variety of ways. For a few individuals, long-term 'case management' involving care planning, monitoring and review may be necessary, but in many instances such continuing involvement would not be needed. It would seem to be desirable that people could obtain some assistance without having to become (even temporarily) clients of a social services department, or having to be recipients of income support. Perhaps a fund, similar to the Family Fund (Bradshaw, 1980), could be set up to help families caring for disabled elderly relatives in a flexible, but not necessarily, continuing way. Certainly, if government policies in general areas such as income support, housing, transport and employment restrict the capacity of some families and elderly people to provide their own care, then the necessity to find and implement the most effective ways to provide services to individuals in need becomes even more urgent.

This chapter has emphasised the centrality of the family and female kin in the provision of care as well as the peripheral and often inadequate contribution of the formal sector. If the role of the statutory services is to provide a safety net – to offer help where no other help exists – then they can be judged as moderately successful in doing so. However, if this is the limit of their role it means that very little is done to *support* the caring activities of families or to overcome the social pressure on women, especially daughters, to care for elderly relatives. Indeed, this is the narrow approach we found in practice. It is to the issue of an alternative role for social services that we turn finally.

9

Conclusion: Towards Shared Care?

The previous chapters have explored the current state of the caring relationship between elderly people and their children. Our primary concerns were to document contemporary family relations in old age and to explore the social and emotional foundations of the caring relationship. Since the family is the main provider of care and tending to the elderly, as well as other family members in need, policy questions about the caring capacity of the community and, specifically, about responding to the rising need for care in the wake of an increasingly aged population should be addressed first to the family. Rather than appealing for increased activity to a nebulous and ill-defined 'community', we believe that a sound policy must be based on a better understanding of the strengths and weaknesses of family care.

Contrary to alarmist speculation about the reduced commitment of families to elderly relatives, we found no evidence of any weakening in the willingness of families (and women in particular) to provide care for elderly relatives. This continuing ascendancy of the family, and within it female kin, is underpinned by two powerful normative beliefs which, in practice, translate into strong pressures on family members to conform. First, there is a prevailing belief that children have a general responsibility to ensure the welfare of their parents in old age. Thus more than four out of five elderly people with principal helpers were receiving help from within the family. Second, there is the assumption of the primacy of women over men, and specifically daughters over sons, as carers within the family. Therefore over half of the principal helpers in our survey were daughters. Together these two universal

243

beliefs underlie the powerful normative construction of the daughter's duty to care for her elderly parents (discussed in detail in Chapters 5 and 6).

Unusually in studies of informal care we were able to assess the effectiveness of this sector in the actual delivery of care to elderly people in need. Thus the majority of those needing care and attention were receiving it (Chapter 4). People with very severe disability were all receiving informal care where it was available and statutory assistance where it was not. So, on the face of it, the family system of care appears to be operating very effectively to deliver tending and support when it is needed.

As far as wider family relationships were concerned we found no evidence whatsoever that the family is breaking up. The long-term trend towards elderly people living alone was matched by the growth of the local extended family form (Chapter 3 and Willmott, 1986) and sustained high levels of contact between elderly people and their children. Thus the myth that elderly people are becoming alienated and isolated from their families appears to be based on a confusion of trends in household formation with those in family cohesion and contact. Although the preference of elderly people was against joint households with their children, they were in favour of maintaining intimacy and close contact. The majority managed to achieve this and a significant minority had very frequent contact with relatives: one in three elderly people were in daily contact with at least one relative. Even when joint households were found these usually had arisen either from the continuance of the elderly person's nuclear family household (children staying with their parents) or from children moving in with elderly parents, though not to provide physical tending but company (often following widowhood) in return for shelter.

Two major conclusions from our research are that the family life of elderly people continues to thrive and that the caring relationship is alive and well (at least in Sheffield). However, policy makers should not be encouraged by this conclusion towards continuing complacency about the family care of elderly. In the first place, despite the rather romantic popular image of family care, it can entail considerable disadvantages for both sides of the caring relationship, but especially those female kin put under enormous social pressure to care. Second, there is evidence of a growing informal care gap, or shortfall, which is not being filled by the formal sector.

Bearing the burden of family care

The social construction of daughters' and other relatives' primacy in caring for elderly relatives in need has profound implications both for those immediately affected and for social care policy. Caring is a social relationship that comprises physical tending and support on the one hand and, on the other, emotional feelings based on affection, reciprocity and duty (Graham, 1983). As we showed in Chapters 4–6, these physical and emotional components of caring are borne primarily (though not exclusively) by women. While there are undoubtedly rewarding aspects of caring for elderly relatives, which might include repayment of past debts and the achievement of self-fulfilment in a caring role, there are also costs. Those may be economic, physical, psychological and social (Nissel and Bonnerjea, 1982; G. Parker, 1985): for example, married women are sometimes forced to give up their careers or jobs to care for elderly parents. In the words of one carer in our survey:

> They both had a bad attack of pneumonia and Father started with Parkinson's disease, and I was working at the Inland Revenue then, and I had to give up that job because it was too trying with them, and another job came into the offing where I had more time. It wasn't as, you know, career minded as the other one but it gave me freer time that I could pop off and see them if they needed my attention, whereas in the Civil Service you can't just walk out when you want, it's a responsible job. (Daughter)

The strong social belief that women should sacrifice their paid employment operates not only across the generations but between potential family carers:

> No doubt about it I was expected to give up my job and look after my mother and father – no question about that you know. [You mean your parents expected it or everyone?] Yes, apart from my husband. Oh yes, my brother thought I . . . yes definitely that I should give up my career. (Daughter)

> [My brother] thinks it's women's work, love, he doesn't think he should do anything . . . There was only me and him, and he's always been brought up that way you see, it didn't matter what I did it was my job to do it, it wasn't his job. (Daughter)

As well as economic costs of care we found plenty of examples of the effects of physical and psychological strain among family carers, as the following four cases indicate.

> It is hard work looking after old people. You know – errands, cleaning, beds – everything that you do in your own home you're doing for him as well, it is really hard work. (Daughter)

> Sometimes things tend to pile on top, you know, as when Mother was ill and one thing and another, I'm sort of trying to sort her out, and the children out, she was ill at the time we were trying to sort my daughter out on her options at University, and all these things ... I'm being pulled in two directions at times. (Daughter)

> She's on my mind quite a lot. I think that's a normal thing though, she could have a fall or anything ... I do take these tranquillisers, I am a nervous person, I do get myself concerned about family things since I've retired. (Daughter)

> I think people like myself who are really ... looking after two homes, yourself you get tired, I mean I'm getting older, feel tired and I don't feel as though, you know, you need a holiday and if somebody could just pop in and take over just for a week or a fortnight. (Daughter)

As illustrated in chapter 8, some carers also felt deprived of a social life or holiday by their caring role.

Of course, these costs are not borne solely by the figuratively broad shoulders of carers; they often cause strains within the carer's own household. The following quotation is from one of the minority of sons caring for an elderly parent: 'It does get you down at times you know. Sometimes I come home and I get on at Mary and the children, you know, because I've had such a day with her, which is not right to the family.'

Even when there are no outward signs of stress or quantifiable costs, one of the most common features of the female caring role is guilt.

You feel so guilty, when you come away, it's awful when I come away, I feel so ... she is sat there and oh ... I try to imagine how bored she must get. (Daughter)

I feel I should be going down there and yet I mean I'd like to go to a night class or a keep fit class or something but I don't quite feel that I should do it. I feel that if I have any spare time I feel that they should get it. (Daughter)

These examples, together with the earlier analyses, indicate that the family (and daughters in particular) are bearing most of the physical and emotional strains that caring can entail. They begin to raise questions about the extent to which the family system of care is operating effectively and fairly and, therefore, whether the normative and official assumption of the primacy of the family in the care of elderly relatives imposes unreasonable burdens on female kin.

If caring can involve considerable costs for carers and their families in what would be widely regarded as the normal family settings exemplified by the majority of our sample, in some circumstances the damage it can cause to either or both sides of the caring relationship raises the question whether, contrary to normative belief, the family should be regarded as the best source of care. Where difficult or strained family relationships are concerned the powerful normative pressure, transmitted in part through social policy and practice, can quite inappropriately force daughters and elderly people into potentially disastrous close physical and emotional relations. There are two distinct ways in which the imposition of family care can become an intolerable burden.

First, prolonged care, particularly for a relative suffering from dementia (Levin, Sinclair and Gorbach, 1985) can turn a previously equable family relationship into a strained and sour one. Thus, as the following quotation shows, the caring relationship may become stripped of feelings of affection and sustained merely by guilt and duty, which are (to say the least) questionable bases for the provision of good quality care to elderly people in need.

Well I think it's just really, you know, I feel I should do, it's just a duty – you know you feel it's a duty. Now I do feel that it's just

a duty and it's not for the love of a parent you know . . . for care
. . . I mean I worry about her and that's what upsets me, I think.
After so long I get really uptight inside because I don't care like
I used to care and I think it causes . . . you know . . . It upsets me
and I get depressed about that because I feel that I should care
but I'm afraid I don't these days and that worries me – that
upsets me more than anything, I think – I feel that the feeling,
you know, most of the feeling that I had for my mother has
vanished. (Daughter)

Second, family relations may have been awkward or strained for
many years. Thus the normative belief system might imply that the
least apropriate family member should adopt the caring role. The
following detailed case study illustrates just such an instance. It
shows the blunt and indiscriminating nature of the widespread
assumption, made by potential service providers from both the
formal and informal sectors, that a daughter is ultimately responsible
for the care of her parents. This case study is not put forward as
typical, but because it illustrates, in extreme form, the difficulty of
contradicting or cutting across this general belief in individual
cases. (Certain minor descriptive details have been changed to
protect the identity of those concerned. By the time of the carer
follow-up interview the elderly person had died.)

Mrs Booth

Mrs Booth (aged 63) lived with her second husband to whom
she had been married for ten years. She had one daughter by her
first husband from whom she was divorced. Mrs Booth had
worked full time as a manageress of a café until she retired.

Mrs Booth's father, Mr Rains, was 90; he was deaf and
becoming increasingly confused and sometimes aggressive. Mrs
Booth felt that the relationship between herself and her father
had never been good. In some respects she felt that she was the
very last person that could help him, partly because of her own
negative feelings towards him, and partly because the fact that
she was his daughter seemed to mean that he felt he had special
licence to ill treat her.

I used to say, 'I can't stand my father' and so I wasn't the best of people to deal with him really because I didn't like him. Simply because I was his daughter he thought he could say what he liked to me. He's always been a bit nasty but the last six months it got very violent, so this is the reason I could have done with some back-up help from some kind of health service because he got too violent for me to deal with.

Despite these factors, Mrs Booth accepted that she had to provide practical assistance to her father, both because her conscience demanded it and because of 'what people might say' if she did not. However, she felt that she, as helper, laboured under the unique disadvantage of being his daughter. Examples of his extreme behaviour towards her included not only physical violence, but also verbal abuse, including swearing and shouting outside her home in the early hours of the morning, writing poison pen letters about her to other relatives as well as writing abusive notes to her, abusing and insulting her husband and daughter, and refusing to give her any money for shopping she bought for him.

Attitudes of other family members

Mrs Booth had two brothers, one of whom had emigrated to Australia. The other lived locally but had absolutely no contact with his father: 'When my brothers came to Mum's funeral, my eldest brother said "Well, neither of them were much good – they didn't do anything for any of us; but the best of the two has gone now." That was Mum, you see. So that was his attitude.'

It was clear that the abusive and aggressive behaviour of Mr Rains had effectively alienated other relatives who might otherwise have helped.

Mother and Dad used to insult them when they went, you see. It was their idea of being funny, like – 'Oh, you have got a big nose, you look like a Jew.' All that kind of thing, you see . . . Well, they're not going to take kindly to two people who insult them like that, and so they didn't go.

Friends and neighbours

After a disastrous attempt at joint living with his daughter and son-in-law, Mr Rains went to live in a council flat. He did not endear himself to his neighbours who actually got up a petition to the council asking for him to be moved. The attitude of neighbours towards Mr Rains' daughter was partly a desire that she should take on responsibility for him which was later coupled with a degree of sympathy for the tremendous problems she had to cope with when she did so.

> They didn't give any help whatsoever because he was naughty. In the night he used to bang about and move the furniture . . . He used to walk about all night and he used to move all the furniture . . . Oh God, the neighbours used to come and fetch me, or they'd ring me up and say 'Your Dad's moving again' and I'd go down there . . . and this would be at 3 o'clock in the morning.

Mrs Booth did receive some informal support. Her husband, despite consistent rejection by Mr Rains, did continue to provide assistance by doing shopping, and helping with shaving, dressing and routine household maintenance. However, it was he who insisted that the joint household should end, because Mr Rains refused to contribute financially towards his keep, and behaved in a variety of other ways which he found unacceptable.

Mrs Booth also received help from two of her own friends, one of whom was a neighbour.

> She used to go with me, because I got that I couldn't go by myself because he was violent, so she used to go with me to hold the fort . . . at night she used to go with me and sort of help me make his bed or get him into bed and get him a cup of tea because he used to be hitting me . . . Mary's a big girl, she's about six foot tall, she used to say 'Come on, if he starts anything I'll clout him.'

The other friend had called in during the evenings when Mrs Booth had gone on holiday.

Formal services

A variety of formal services became involved in a number of ways, and it was clear to Mrs Booth that they, like Mr Rains' neighbours, also considered that she was, or should provide, the solution to the problems associated with her father, despite a number of attempts on her part to dispute this assumption.

The police. The police were involved in two ways: first, through Mr Rains' neighbours, and second because Mr Rains went for long walks and became lost and disorientated and was then brought 'home' to his daughter.

> He was capable of walking about. Now he could walk miles ... in fact, the police brought him back numerous times because he'd got lost.

> The people above [neighbours] fetched the police numerous times to him. The police used to come here and used to say 'What are you going to do about your father – can't you get him anywhere?' and I said 'Well you try to get him somewhere. You try to do something about it.' It would appear that the onus is thrown from one person to another and to another. You've got to see Mrs Somebody and Mrs Somebody's got to do this and that, and Mrs Somebody [Else] is in charge of home helps and I'll say 'Well, *who* is going to *do* something?'

Social services. Mrs Booth's initial attempts at obtaining some help in dealing with her father were unsuccessful.

> He could come up here umpteen times a day and because he could do that they said 'He's quite capable of doing that, he's not incapacitated in any way, he's not crippled, he's not bedfast, he's not incontinent and therefore you can deal with it', which is very unfair.
> I know that it's a problem because there isn't enough money, is there, from the state for these things? And, I suppose the state think that the family should be responsible for their old people, but sometimes – in my case – it was too

much for me, and there's no other part of the family to take charge or to help, so I think there's not enough back-up help and not enough interest in old people.

Eventually, when she wanted to go on holiday with her husband and daughter, Mrs Booth renewed her attempts to obtain assistance or at least relief help:

When I was going on my holidays, I had to fight for help; well, for the warden service I practically had to fight for it. I even rang ... my local MP and asked him to intervene if possible to find somebody to take charge of Dad while I went on holiday.

It was finally agreed that warden service would be provided for two weeks of holiday cover only:

but the warden herself said at the end of the fortnight that she would put a report in that actually I needed help all the time, that he was too much for me to manage by myself. Through the warden putting the report in, and having a talk, because apparently they have these meetings, the wardens ... she suggested to Mrs P. [organiser] that it would be better for me, because at the time I wasn't so well ... she said 'Mrs Booth could do with this help, just to relieve her from having to go down and get her Dad's breakfast ready' ... we tried for the meals on wheels but at the time I was told that there was too many to deal with as it was, he would have to wait.

However, for a period, warden services were provided in the mornings and this was a considerable help to Mrs Booth, although she had first the task of persuading her father to accept such help:

At first he said he wouldn't have anybody, and if anybody went in his home he would throw a bucket of water over them, and all this kind of talk. And I said 'Look Dad, if I was to be taken ill and go into hospital, or if I was to die, who are you going to be dependent on? Your sons don't want to know you, you have no one else. These ladies, if anything was to happen to me, would see to you,' and he began to come round to it that way.

However, although Mrs Booth appreciated the help, it was not always reliable:

> They were very, very kind, but ... I must say that I think they're overworked and too many people to see to, so that they can't give any individual attention at all, so I had to go down. Sometimes they forgot Dad and he wasn't capable of getting anything for himself, so I had to go and make sure he'd got something to eat and make him some tea.

Nevertheless, there were ways in which the involvement of statutory workers was invaluable, precisely because they were *not* family members:

> I used to fetch his shopping and say 'Dad, come along and give me some money for your shopping' and he used to say 'I'm not giving you any money' ... very often I used to have to ask the ladies that came from the warden service – I used to have to ask them to ask him for the money for the groceries, as if they'd paid for them, and he'd give them the money.
> He accused me of stealing from his home, and trying to poison him and trying to do away with him ... I was having to leave him so many tablets on a piece of paper because if I gave them him he used to say 'You're trying to poison me' ... then I got the warden going at night to give him his tablets.

Unfortunately the situation deteriorated, and Mr Rains' behaviour became more difficult, although he still reserved most of his violence and abuse for his daughter:

> He used to call me the most filthy names – 'cow' and all sorts of things, and he used to be hitting me; when I used to go he used to hit me. About a month before he died I had to tie him to the chair with his braces, he was so awfully violent, and he got to walking about with a hammer in his pocket.

News of this behaviour reached the Organiser of Domiciliary Care and her reaction was swift: .

> That's when the back-up help was refused. The warden services organiser, Mrs P., cancelled all warden services,

cancelled everybody going in ... she said 'Well, because of
this, because of the violent streak in your father, I'm taking
off all help, all back-up help; you won't have anyone going in
'cos if they do and anything happens to them, I'm responsible.' So I didn't get any help.

In vain, Mrs Booth tried to explain that she did not think that
her father would hit anyone (apart from herself): 'I said, "I'm
his daughter and he feels he can hit me when he likes."'

Fortunately (from Mrs Booth's point of view) the warden
herself, who had first-hand knowledge of the problem, proved
willing to step outside her formal role and to simply disregard
her superior's instructions.

The warden herself, she came up to see me, she said, 'Look,
Janice, because of the problems you've got, I'll go in because
I know how to handle him,' but she said, 'Don't tell Mrs P.,
don't tell anyone. I'll do it off my own bat and if anything
happens to me, I'll have to take my own consequences.'

Mr Rains expressed consistent opposition to the idea of
residential care:

I always promised I would never ever let him go in a home.
He used to say 'Don't let them put me in an old man's home,
will you?' and I used to say 'No, no, while ever I'm alive you'll
stay with me.' Well, gradually, as I say, we were trying to get
him ... to go permanently, but I don't really think he would
have done. I would have had to have had him here.

Health services.   Mrs Booth had consulted her GP (who was
also her father's GP) on a number of occasions. She suffered
from some physical health problems which she described as
'kidney trouble' but also received treatment for 'nerves'. Several
years before, whilst caring for both her parents, she had felt
herself to be at breaking point: 'It began to be a big, big burden
and I thought, I shall make ill of myself. And this is what I said
to Doctor A. "If I don't get some help I feel that I shall do
something to myself."'

It seems that the GP did not arrange for any practical

assistance but he did refer Mrs Booth for psychotherapy. Mrs Booth perceived this treatment as most helpful:

It was the fact that I was sort of bottling everything up inside and I wasn't able to say anything, 'cos families don't understand ... you can't talk to families, plus the fact that my family were not interested ... he helped quite a lot because I was able to talk it all out ... I told him 'You've helped quite a lot just by the mere fact that you understand the problem and you're giving me some help just by talking to me,' and I got over it.

At the time of his death, Mr Rains was due to enter a psychogeriatric ward for assessment, with a view to his placement in a day centre. Mrs Booth commented on her father's changed behaviour in the presence of the doctor: 'The funny part about it was that each time the doctor came Dad was all right – very lucid and OK. Then as soon as he'd gone the pantomime used to start, and even the warden said, "You know, the doctor ought to be here when he's carrying on like this." '

Mrs Booth's one visit to the geriatric ward was enough to convince her that she could never allow her father to stay in such a place; however, in the event, Mr Rains was taken ill the day before his proposed admission and this in fact caused considerable problems:

by about 9 o'clock at night he'd got that we [carer and husband] couldn't control him at all; we were trying to hold him down, he was violent, he was shouting and raving, and trying to get outside, running out in his pyjamas and wetting all over the place. So we sent for the doctor, who came in the evening, and he tried until about 10 o'clock, a solid hour, in a neighbour's house opposite to get him into somewhere. He said, 'we must get him in somewhere'. No one would have him because he was the patient of this chap who was taking him into the hospital the next day, you see, for an assessment.

The GP gave an injection and tablets which he predicted would cause Mr Rains to sleep 'all night and most of the day' and left instructions that he should be called out if trouble recurred. In fact Mr Rains slept for about an hour and then began again. A neighbour, on being disturbed by the noise at about 3 o'clock, offered to call out the doctor again (Mr Rains had no telephone). The doctor, from a deputising service, arrived at about 6 o'clock by which time Mr Rains had been asleep for about an hour. In the morning a GP from the practice called and rebuked Mrs Booth for failing to cancel the request for the doctor once her father fell asleep, pointing out that a fee was charged to the practice for such calls. Mrs Booth was disinclined to show much contrition. She described her response to this comment as 'a bit sharp'. Mr Rains was admitted to the ward where he was due to be assessed and died later that day.

Aftermath

> I've got a guilt complex now I must admit. Because, after Dad died, oh for weeks and weeks I couldn't do anything but cry. And I couldn't stand my own bedroom 'cos Dad used to come and throw all things at the bedroom window in the middle of the night. In fact the week before he died he threw the shovel through the window – he brought the shovel with him and threw it through the window. We had a terrible, terrible time with him.
>
> At first I couldn't sleep when Dad first died. I couldn't sleep. I was down here, wandering round but that was my guilt complex, and I explained that to Doctor A. and he said, 'It's surprising how many people do suffer from this, but knowing you, and knowing how your Father was, I think you did all you could.' Of course, the wardens all said that and all the neighbours said that which was a good boost for me. They all said, 'Well, we think you did marvellous, you did the best you could, 'cos we all knew what an old bugger your dad was.'

This study illustrates many of the limitations of current welfare provision, formal and informal. Although there is a general presumption that family care is superior to state care because it is rooted in pre-existing informal relationships, this example reinforces the contention that families may engender both the best and the worst of relationships, and that to be a close relative, in particular a child, *can* be a unique disadvantage as well as (more usually) an advantage in dealing with a particular elderly person.

Operation of the informal sector

It is of note that at least some of those 'expected' to care – sons, relatives, neighbours – did not do so, because they felt no sense of debt, but rather the reverse, towards the potential recipient. Their attention was focused upon the daughter, whom they wished to take responsibility and who was vulnerable to the pressure of others' expectations, although she herself felt little individual-level obligation towards her father. The informal help which was available was that 'owed' to the daughter herself: the obligations of her spouse and her friends to give her assistance. Her own daughter had the care of a young child as a prior obligation, but did occasionally provide help, although she too had received a share of abuse from her grandfather throughout her life.

Those informal sector members who had rejected the elderly person and insisted on his daughter assuming responsibility were prepared to acknowledge the difficulty of the problem and the strain on the carer once the problem had disappeared. At this stage the daughter received the rewards of social approval for an obligation discharged from all concerned.

The attitude of the elderly person towards his daughter and other relatives was worse than his attitude towards other helpers. His daughter experienced more difficulty in dealing with him than did individual agents of the state.

Operation of the formal sector

Formal sector service providers all assumed the primary responsibility of the daughter, and failed to assess the difficulties involved as a whole, confining themselves to refusal of a specific service (domiciliary service) on the grounds of insufficient physical disability. Upon forced close acquaintance with the problems, the fieldworkers at the lowest level of the hierarchy were persuaded of the shortfall in help, and argued that it should be provided. This help was useful although delivery was unreliable and not well co-ordinated with the daughter's help. However, the involvement of non-informal helpers was successful in overcoming some problems.

Ironically, a worsening of the situation led to the withdrawal of statutory help because bureaucratic considerations outweighed the meeting of needs, and only the actions of an individual worker who stepped outside her formal role and helped 'despite the system' provided any relief to the carer.

The GP had been supportive to Mrs Booth but did not seem to have played any role in securing any practical assistance; and neither was he able, despite considerable efforts, to secure hospital admission when required. The deputising service did not operate satisfactorily.

This is undoubtedly an extreme case, in which many negative elements have occurred together by chance, but there is research evidence to suggest that similar features do occur in other cases. There has been considerable discussion about the general failure by statutory workers to assess the overall situation of elderly people, but instead to narrowly assess in relation to need for specific services only (see Goldberg and Connelly, 1982, p. 55–7) and there is evidence (Jones, Victor and Vetter, 1983) that elderly people suffering from mental disturbances or mental illness are less likely to be offered domestic assistance than those suffering physical disability. There is also evidence that carers reporting a difficult past relationship with the elderly person suffer more stress (Gilleard *et al.*, 1984; Levin, Sinclair and Gorbach, 1986) than those who report a good past relationship. Allocation procedures for domiciliary services which restrict help to people without local daughters are known to operate (A. I. Harris, 1968), and may operate informally even if no such formal policy exists.

Moreover, there is a great deal of apparently inexplicable variation in the way in which GPs respond to elderly patients (Wilkin *et al.*, 1984) and in the degree to which they refer people on for other services. There is a particularly acute shortage of geriatric hospital places in Sheffield, and the shortcomings of deputising services, which may now have been improved, were well known.

It should be crystal clear from Mrs Booth's experience that, apart from the narrowest concern with preventing public expenditure, it makes little sense to base the care of vulnerable elderly people on this sort of antagonistic relationship. Certainly the quality of care provided within this context – an issue that attracts official and media scrutiny in the formal sector but little or no attention in the informal sector – may not be very high. Furthermore, the provision of care and tending can be physically and emotionally bruising for the carer. Yet, as we have seen, the dominant assumption of those in both the formal and informal sectors was that the daughter was the right person to care, and the strength of this norm may be gauged by the fact that the daughter herself was also persuaded, despite her low regard for her father. The earlier quotation (p. 248), in which this duty was not openly questioned as Mrs Booth had done, showed that the imposition of a caring responsibility over a long period can destroy the bonds of affection on which the caring relationship is partly based.

These instances of the wholly inappropriate and dysfunctional application of a generalised normative belief – by informal carers, policy makers and practitioners alike – and the considerable burdens that family carers can, therefore, be forced to bear lead us to the firm conclusion that it must be made more socially acceptable for families *not* to care or not to do so alone. It was clear that, in a significant minority of cases, there was no love or affection for the relative being cared for and not even a personalised sense of obligation, but only external compulsion. This suggests an important role for social policy in both creating services and practices intended to supplement or substitute for family care and, equally importantly, in questioning the normative basis of family care. We will return shortly to the practical implications of this prescription, but before doing so it is important to refer back to the existing shortfall in the need for care on the part of disabled elderly people.

The care gap

As we saw in Chapter 1 various demographic and social changes are reducing the pool of potential family carers (Ermisch, 1983; Walker, 1985). At present the surest guarantee of receiving family care in old age is to have at least one daughter, but with fewer children the likelihood of giving birth to a girl is reduced. Also the growth of dispersed extended families resulting from occupational and geographical mobility will inhibit the ability of daughters to care for elderly relatives (Willmott, 1986). Another potential challenge to the traditional pattern of family care, so evident in our research, comes from the increasing participation of women in the labour market. Although there was no suggestion that daughters in our sample were choosing careers instead of care, there was no doubting the explicit conflict between the two and the resulting strain that this imposed on those attempting to carry out both roles. It remains an open question whether or not daughters will continue to provide care under such stress – and we have already indicated that this can undermine the affect base of the caring relationship – but we have no doubt that they should not be expected to do so.

It seemed that daughters-in-law might be choosing not to provide care if they were in full-time work, and that in such circumstances their husbands did not provide a compensating increase in domestic assistance for elderly people. No positive association was evident for men between unemployment and the provision of help to elderly parents. Indeed, the reverse appeared to be the case, with only one in 19 unemployed sons providing any practical help at all, compared with one in four of all sons in full-time work.

The dominant caring relationship among Sheffield families was built on the local extended family form. Even in the traditionally low external migration setting of Sheffield, however, this pattern is under some threat from housing and relocation policies (three out of five elderly people who had moved in the last 20 years gave the demolition of their home as the main reason), unemployment and the need to move to find employment, and the removal of bus fare subsidies which were an important aid to frequent contact between elderly people and their relatives. In other parts of the country, particularly London, the local extended family is less prevalent (Willmott, 1986). The bonds of affection, reciprocity and respect that hold the extended family together may be undermined to some extent by the increasing tendency in industrial societies to denigrate the old and devalue their contribution in formal, secondary relations, particularly in the labour market (Walker, 1981b).

Now we turn from speculation about the future of the extended family to hard evidence about the existing care gap. Although female kin were fully engaged when required in care and tending, there was clear evidence of shortfalls in the care being provided. The effectiveness of the family system of care in delivery services to those in need cannot be gainsaid: 97 per cent of those with a 'very high' need for care were receiving 'high' levels so the majority of those in need of care were getting it. However, one-quarter of those with 'high' need were receiving only medium inputs of different forms of care, and one in six in substantial need of care and tending were not receiving any help. In other words, elderly people in need were either not receiving help with some personal and household tasks or they were not getting sufficient help.

Areas where specific unmet needs were identified, by objective and subjective means, included help with chiropody, occasional help with heavy housework, laundry and shopping, and climbing stairs. In addition decorating and gardening were mentioned as needs not being met. These gaps in informal provision were not being filled by the formal or voluntary sectors. Indeed, there was a significant shortfall in formal care services in relation to need: one-third of home help users identified a felt shortfall in home help tasks. Moreover, there was a firm belief on the part of family carers that an informal rationing system was in operation so that the home help service tended to favour those living alone and rarely went to those living with relatives (see Chapter 8).

As well as a considerable shortfall in care and tending we discovered a clear gender division in the receipt of both formal and informal care. So, for example, men were more likely than women to get assistance with housework tasks such as laundry. This meant that elderly men were often the recipients of an 'excess' of care – due primarily to the activity of female spouses – whereas women were more likely to suffer a shortfall.

Our primary concern has been with the family care of elderly people but, of course, there is a significant minority of elderly people with no living relatives, especially children, or none living nearby. This group cannot be left to rely on the informal sector and may require some special attention from policy makers, particularly the 7 per cent we indicated as severely isolated in Chapter 3 (which is likely to be an underestimate of the national picture).

Towards shared care?

This analysis of the unequal and unfair imposition of the duty to tend and care on daughters and other female kin and the costs that this can entail for both sides of the caring relationship, together with the questions we have raised about the existing and potentially widening care gap, point the way to the need for an alternative approach to the care of elderly people. The most common response on the part of policy analysts in recent years has been to propose various forms of 'shared' care, or a 'care-partnership' or 'interweaving' (Bayley, 1982) between the informal and formal sectors. Before looking in more detail at what this might consist of it is important to note that there are two main alternatives to the policy of shared care.

First, there is the policy pursued by the Conservative governments from 1979, one important aspect of which is to encourage greater reliance on the informal sector itself. Thus, in the now famous words of the 1981 White Paper on the elderly: 'care *in* the community must increasingly mean care *by* the community' (DHSS, 1981a, p. 3). This policy comprises two main elements. On the one hand, already minimal domiciliary provision has been purposely reduced in relation to the growing need among the population aged 75 and over (Walker, 1985a; Social Services Committee, 1986). A major official justification for these cuts in local authority expenditure is the availability of a large informal sector of care (Social Services Committee, 1980, pp. 99–100). On the other hand, ministers have been appealing to the wider 'community' to provide an increased input and have devoted comparatively small sums of money to several initiatives – such as the Helping the Community to Care initiative – designed to encourage it to do so. As our research has demonstrated, the fundamental flaw in this approach is that it is based, at best, on an overoptimistic view of the existing and potential contribution of the wider community and is, therefore, bound to increase the burden on family carers. Similar caution is required with regard to the now fashionable concept of 'natural' helping networks (Collins and Pancoast, 1976; Froland *et al.*, 1981; Wenger, 1984, p. 188). The description 'natural' is misleading because it conceals relationships, dependencies and responsibilities which are *socially* constructed – such as the gender division of labour in tending – and therefore amenable to social policy (Walker, 1985b, p. 52).

Second, it has been proposed that the public sector residential services should take over a substantial amount of the care of elderly people currently provided by the family. Some feminists, doubting the feasibility of the social and economic changes necessary to establish gender equality in caring, have suggested that residential care represents a preferable alternative as far as female carers are concerned (Dalley, 1983; Finch, 1984; Waerness, 1986). This approach is based on the erroneous assumption that the primary conflict in the social construction of the caring role is between female carers and elderly people (most of whom are themselves female). In fact the primary division is between both carers and elderly people on the one side and the (patriarchal) state, which is failing to ensure adequate support for either, on the other side. Also, proponents of this attempt to rehabilitate the concept of the residential institution apparently do not take into account the long history of research which demonstrates the inhibiting and dependency-creating nature of residential care (for reviews, see Townsend, 1981a, 1981b). In other words this approach is one-sided – emphasising the needs of carers and ignoring those of elderly people – and does not reflect the perceptions of those actually engaged in caring relationships. Thus seven out of ten elderly people in our sample either rejected residential care or regarded it as a last resort. At the same time nearly six out of ten carers also rejected the idea. Moreover, the critique of the family and the ideology of 'familism' on which it is based tends to be culturally specific, ignoring black women whose family experience may not fit the stereotype (Carby, 1982).

Both of these alternatives entail unacceptable costs for either female carers or elderly people. Yet, as we have argued previously, the status quo is equally untenable. This conclusion has led a number of policy analysts to propose a greater sharing of caring tasks and responsibilities between the formal and informal sectors (Moroney, 1976, 1986; Land and Parker, 1978; R. Parker, 1981; Bayley, 1982; Walker, 1982a). For example, one of us has argued previously for the introduction of community care policies which support and share the caring activities of families. Such a policy 'should not put women under a greater obligation than men to provide care and . . . as far as possible, it should actively encourage men to provide care' (Walker, 1982a, p. 37). The aim of this proposal was not to establish sex equality, since this would rest on social and economic changes outside the realm of the division of labour in caring, but rather to attempt to ensure that sex inequality in caring is not reinforced.

Is this goal of shared care feasible? The difficulties must not be underemphasised. According to R. Parker (1981, p. 24):

> Sharing care may be a much more difficult undertaking than is generally believed. 'Sharing' has an attractive sound to it; it is commendable. That does not mean to say that it is easily realised. It may be hard to achieve emotionally and, practically, it may be exceedingly complicated to organise.

What little evidence there was of interweaving or shared care in our survey primarily concerned relatives, or relatives and the wider informal sector rather than the formal and informal sectors. There were, in fact, very few subsidiary carers; in most cases there was only one person doing the bulk of the caring work. The most common cases of support were relatives helping other relatives: threeout of four carers providing secondary help with heavy shopping came into this category. In common with previous research (Wenger, 1984) we found that neighbours and friends were rarely engaged in personal care tasks as principal helpers, but they did provide important back-up help in some of the less personal activities – such as shopping – where one in four second helpers were neighbours or friends. Furthermore, there was some indication of the care of the severely disabled being shared within the informal sector, but again this usually related to household management tasks such as shopping (two-thirds of carers of the severely disabled received help in doing the elderly person's shopping).

Although shopping was an activity where men (for example, the spouses of carers) played some role, there was not much evidence of significant sharing across gender lines. Women dominated in the provision of care – except in gardening and decorating – but the variations in the contributions of women and men of 4:1 in doing heavy shopping and 22:1 in doing laundry suggest that men were able to choose where they provided help. As far as the personal tending activities that can impose the greatest strains on carers were concerned – tasks such as washing and bathing elderly people – all non-spouse relatives engaged in such tending were either daughters or daughters-in-law.

The relative lack of practical examples of care being shared between formal and informal sectors may be attributed in part to inhibitions in both sectors. As we argued in Chapter 2, resistance to developing supportive public services on the part of policy makers is based on the individualistic ideology that care must be primarily family-based rather than collectively provided. Fears are commonly expressed about undermining the foundations of family care and creating a flood of demands for public expenditure. Historical and contemporary research (including our own) has demonstrated that, contrary to these fears, social services have not weakened the commitment of the family to care (Moroney, 1976; Anderson, 1977; Brody, 1981). What is clear, however, is that the primacy of the family's burden of care has devolved unfairly on female kin. Moreover, when a duty to care is imposed on families, either directly as under the nineteenth-century household means test or indirectly by the failure to provide alternatives, this can be dysfunctional.

There is also resistance to shared care on the part of the family, though arguably this would be easier to overcome than the ideological resistance on the part of the state. In common with previous research, elderly people in our sample often preferred informal care to other forms, and especially preferred female kin (Brody, Johnson and Fulcomer, 1984). But there is some evidence that younger generations are more receptive to men and women sharing care within the family (Brody, 1983). Elderly people have usually been living independently all their lives and, therefore, dependency and help are often difficult to accept (Hazan, 1980), which in turn makes sharing care more difficult to achieve.

As well as these structural barriers to shared care – which are both to a significant degree based on the same normative construction of the natural caring role of the family, and women in particular – there is a range of practical problems which beset any attempt at sharing care. These include the danger of colonisation by the formal of the informal; the differing nature, organisation and goals of the two sectors (the one based on the emotional ties of kinship and friendship, the other based on the rational contracts of bureaucratic organisation); the lack of co-terminosity between the boundaries and responsibilities of the two sectors; the different knowledge base, resources and time commitments that each sector brings to bear on the caring task; and the different political and ideological concerns of the two sectors (for a full review of these problems, see Froland, 1980; Bayley, 1982; Willmott, 1986, pp. 110–11; Bulmer, 1987, pp. 188–201). In view of these potential problems and the considerable structural barriers in the way of change, any programme for initiating policy development towards shared care must be a cautious one.

We have reviewed the arguments that informal care is qualitatively superior to formal care, as well as being cheaper in terms of public expenditure. Acceptance of the first point has to be qualified both by the observation that not all informal networks are supportive, and also by the specification of exactly which aspects of informal care do have that special quality which makes it so difficult to provide substitutes through the formal sector. It is argued that a concern with cost-cutting leads emphasis to be placed upon generating, from the informal sector, precisely those aspects of care (practical help) which *are* substitutable, without consideration of the fact that this may well reduce the supply of those particular social and emotional benefits which informal relationships are uniquely well equipped to provide.

The foregoing argument illustrates one way in which the very use of the term 'sector' in discourse on informal care reflects an implicit economic model of the production and distribution of welfare which can be misleading in several important respects. At the level of organisation, whilst statutory and voluntary sectors can relate formally through joint committees, meetings of officers and similar mechanisms, the formal sector can only relate to the informal sector at the level of particular individuals because the so-called informal sector exists in a different form for each individual. This is not to suggest that there can be no general policy towards informal care: such policies (for example, a refusal to provide domestic assistance of elderly people with local daughters) already exist in some areas. However, we would argue that the keynote of the approach of the formal sector to informal care must be a much greater *flexibility* of response in order to enable it to reflect the operation of informal care as we have demonstrated it is delivered: within the structure of a set of generally accepted rules to which a great many exceptions and variations are allowed in practice.

These considerations seem to us to imply strong support for policies and practices which involve the devolution of control over resources to front-line workers so that they can be allocated in different ways as appropriate for individuals. However, we see no reason why control should necessarily have to remain with professional workers so that assistance is always 'in kind'. To a limited extent, individuals have in the past been able to make their own decisions about what would be helpful to them and apply for assistance (for example, under the Chronically Sick and Disabled Persons Act), or special social security payments such as the attendance allowance. We would argue that greater priority should be given to providing forms of assistance which would contribute to what might be seen as 'informal network maintenance'; that is, assistance which would enable interactions with other in the network which were not directly tied to the fulfilment of a specific practical need. This could be cheaper and more effective than a specific service: for example, transport to enable an elderly, disabled woman to regularly visit her equally disabled elderly sister might make a much greater contribution to her well being than regular transport to day care; free telephone installation might enable housebound elderly people to continue to play an active role in their social network, and to continue to maintain and strengthen relationships by ensuring that direct support is only one of their functions; local authorities and housing associations could give a degree of priority to those wishing to be housed near relatives (in some cases perhaps financial assistance could be given with moving house); carers of elderly people could, and should, receive regular relief care so that they can engage in activities vital to informal network maintenance, such as visiting their own children and grandchildren. Also, forms of practical help could be given to carers in order to assist them in their caring tasks, and this might include domestic assistance in their home, a telephone to facilitate contact, or direct payments to enable them to give up work; nothing should be ruled out *a priori*. Community Care Grants from the Social Fund under the Thatcher government's social security reforms, embodied in the 1986 Social Security Act (operating from April 1988), might at first seem to offer a hopeful way forward in respect of flexibility and individual freedom to apply. Unfortunately, the extremely severe cash limits on this aspect of the Fund, and the instructions to officers to consider all other sources of support for people, make it clear that the underlying orientation is towards the family as an alternative *source* of support in the context of the overall aim of cost-cutting.

Furthermore, carers are the only major group in need not specifically recognised by a special premium under the income support scheme. This means that carers are worse off under the new social security scheme than they were prior to April 1988 when they were entitled to the long-term rate of supplementary benefit. This is a policy which seems to be completely at odds with both the Thatcher government's rhetoric about carers and the community care emphasis in the Social Fund.

An agenda for shared care

The fundamental principles upon which a policy of shared care should be based are that neither families nor female kin should be put under any external obligation to care for elderly relatives and, if they choose to do so, the expectation must be that supportive formal services will be available on demand to assist them. Families have been left to themselves to organise and deliver care. This burden has fallen largely on daughters, often single-handed and with little sustained formal support. Policy makers have legitimated non-intervention by the excuse that it is the family's responsibility. But a genuine commitment to shared care implies the provision of resources to supplement and,where necessary, substitute for family care. The policy would be aimed at supporting the caring activities of family and other informal carers while not exploiting their willingness to care. What are the critical points at which change must be initiated to promote a policy of shared care?

In the first place, it is important to recognise the structural limitations of the family system of care and informal support networks. They are unable to establish *rights* to support; it is only the public sector which can implement and secure rights. They are relatively powerless, furthermore, in the face of major social deprivation and poverty. This reminds us of the interconnectedness of economic and social policies and that policies in the formal economy, resulting in unemployment and economic insecurity, can militate against the creation of caring relationships. In Garbarino's (1983, p. 26) terms, 'Economic inadequacy ... jeopardises relationships.' It is unlikely that an increasing amount of care will be provided by the community without economic and social policies to care *for* the community (Walker, 1982a). Thus government intervention through the public sector is critical in both creating the general economic security on which caring relationships might be successfully founded and also in the provision of direct supportive home care services. Unfortunately, the present trend of policy towards the residualisation of the personal social services is likely to restrict the availability of support services (Walker, 1988).

Second, change is required in the organisation and operation of the formal services. In order to overcome the rigid division between the formal and informal sectors it might be helpful to think more in terms of 'social support networks' than informal support networks (Whittaker and Garbarino, 1983). Social support networks are not necessarily 'natural' and may be created to fill a specific need. They may comprise *both* formal and informal helpers, or professional and non-professional personnel. This broader concept of support networks encourages policy makers to perceive care in the form of a partnership between people with different skills. It also prevents the entirely unjustified conflation of 'informal' network with 'support' network, given that informal networks may not be supportive. This purposive integration of informal carer and professional has also been referred to as a 'care partnership' (Allen, 1983) and 'sensitive interweaving' (Bayley, 1980). According to Wenger (1984, p. 192): 'This approach calls for a more integrated perspective of service provision where the personnel of different agencies adopt a co-operative stance, sharing tasks and information in order to provide a cohesive support package.'

At the present it is rare for the formal and informal sectors to co-operate, let alone interweave, and there is no choice for many carers between total responsibility and no responsibility in care. However, in recent years a wide range of important innovations in the community-based care of elderly people have been developed, the best known examples of which include the Kent Community Care Scheme (Qureshi, 1985; Challis and Davies, 1986) and the Dinnington Project (Bayley *et al.*, 1981). Evaluations of these and other similar schemes have shown that it is possible to organise informal or quasi-informal helpers to provide care for elderly people in their own homes who might have been admitted to an old people's home, at no extra cost to the social services department (for summary cost comparisons of a wide range of schemes, see Tinker, 1984).

Of course, given the high cost of residential care, it is not difficult to understand the appeal of schemes which appear to offer a better quality of care for lower cost. However, even though there is obvious potential for the extension of such schemes to other groups, it remains to be seen whether such extensions, which could well improve quality, will be supported when their cost advantages are not so obvious.

While various experimental projects provide grounds for optimism about increasing the sensitivity of the formal sector to informal care networks, there is not much evidence so far of a fundamental change in the social division of caring tasks within such schemes. It is still women in the informal sector who provide the vast bulk of care. The way is open, therefore, for schemes which specifically set out to involve men in caring. Furthermore, there is little evidence of changes in traditional roles *within* the state social services. This is precisely the intention of an innovatory form of social service provision that has started recently in the city of Sheffield. Neighbourhood Support Units are intended to replace both residential care and traditional day and community care services and personnel with flexible community support services aimed at keeping people independent in their own homes (MacDonald, Qureshi and Walker 1984). This is one of the few examples of a proposed expansion in collective home care services, and it has suffered set-backs in its development because of the cost of its implementation and the restrictions placed on local authority spending by the government. This emphasises the point that sharing care between the formal and informal sectors is not a cheap option.

Third, change must be initiated in professional values and attitudes within the formal sector if a partnership between the formal and informal sectors is to be developed. This does *not* mean that there is necessarily a conflict between a policy to encourage social support networks and professional values (Whittaker, 1983, p. 61). It is primarily a matter of increasing the accountability of professionals rather than believing that it is possible to deprofessionalise the social services entirely. Although a long-term goal would be the socialisation of the health and social services to transform the experience of welfare from a passive one (as clients or patients) to active participation in the definition of need and policy responses to it, there will always be an important role for professional groups. Professional and informal helping should be seen as necessary and potentially complementary elements in social support and care.

Fourth, a new approach to the provision of community care services is required. Thus it is important to reorientate policy makers and formal service providers away from a short-term, casualty perception of need towards a longer-term strategy of prevention. The function of responsible social services should not be confined to the management of stress. Instead of concentrating on coping strategies they should be directed at *preventing* the causes of social breakdown and distress.

Finally, the goal of shared care must not divert attention from the need to share care *within* the family. Major social and ideological changes are required to overcome the normative designation of women as carers and the moral imperative on them to care. In the absence of policies to overcome gender inequalities in society as a whole, the best that can be hoped for are social care policies which do not put women under a greater obligation than men to provide care. A start can be made in this direction by ensuring that the availability of female kin is not a criterion for rationing formal care, and that sufficient social services are available to facilitate a choice for female kin

*   *   *   *   *

A clear danger associated with any study of family care is that it might be misinterpreted as a eulogy of the caring relationship. We have shown, in fact, that the family can provide the very best and the very worst setting for the care of elderly people. The strengths and limitations of family care should by now be obvious: the social construction of the primary caring role of the family and female kin, or the ideology of 'familism' (Barrett and McIntosh, 1982; Dalley, 1988) means that in practice the main burden of care is borne by women. Yet the family system of care has the great strengths of flexibility, informality and making people feel *cared for* (P. Abrams, 1978a; Graham, 1983). There can be no doubt that, as presently constituted, the family caring relationship entails unacceptable costs for (female) carers. An alternative approach is urgently needed, not only to relieve female kin from their primary responsibility but also to meet the growing needs of the elderly population. Shared care, based on an enlarged collective home-care service, would meet the expressed demands of elderly people and carers, avoid the increase in dependency associated with residential forms of care, and would be the best expression of the responsibility of society as a whole to care for its elderly citizens in need.

Appendix: Methodology

435 names and addresses were initially selected randomly from the lists of six different practices included in the age/sex register, in such a way as to ensure that the proportions of people living in different areas of the city were consonant with a representative distribution derived from a cluster analysis of Sheffield wards based on census data (Drew, 1980). (Patients aged 75 or more are listed separately because a higher capitation fee is paid to doctors for such older patients.) Of course, the individual practices concerned were fully consulted, and able to satisfy themselves about the aims of the research and the questions which would be asked before their lists were used.

There is relatively little research on the adequacy of doctors' lists as a sampling frame. The picture is undoubtedly variable throughout the country. Isaacs and Neville (1976) considered that such lists covered the vast majority of the population (95 per cent), and a small-scale census in Aberdeen found that the Aberdeen index excluded about 10 per cent of the population, although GPs' own lists excluded only about 5 per cent (Ford, personal communication). However, it seems that lists have been found to include a high proportion of people who are no longer living, and this is obviously a particular problem among older age groups where death rates are higher. For example, a quarter of those elderly people on the lists of GPs in the Dinnington area were found to be deceased (Seyd, Tennant and Bayley, 1985).

The list obtained from the Sheffield Central Register was checked against the Electoral Register and, where discrepancies occurred, the lists of the individual GPs were checked for an up-to-date address. The Sheffield central index showed a comparatively high degree of accuracy; indeed, the numbers of patients who were deceased was no more than would have been expected in the course of a year in that particular age group. Table A.1 shows a detailed breakdown of the original sample and the final response rate.

Where interviewees were too ill or infirm to give or complete an interview, a shortened interview could be sought from a proxy such as a friend or relative. Despite this, of the 306 interviews seven could not be regarded as complete and had to be excluded from parts of the detailed analysis. Eight interviews were given by proxy.

273

Table A.1   *Original and achieved samples of elderly people*

1	Issued sample	435
2	*Out-of-scope elements*	
	Deceased	15
	Moved into residential care	8
	Moved away or house demolished	24
	Mistakenly included (e.g. not over 74)	4
3	*In-scope elements*	384
4	*Non-response*	
	Refusal	54
	Too ill or infirm (no proxy)	17
	Could not be contacted	
	(after 6 call backs)	6
	Total non-response	77
5	Interviews obtained	306
6	Response rate	80%

The follow up sample of carers

There was one instance in which a person was identified as a carer to two different elderly people, and was therefore interviewed in relation to both. Strictly speaking, therefore, the total number of interviews with carers was 57. There is a double level of refusal in a screening procedure of the kind used here, and it will be evident from Table A.2 that interviews were obtained with at least one carer outside the household in just over half the instances in which such carers were identified (a response rate of 75 per cent among the carers whom we were able to approach).

Table A.2   *Original and achieved samples of carers*

		Number of elderly people
Out-of-household carer(s) identified		103
Address not known to respondent	6	
Address refused	20	
Total respondents who gave addresses		77
Carer could not be traced		
(e.g. address inadequate, demolished)	8	
Carer refused interview	16	
Interview obtained with at least		
one carer		53
Interview obtained with 2 carers	5	
Total carer interviews		58

Representativeness of carer sample

It has been made clear that the sample of carers consisted only of persons living outside the elderly person's household, and to that extent is not representative of all persons giving informal assistance to elderly people in Sheffield. Accepting this limitation it is important to gain some idea of the extent to which the carers interviewed may be regarded as representative of all those providing care from outside the household. Two aspects of representativeness will be considered: first, whether there was any difference between those elderly people for whom a carer interview was and was not obtained; and second, whether the carers interviewed were similar to all those relatives identified as providing assistance from outside the household.

Table A.3 shows the household type of the 103 elderly people who were receiving help from outside the household compared with the remainder of the sample.

Table A.3 *Percentage of elderly people receiving care from outside the household according to household type*

Household type	Receiving care from outside household	Rest of sample	Total
Lives alone	75.7	39.4	51.6
Married couple	15.5	39.9	31.7
Other	8.7	20.7	16.7
Total	100	100	100
Number	103	203	306

It was no surprise to find that help from outside the household went overwhelmingly to elderly people living alone.

The most noticeable difference beween those elderly people for whom at least one carer was interviewed and the target group as a whole was the underrepresentation of elderly people living with someone other than a spouse. Although elderly people sharing a household with others but also receiving help from someone outside of the household are not found very frequently, it seems that interviews with carers were particularly unlikely to be obtained in such instances. Thus, out of a total of nine households where the elderly person was living with someone other than a spouse (for example, a sibling) and receiving assistance from someone outside the household, only one carer was interviewed. This compares with more than half and nearly two-thirds respectively for interviews obtained with carers of elderly people living alone and in married couples. Interviews were more likely to be obtained if the elderly person was female than male, and also more likely if the elderly person was married. This suggests that men were more reluctant to pass on the names and addresses of caring relatives and that, perhaps, elderly people in married couples felt less uncertain than others about doing so, although we did not pursue these conjectures.

Bibliography

Abrams, M. (1978) *Beyond Three Score and Ten*, Age Concern, Mitcham.

Abrams, M. (1980) *Beyond Three Score and Ten: A Second Report on a Survey of the Elderly*, Age Concern, Mitcham.

Abrams, P. (1977) Community Care: some research problems and priorities, *Policy and Politics*, 6, 2, 125–21.

Abrams, P. (1978a) *Neighbourhood Care and Social Policy*, Volunteer Centre, Berkhamsted.

Abrams, P. (1978b) *Work, Urbanism and Inequality*, Weidenfeld & Nicolson, London.

Abrams, P. (1980) 'Social Change, Social Networks and Neighbourhood Care', *Social Work Service*, 22, 12–23.

Allen, I. (1983) *Short Stay Residential Care for the Elderly*, Policy Studies Institute, London.

Anderson, M. (1971) *Family Structure in Nineteenth-Century Lancashire*, Cambridge University Press.

Anderson, M. (1977) 'The Impact on the Family Relationships of the Elderly of Changes since Victorian Times in Governmental Income Maintenance', in E. Shanas and M. Sussman (eds), *Family, Bureaucracy and the Elderly*, Duke University Press, Durham, NC.

Barclay Committee (1982) *Social Workers: Their Role and Tasks*, Bedford Square Press/National Council for Voluntary Organisations, London.

Barker, J. (1983) *Volunteer Bereavement Counselling Schemes: A Report on a Monitoring Exercise*, Age Concern Research Publications, Mitcham.

Barrett, M. (1978) *Women's Oppression Today: Problems in Marxist Feminist Analysis*, Verso, London.

Barrett, M. and McIntosh, M. (1982) *The Anti-Social Family*, Verso, London.

Bayley, M. (1973) *Mental Handicap and Community Care*, Routledge & Kegan Paul, London.

Bayley, M. (1980) 'Neighbourhood Care and Community Care: A Response to Philip Abrams', *Social Work Service*, 26, 4–9.

Bayley, M. (1982) 'Helping Care to Happen in the Community', in Walker (1982a) 179–69.

Bayley, M., Parker, P., Seyd, R. and Tennant, A. (1981) *Origins,*

Strategy and Proposed Evaluation (The Dinnington Project), Department of Sociological Studies, University of Sheffield.

Bayley, M., Seyd, R., Tennant, A. and Simons, K. (1983) 'What Resources does the Informal Sector Require to Fulfil its Role?' in *The Barclay Report: Papers from a Consultative Day*, Paper No. 15, NISW, London, 5–45.

Bebbington, A. C. (1980) 'Changes in the Provision of Social Services to the Elderly in the Community over Fourteen Years', *Social Policy and Administration*, 13, 2, 114–23.

Bebbington, A. C. (1981) 'Appendix' in E. M. Goldberg and S. Hatch (eds), *A New Look at the Personal Social Services*, PSI, London.

Beresford, P. and Croft, S. (1984) 'Welfare Pluralism: The New Face of Fabianism', *Critical Social Policy*, 9 (Spring), 19–39.

Black, J. A., Bowl, R., Burns, D., Critcher, C., Grant, G. N. and Stockford, R. (1983) *Social Work in Context: A Comparative Study of Three Area Social Work Teams*, Tavistock, London.

Blau, P. (1964) *Exchange and Power in Social Life*, Wiley, New York.

Blau, P. (1968) *The Dynamics of Bureaucracy* (2nd edn), Chicago University Press.

Blau, Z. S. (1973) *Old Age in a Changing Society*, New Viewpoints, New York.

Bosanquet, N. (1983) *After the New Right*, Heinemann, London.

Bowl, R. (1986) 'Social Work with Old People', in Phillipson and Walker, 128–45.

Boyd, R. V. and Woodman, J. A. (1978) The Jekyll-and-Hyde Syndrome: an example of disturbed relations affecting the elderly. *The Lancet*, No. 8091, 671–2.

Bradshaw, J. (1980) *The Family Fund: an initiative in social policy*, Routledge & Kegan Paul, London.

Brody, E. M. (1981) 'Women in the Middle' and 'Family Help to Older People', *The Gerontologist*, 21, 5, 471–9.

Brody, E. M. (1983). 'Women's Changing Roles and Help to Elderly Parents: Attitudes of Three Generations of Women', *Journal of Gerontology*, 38, 5, 597–607.

Brody, E. M., Johnson, P. T. and Fulcomer, M. C. (1984) 'What should Adult Children do for Elderly Parents?', *Journal of Gerontology*, 39, 6, 736–46.

Brown, G. and Harris, T. (1978) *Social Origins of Depression: A Study of Psychiatric Disorder in Women*, Tavistock, London.

Bulmer, M. (1987) *The Social Basis of Community Care*, Allen & Unwin, London.

Butcher, H. and Crosbie, D. (1978) *Pensioned Off*, University of York/Cumbria Community Development Project, York.

Cantor, M. (1979) 'Neighbours and Friends: An Overlooked Resource in the Informal Suport System', *Research in Ageing*, 1, 4, 434–63.

Caplan, G. (1974) *Social Support and Community Mental Health*, Basic Books, New York.

Carby, H. (1982) 'White Women Listen! Black Feminism and the Boundaries of Sisterhood' in Centre for Contemporary Cultural Studies (1982) *The Empire Strikes Back: Race and Racism in 70s Britain*, Hutchinson, London, pp. 212–35.

Carpenter, M. and Paley, J. (1984) 'Getting What They Ask For', *Community Care*, 8 March, 25–6.

Carver, V. and Rodda, M. (1978) *Disability and Environment*, Schocken Books, New York.

Challis, D. and Daviés, B. (1985) 'Long-term Care for the Elderly: The Kent Community Care Scheme', *British Journal of Social Work*, 15, 6, 563–79.

Challis, D. and Davies, B. (1986) *Case Management in Community Care*, Gower, Aldershot.

Challis, D. and Knapp, M. (1979), *An Examination of the PGC Morale Scale in an English context*, Personal Social Services Research Unit discussion paper 168. University of Kent, Canterbury.

Chappell, N. L. (1983) 'Informal Support Networks among the Elderly' *Research on Ageing*, 5, 1, 77–99.

Charlesworth, A., Wilkin, D. and Durie, A. (1984) *Carers and Services: A Comparison of Men and Women Caring for Dependent Elderly People*, EOC, Manchester.

Checkland, S. G. and Checkland, E. O. A. (eds) (1974) *The Poor Law Report of 1834*, Penguin Books, Harmondsworth.

Cole, D. with Utting, J. (1962) *The Economic Circumstances of Old People*, Codicote Press, Welwyn.

Collins, A. H. and Pancoast, D. L. (1976) *Natural Helping Networks*, National Association of Social Workers, Washington, DC.

Connor, K. A., Powers, E. S. and Bultena, G. L. (1979) 'Social Interaction and Life Satisfaction', *Journal of Gerontology*, 34, 16–121.

DHSS (1975) *The Census of Residential Accommodation 1970: 1 – Residential Accommodation for the Elderly and for the Younger Physically Handicapped*, HMSO, London.

DHSS (1978) *A Happier Old Age*, HMSO, London.

DHSS (1981a) *Growing Older*, Cmnd. 8173, HMSO, London.

DHSS (1981b) *Care in the Community*, HMSO, London.

Dalley, G. (1983) 'Ideologies of Care: A Feminist Contribution to the Debate', *Critical Social Policy*, 8, 72–81.

Dalley, G. (1988) *Ideologies of Caring*, Macmillan, London.

Deeping, E. (1979) *Caring for Elderly Parents*, Constable, London.

Disability Alliance (1975) *Poverty and Disability*, Disability Alliance, London.

Dono, J. Falbe, C., Kail, B., Litwak, E., Sherman, R. and Siegel, D. (1979) 'Primary Groups in Old Age: Structure and Function', *Research on Ageing*, 1, 4, 403–33.

Drew, D. (1980) *A Classification of Residential Neighbourhoods of Sheffield using Cluster Analysis*, Research report MS/23, Department of Maths, Stats and OR, Sheffield City Polytechnic.

EOC (1980) *The Experience of Caring for Elderly and Handicapped Dependents*, EOC, Manchester.

Ermish, J. (1983) *The Political Economy of Demographic Change*, Heinemann, London.

Estes, C. L. (1979) *The Ageing Enterprise*, Jossey-Bass, San Francisco.

Fengler, A., Danigelis, N. and Little, V. (1983) 'Later Life Satisfaction and Household Structure: Living with Others and Living Alone', *Ageing and Society*, 3, 357–77.

Finch, J. (1984) 'Community Care: Developing Non-Sexist Alternatives', *Critical Social Policy*, 9, 6–18.

Finch, J. and Groves, D. (1980) 'Community Care and the Family: A Case for Equal Opportunities?', *Journal of Social Policy*, 9, 4, 487–514.'

Finch, J. and Groves, D. (eds) (1983) *A Labour of Love: Women, Work and Caring*, Routledge & Kegan Paul, London.

Finkelhor, D., Gelles, R., Hotaling, G. and Straus, M. (1983) *Dark Side of Families: Current Family Violence Research*, Sage, Beverly Hills.

Flandrin, J. L. (1979) *Families in Former Times*, Cambridge University Press.

Foster, P. (1983) *Access to Welfare*, Macmillan, London.

Fowler, N. (1984) Speech to the Joint Social Services Annual Conference, Thursday 27 September.

Froland, C. (1980) 'Formal and Informal Care: Discontinuities on the Continuum', *Social Service Review*, 54, 4, 572–87.

Froland, C., Pancoast, D., Chapman, N. and Kimboko, P. (1981) *Helping Networks and Human Services*, Sage, Beverly Hills.

Garbarino, J. (1983) 'Social Support Networks – RX for the Helping Professionals', in Whittaker and Garbarino (1983), 3–32.

Gelles, R. (1983) 'An Exchange/Social Control Theory', in Finkelhor *et al.*, (1983).

Gilleard, C. J., Belford, H., Gilleard, E., Whittick, J. E. and Gledhill, K. (1984) 'Emotional Distress amongst The Supporters of the Elderly Mentally Infirm', *British Journal of Psychiatry*, 145, 172–7.

Gladstone, F. (1979) *Voluntary Action in a Changing World*, Bedford Square Press, London.

Goldberg, E. and Connelly, N. (1982) *The Effectiveness of Social Care for the Elderly*, Heinemann, London.

Goldberg, E. and Warburton, W. (1979) *Ends and Means in Social Work*, George Allen & Unwin, London.

Goldfarb, A. I. (1965) 'Psychodynamics and the Three-Generational Family', in Shanas and Streib (1965), Social Structure and the Family: Generational Relations, Prentice Hall, Englewood Clifs, N.J.

Gottlieb, B. (1981) *Social Networks and Social Support*, Sage, Beverly Hills.

Graham, H. (1983) 'Caring: A Labour of Love', in Finch and Groves (1983), 13–30.

Green, S., Creese, A. and Kanfert, J. (1979) 'Social Support and Government Policy on Services for the Elderly', *Social Policy and Administration*, 13, 3, 210–218.

Hanley, I. and Baikie, E. (1984) 'Understanding and Treating Depression in the Elderly', in Hanley and Hodge (1984).

Hanley, I. and Hodge, J. (1984) *Psychological Approaches to the Care of the Elderly*, Croom Helm, London.

Harris, A. I. (1968) *Social Welfare for the Elderly*, Government Social Survey, I, HMSO, London.

Harris, A. I., Cox, E. and Smith, C. R. W. (1971) *Handicapped and Impaired in Great Britain*, Part I, HMSO, London.

Hatch, S. (1980) *Outside the State*, Croom Helm, London.

Hazan, H. (1980) *The Limbo People: A Study of the Constitution of the Time Universe Among the Aged*, Routledge & Kegan Paul, London.

Health Advisory Service (1983) *The Rising Tide*, DHSS, London.

Hendricks, J. and Hendricks, C. D. (1977) *Ageing in Mass Society*, Winthrop, Cambridge, Mass.

Henwood, M. and Wicks, M. (1984) *The Forgotten Army: Family Care and Elderly People*, Family Policy Studies Centre, London.

Hirsch, F. (1977) *Social Limits to Growth*, Routledge & Kegan Paul, London.

Hunt, A. (1968) *Women's Employment*, I, HMSO, London.

Hunt, A. (1978) *The Elderly at Home*, HMSO, London.

Hurley, B. and Wolstenhome, L. (1979) *The Home Help Study: A Summary of Findings and Implications*, Bradford Social Services Department.

Isaacs, B., Livingstone, M. and Neville, Y. (1972) *Survival of the Unfittest: A Study of Geriatric Patients in Glasgow*, Routledge & Kegan Paul, London.

Isaacs, B. and Neville, Y. (1976) *The Measurement of Need in Old People*, Scottish Health Service Studies No. 34, Scottish Home and Health Department, Edinburgh.

Jahoda, M. (1979) 'The Impact of Unemployment in the 1930s and 1970s', *Bulletin of the British Psychological Society*, 32, 309–14.

Jenkin, P. (1981) *The Guardian*, 8 April.

Johnson, M. L. (1972) 'Old and Young in the Family: A Negotiated Arrangement', paper given at the British Society for Social and Behavioural Gerontology Conference.

Johnson, M. L. (1981) 'Community Care for Elderly People: A Case Study in Symbolic Social Policy', Paper given at The International Congress of Gerontology, July, Hamburg.

Johnson, N. (1987) *The Welfare State in Transition*, Wheatsheaf, Brighton.

Jones, D. A., Victor, C. R. and Vetter, N. J. (1983) Carers of the Elderly in the Community, *Journal of the Royal College of General Practitioners* 33, 707–10.

Joshi, H. (1987) 'The Cost of Caring' in C. Glendinning and J. Millar (eds), *Women and Poverty in Britain*, Wheatsheaf, Brighton, 112–133.

Kalish, R. A. (1969) *The Dependencies of Old People*, Ann Arbor, Michigan.

Kohen, J. A. (1983) 'Old But Not Alone: Informal Supports among the Elderly by Marital Status and Sex', *The Gerontologist*, 23, 1, 57–63.

Kreps, J. (1977) 'Intergenerational Transfers and the Bureauracy', in E. Shanas and M. Sussman (eds), *Family, Bureaucracy and the Elderly*, Durham, NC: Duke University Press.

Land, H. (1978) 'Who Cares for the Family?', *Journal of Social Policy*, 7, 3, 357–84.

Land, H. and Parker, R. (1978) 'Family Policy in the UK', in S. Kamermann and A. Kahn (eds), *Family Policy: Government and Families in Fourteen Countries*, Columbia University Press, New York, 331–66.

Lawton, M. P. (1972) 'The Dimensions of Morale' in D. P. Kent, R. Kastenbaum and S. Sherwood (eds), *Research Planning and Action for the Elderly*, Behavioural Publications, New York.

Lawton, M. P. (1975) 'The PGC Morale Scale: A Revision', *Journal of Gerontology*, 30, 85–9.

Lee, G. and Ellithorpe, E. (1982) 'Intergenerational Exchange and Subjective Well-Being among the Elderly', *Journal of Marriage and the Family*, February 1982, 217–24.

Levin, E., Sinclair, I. and Gorbach, P. (1983) *Supporters of Confused Elderly Persons at Home*, NISW, London.

Levin, E., Sinclair, I. and Gorbach, P. (1986) *Families, Services and Confusion in Old Age*, Allen & Unwin, London.

Litwak, E. and Meyer, H. (1966) 'A Balance Theory of Co-Ordination between Organisations and Community Primary Groups', *Administrative Science Quarterly*, 11, 1, 31–58.

Litwak, E. and Szelenyi, I. (1969) 'Primary Group Structures and their Functions: Kin, Neighbours and Friends', *American Sociological Review*, 34, 465–81.

Lopata, H. Z. (1979) *Women as Widows: Support Systems*, Elsevier, New York.

MacDonald, R., Qureshi, H. and Walker, A. (1984) 'Sheffield Shows the Way', *Community Care*, 18 October, 28–30.

Marsden, D. and Duff, E. (1975) *Workless*, Penguin, Harmondsworth.

Martin, J. and Roberts, C. (1984) *Women and Employment: A Lifetime Perspective*, HMSO, London.

Ministry of Health (1963) *Health and Welfare: The Development of Community Care*, Cmnd., 1973, HMSO, London.

Moen, E. (1978) 'The Reluctance of the Elderly to Accept Help', *Social Problems*, 25, 293–303.

Mooney, G. A. (1978) 'Planning the Balance of Care of the Elderly', *Scottish Journal of Political Economy*, 25, 2, 149–64.

Moore, J. (1987) Speech to the Conservative Political Centre, Saturday, 26 September.

Moroney, R. M. (1976) *The Family and the State*, Longman, London.

Moroney, R. M. (1986) *Shared Responsibility: Families and Social Policy*, Aldine, New York.

Morris, L. (1985) 'Renegotiation of the Domestic Division of Labour in the Context of Male Redundancy' in Roberts B., Finnegan R. and Gallie D. (eds), *New Approaches to Economic Life*, Manchester University Press, Manchester.

Nissel, M. and Bonnerjea, L. (1982) *Family Care of the Handicapped Elderly: Who Pays?*, PSI, London.

Norman, A. (1980) *Rights and Risk*, National Corporation for The Care of Old People, London.

OPCS (1973) *General Household Survey 1972*, HMSO, London.

OPCS (1981) *General Household Survey 1980*, HMSO, London.

OPCS (1982) *General Household Survey 1981*, HMSO, London.

Oliver, J. (1983) 'The Caring Wife', in Finch and Groves (1983), 72–85.

Parker, G. (1985) *With Due Care and Attention*, Family Policy Studies Centre, London.

Parker, R. (1981) 'Tending and Social Policy', in E. M. Goldberg and S. Hatch (eds), *A New Look at the Personal Social Services*, PSI, London, 17–32.

Phillipson, C. and Walker, A. (1986) (eds) *Ageing and Social Policy: A Critical Assessment*, Gower, Aldershot.

Pinker, R. (1979) *The Idea of Welfare*, Heinemann, London.

Powers, E. A. and Bultena, G. L. (1976) 'Sex Differences in Intimate Friendship of Old Age', *Journal of Marriage and the Family*, 38, 739–47.

Qureshi, H. (1985) 'Exchange Theory and Helpers on The Kent Community Care Scheme', *Research, Policy and Planning*, 3, 1, 1–9.

Rea-Price, J., Stevenson, O., Walker, A., Laming, H., Leat, D. and Allen I. (1987) *The Future Role of Social Services Departments*, PSI, London.

Rosenmayer, L. and Kockeis, E. (1963) 'Propositions for a Sociological Theory of Ageing and the Family', *International Social Service Journal*, 15, 3, 410–26.

Rosow, I. (1967) *Social Integration of the Aged*, Free Press, New York.

Rossiter, C. and Wicks, M. (1982) *Crisis or Challenge? Family Care, Elderly People and Social Policy*, Study Commission on the Family, London.

Rowlings, C. (1981) *Social Work with Elderly People*, Allen and Unwin, London.

Sainsbury, P. and Grad de Alarcon, J. (1971) 'The Psychiatrist and the Geriatric Patient', *Journal of Geriatric Psychiatry*, 4, 1, 23–41.

Sainsbury, S. (1973) *Measuring Disability*, Bell, London.

Scott, J. P. (1983) 'Siblings and Other Kin' in T. H. Brubaker (ed.) *Family Relationships in Later Life*, Sage, London, 47–62.

Seyd, R., Tennant, A. and Bayley, M. (1983) *The Home Help Service*, Working Paper No. 6 (The Dinnington Project), Department of Sociological Studies, University of Sheffield.

Seyd, R., Tennant, A. and Bayley, M. (1985) *Old and Alone*, Working Paper No. 10 (The Dinnington Project), Department of Sociological Studies, University of Sheffield.

Shanas, E. (1962) *The Health of Older People*, Harvard University Press, Cambridge, Mass.

Shanas, E. (1973) 'Family – Kin Networks and Aging in Cross-Cultural Perspective', *Journal of Marriage and the Family*, 35, 505–11.

Shanas, E. (1979) 'Social Myth as Hypothesis: The Case of the Family Relations of Old People', *The Gerontologist*, 19, 169–74.

Shanas, E. and Streib, G. (eds) (1965) *Social Structure and the Family: Generational Relations*, Prentice-Hall, Englewood Cliffs, NJ.

Shanas, E., Townsend, P., Wedderburn, D., Henning, F., Milhof, P. and Stehouwer, J. (1968) *Old People in Three Industrialised Societies*, Routledge & Kegan Paul, London.

Showler, B. and Sinfield, A. (1981) (eds) *the Workless State*, Blackwell/Martin Robertson, Oxford.

Sinclair, I., Crosbie, D., O'Connor, P., Stanforth, L. and Vickery, A. (1984) *Networks Project: A Study of Informal Care Services and Social Work for Elderly Clients Living Alone*, NISW Research Unit, London.

Social Services Committee (1980) *The Government's White Papers on Public Expenditure: The Social Services* 11 (HC 702), HMSO, London.

Social Services Committee (1986) *Public Expenditure on the Social Services*, I (HC 387), HMSO, London.

Social Services Committee (1988) *The Government's White Papers on Public Expenditure: The Social Services*, II (HC 702), HMSO, London.

South Yorkshire County Council (1979) *Household Survey 1977*, Barnsley.

Stevenson, O. and Parsloe, P. (1978) *Social Services Teams: The Practitioners' View*, HMSO, London.

Supplementary Benefits Commission (1978) *Annual Report 1977*, HMSO, London.

Taylor, R. and Ford, G. (1983) 'Inequalities in Old Age: An Examination of Age, Sex and Class differences in a Sample of Community Elderly', *Ageing and Society*, 3, 2, 183–208.

Teeland, L. (1978) *Keeping in Touch: The Relations Between Old People and their Adult Children*, University of Gotenberg, Department of Sociology Monograph 16.

Thatcher, M. (1981) Speech to WRVS National Conference 'Facing the New Challenge', Monday 19 January.

Tinker, A. (1981) *The Elderly in Modern Society*, Longman, London.

Tinker, A. (1984) *Staying at Home: Helping Elderly People*, HMSO, London.

Titmuss, R. M. (1955) 'Age and Society: Some Fundamental Assumptions' in *Old Age in the Modern World*, Report of the Third Congress of International Association of Gerontology, Livingston, Edinburgh, 46–9.

Titmuss, R. M. (1963) *Essays on the Welfare State* (2nd edn) Allen & Unwin, London.

Tobin, S. S. and Lieberman, M. A. (1976) *Last Home for the Aged*, Jossey-Bass, London.

Townsend, P. (1962) *The Last Refuge*, Routledge & Kegan Paul, London.

Townsend, P. (1963) *The Family Life of Old People*, Penguin, Harmondsworth (first published 1957).

Townsend, P. (1979) *Poverty in the United Kingdom,* Pelican, Harmondsworth.

Townsend, P. (1981a) 'The Structured Dependency of the Elderly: the Creation of Social Policy in the Twentieth Century', *Ageing and Society*, 1, 1, 5–28.

Townsend, P. (1981b) 'Elderly People with Disabilities', in Walker and Townsend (1981), 91–118.

Townsend, P. and Tunstall, S. (1968) 'Isolation, Desolation and Loneliness', in Shanas *et al.*, (1968), 258–87.

Townsend, P. and Tunstall, S. (1973) 'Sociological explanation of the lonely', in P. Townsend, *The Social Minority*, Allen Lane, London.

Townsend, P. and Wedderburn, D. (1965) *The Aged in the Welfare State*, Bell, London.

Troll, L. E. (1971) 'The Family of Later Life: A Decade Review', *Journal of Marriage and the Family*, 33, 263–90.

Tunstall, J. (1960) *Old and alone*, Routledge & Kegan Paul, London.

Ungerson, C. (1983a) 'Why Do Women Care?' in Finch and Groves (1983), 31–50.

Ungerson, C. (1983b) 'Women and Caring: Skills, Tasks and Taboos', in E. Gamarinkow, D. Morgan, J. Purvis and D. Taylorson (eds), *The Public and the Private*, Heinemann, London, 62–77.

US Bureau of the Census (1983) *Statistical Abstract of the United States: 1984* (104th edn), US Government Printing Office, Washington, DC.

VanKrieken, R. (1980) 'The Capitalist State and the Organisation of Welfare: An Introduction', *The Australian and New England Journal of Sociology*, 16, 3, 23–35.

Vaswani, N., Parker, C. and Mitchell, K. (1978) *OR study of the Care of the Elderly in Calderdale: Report of the Operational Research Service of the DHSS'*, ORS Note 41/77, March. DHSS, London.

Vaughan-Morgan, J. *et al.*, (1952) *The Care of Old People*, Conservative Political Centre, London.

Verbrugge, L. M. (1984) 'Longer Life but Worsening Health? Trends in Health and Mortality of Middle-Aged and Older Persons', *Milbank Memorial Fund Quarterly*, 62, 3, 516–19.

Vladek, B. C. (1980) *Unloving Care: The Nursing Home Tragedy*, Basic Books, New York.

Wade, B. and Finlayson, J. (1983) 'Drugs and the Elderly', *Nursing Mirror*, 4 May, 17–21.

Wade, B., Sayer, L. and Bell, J. (1983) *Dependency with Dignity*, Bedford Square Press, London.

Waerness, K. (1986) 'Informal and Formal Care in Old Age?', paper presented to the XIth World Congress of Sociology, New Delhi.

Walker, A. (1976) *Living Standards in Crisis*, Disability Alliance, London.

Walker, A. (1980) 'The Social Creation of Poverty and Dependency in Old Age', *Journal of Social Policy*, 9, 1, 45–75.

Walker, A. (1981a) 'Community Care and the Elderly in Great Britain: Theory and Practice', *International Journal of Health Services*, 11, 4, 541–57.

Walker, A. (1981b) 'Towards a Political Economy of Old Age', *Ageing* and Society, 1, 1, 73–94.

Walker, A. (1981c) 'Social Policy, Social Administration and the Social Construction of Welfare', *Sociology*, 15, 2, 225–50.

Walker, A. (ed.) (1982a) *Community Care: The Family, The State and Social Policy*, Blackwell/Martin Robertson, Oxford.

Walker, A. (1982b) 'The Meaning and Social Division of Community Care' in Walker (1982a), 13–39.

Walker, A. (1982c) 'Dependency and Old Age', *Social Policy and Administration*, 16, 2, 115–35.

Walker, A. (1982d) 'Why we Need a Social Strategy', *Marxism Today*, September, 26–31.

Walker, A. (1982e) 'The Social Consequences of Early Retirement', *The Political Quarterly*, 53, 1, 61–72.

Walker, A. (ed.) (1982f) *Public Expenditure and Social Policy*, Heinemann, London.

Walker, A. (1983a) 'Care for Elderly People: A Conflict Between Women and the State', in Finch and Groves (1983), 106–28.

Walker, A. (1983b) 'A Caring Community', in H. Glennerster (ed.), *The Future of the Welfare State: Remaking Social Policy*, Heinemann, London, 157–72.

Walker, A. (1983c) 'Social Policy and Elderly People in Great Britain: The Construction of Dependent Social and Economic Status in Old Age', in A. Guillemard (ed.), *Old Age and the Welfare State*, Beverly Hills, Sage, 143–67.

Walker, A. (1984a) 'Conscription on the Cheap: Older Workers and the State', *Critical Social Policy*, 11 (Winter), 103–10.

Walker, A. (1984b) 'The Political Economy of Privatisation', in J. Le Grand and R. Robinson (eds), *Privatisation and the Welfare State*, Allen & Unwin, London, 19–44.

Walker, A. (1984c) *Social Planning*, Blackwell/Martin Robertson, Oxford.

Walker, a. (1985a) 'Care of Elderly People' in R. Berthoud (ed.), *Challenges to Social Policy*, Gower, Aldershot.

Walker, A. (1985b) 'From Welfare State to Caring Society? The Promise of Informal Support Networks', in Yoder, Jonker and Leaper (1985), 41–58.

Walker, A. (1985c) *The Care Gap: How can Local Authorities Meet the Needs of the Elderly?*, Local Government Information Unit, London.

Walker, A. (1985d) 'Early Retirement: Release or Refuge from the Labour Market?' *The Quarterly Journal of Social Affairs*, 1, 3, 211–29.

Walker, A. (1985e) 'Making the Elderly Pay', *New Society*, 18 April,- 76–8.

Walker, A. (1986a) 'Community Care: Fact and Fiction', in P. Willmott (ed.), *The Debate About Community: Papers from a Seminar on 'Community' in Social Policy*, PSI, London, 4–15.

Walker, A. (1986b) 'Pensions and the Production of Poverty in Old Age', in Phillipson and Walker (1986), 184–216.

Walker, A. (1987a) 'Enlarging the Caring Capacity of the Community:

Informal Support Networks and the Welfare State', *International Journal of Health Services*, 17, 3, 369–86.

Walker, A. (1987b) 'Clients, Consumers or Partners? Privatisation and User Participation in the Social Services', paper presented to Seminar on 'The Position and Participation of Clients – A key Question in Advancing Social Policy', Helsinki, September.

Walker, A. (1987c) 'The Growth of Poverty among the Elderly Population and the Reasons for Low Take-Up of Benefits' in Age Concern Scotland, *Poverty and Older People*, Edinburgh, 8–20.

Walker, A. (1988) 'Tendering Care', *New Society*, 22 January, 18–19.

Walker, A., Noble, I. and Westergaard, J. (1985) 'From Secure Employment to Labour Market Insecurity', in Roberts B., Finnegan, R. and Gallie, D. (eds), *New approaches to Econonomic Life*, Manchester University Press, 319–37.

Walker, A. and Laczko, F. (1982) 'Early Retirement and Flexible Retirement', in House of Commons Social Services Committee, *Age of Retirement* (HC 26–II), HMSO, London, 211–29.

Walker, A. and Townsend, P. (1976) *Assessing the Severity of Disability: Three Pilot Studies*, DHSS, London.

Walker, A. and Townsend, P. (eds) (1981), *Disability in Britain*, Martin Robertson, Oxford.

Walker, A., Winyard, S. and Pond, C. (1983) 'Conservative Economic Policy: The Social Consequences', in D. Bull and P. Wilding (eds), *Thatcherism and the Poor*, Child Poverty Action Group, London.

Walker, C. (1984) *The Reform of the Supplementary Benefit Scheme*, Leeds University, Department of Social Policy and Health Services Studies.

Walker, R., Lawson, R. and Townsend, P. (1984) *Responses to Poverty: Lessons from Abroad*, Heinemann, London.

Webb, A., Day, L. and Weller, D. (1976) *Voluntary Social Service Manpower Resources*, Personal Social Services Council, London.

Webb, A. and Wistow, G. (1982) *Whither State Welfare?*, Royal Institute of Public Administration, London.

Weiss, R. (1973) *Loneliness – The Experience of Emotional and Social Isolation*, MIT Press, Boston, Mass.

Weiss, R. (1974) 'The Provisions of Social Relationships' *in* S. Rubin (ed.), *Doing Unto Others*, Prentice-Hall, Englewood Cliffs, NJ.

Wenger, C. (1984) *The Supportive Network*, Allen & Unwin, London.

West, P. (1984) 'The Family, the Welfare State and Community Care: Political Rhetoric and Public Attitudes', *Journal of Social Policy*, 13, 4, 417–46.

West, P., Ilsley, R. and Kelman, H. (1984) 'Public Preferences for the Care of Dependency Groups', *Social Science and Medicine*, 18, 4, 287–95.

Whittaker, J. K. (1983) 'Mutual Helping in Human Service Practice' in Whittaker and Garbarino (1983), 33–72.

Whittaker, J. K. and Garbarino (eds) (1983) *Social Support Networks: Informal Helping in the Human Services*, Aldine, New York.

Wicks, M. (1982) 'Community Care and Elderly People', in Walker (1982a), 97–117.

Wilkin, D. (1986) 'The Mix of Lucid and Confused Residents' in Judge K. and Sinclair I. (eds) *Residential Care for Elderly People*, HMSO, London.

Wilkin, D., Metcalfe, D. H. H., Hallam, L., Cooke, M. and Hodgkin, P. K. (1984) 'Area Variations in the Process of Care in Urban General Practice', *British Medical Journal*, 289, 229–32.

Williams, I. (1979) *The Care of the Elderly in the Community*, Croom Helm, London.

Willcocks, D. M. (1984) 'Consumer Research in Old People's Homes', *Research Policy and Planning*, 2, 1, 13–18.

Willmot, P., (1986) *Social Networks, Informal Care and Public Policy*, PSI, London.

Wilson, E. (1982a) 'Women, the "Community" and the "Family"', in A. Walker (1982), 40–55.

Wolfenden, (1978) *The Future of Voluntary Organisations: Report of The Wolfenden Committee*, Croom Helm, London.

Yoder, J. A., Jonker, J. M. L. and Leaper, R. A. B. (1985) (eds) *Support Networks in a Caring Community*, Martinus Nijhoff, Dordrecht.

Index

288